TRAVELLERS' BRITAIN

Arthur Eperon is one of the most experienced and best known travel writers in Europe. Since leaving the RAF in 1945 he has worked as a journalist in various capacities often involving travel. He has concentrated on travel writing for the past ten years and contributed to many publications including *The Times, Daily Telegraph, Sun, Woman's Own, Popular Motoring* and the *TV Times*. He has appeared on radio and television and for five years was closely involved in Thames Television's programme *Wish you were here*. Author of bestselling *Travellers' France* and *Travellers' Italy*, he now turns to the country he knows best – Britain.

Also by Arthur Eperon
in Pan Books

Travellers' France
Travellers' Italy

Travellers'

Arthur Eperon

Britain

Introduction by Cliff Michelmore
Maps and drawings by Ken Smith

Pan Original
Pan Books in association with the British Broadcasting Corporation

Acknowledgements

My sincere thanks to thousands of viewers of BBC's *Holiday* programme who sent us their own choice of hotels and restaurants. I am sorry that some are not in this book – they just did not fit into our routes.

My thanks, too, to all members of the BBC *Holiday* programme team, including Audrey Barnes who spent lonely hours with her knees under driving wheels, hotel dining tables and her desk. Without her, the book would have been a year late.

Also to my wife, travel-writer Barbara Clegg, and a small band of enthusiastic eaters and drinkers who 'spied' for me on a number of hotels and restaurants I could not revisit.

My thanks to staff of the English, Welsh and Scottish Tourist Boards and the area boards for enthusiastic and efficient help, and my old friend John East of the English Tourist Board who was on the phone the day after *Travellers' Italy* was published suggesting England as a good subject for the next book, then added a lot of help.

Having retired my Ford Capri after 129,000 miles, I have used a Rover 2600, which is piling up mileage like Ian Botham collecting runs, without a hiccup so far.

Arthur Eperon

First published 1981 by Pan Books Ltd,
Cavaye Place, London SW10 9PG
in association with the British Broadcasting Corporation
© Arthur Eperon 1981
Introduction © Cliff Michelmore 1981
ISBN 0 330 26559 8
Typeset by Input Typesetting Ltd, London SW19 8DR
Printed in Great Britain by Morrison & Gibb, Edinburgh

Contents

Introduction

by Cliff Michelmore

Life for me is one long holiday, trekking in Tibet,
playing golf on the Algarve, driving at leisure along the
breathtakingly beautiful Scenic Highway on the west
coast of America or stretching out on the deck of a
yacht cruising through the Greek islands. Now that is
the general impression people have, as the result of
my introducing the BBC *Holiday* programme all these
years, and it is no good seeking to correct such a
distorted view of the life of anyone connected with
writing or talking about travel and holidays. I mention
this because there is another side to the job and that
concerns the time and effort spent in researching,
inquiring and investigating travel. Which is what this
book and its author are all about. Arthur Eperon has
already led many of us down the side roads of France
and Italy and here he has, happily, turned his
attentions to Britain.

Arthur is one of those rare travellers who have the
remarkable ability to encourage you to try other routes,
find hidden corners and come upon the unexpected; to
travel hopefully. He also has a finely tuned, discerning
palate and a nose for good wine which makes him an
admirable travelling companion in person or, as with
his *Traveller*s' books, by proxy. There is that assurance
that the routes he has explored have been covered
with admirable care, and attention paid to your
creature comforts as well. The routes he has chosen
are all interlinked so that you can map out your own
choice drifting first east, or north, and then on, as
whim and weather dictate.

If you are among those whose idea of a motoring
holiday is to pack the car with four children, grandma,
five suitcases, the dog, the budgerigar, three
deckchairs and the portable television set and say isn't
it nice to get away, then I should warn you that this
book is not for you. If you want to do the grand tour of
London, Oxford, Stratford, Edinburgh and St Andrews

stopping five-star all the way then you too must look elsewhere for your inspiration, for you will not find it in *Travellers' Britain*. This is for those of us who love to drift and meander around our country looking into country cottage gardens with high-spiked lupins and hollyhocks, heavily scented roses and wallflowers, admire the evenly spaced rows of vegetables and enjoy the hedgerows that have been left us even after the onslaught of the pesticides and mechanical hedge-trimmers. For they are still there if you care to look and are prepared to give yourself time to see them.

I am often asked – ten times a day on average – where I would go for my ideal holiday, and I must confess that, given the choice, I would follow some of the tracks set out in this book and use them as starting points for a little personal exploration. The wide-skyed landscape of East Anglia, the well-groomed beetle-browed thatched cottages of the New Forest, the glow of Cotswold stone in the early morning or late evening, or the serene dignity and almost wild abandon of the rivers and dales of Derbyshire and Yorkshire are among some of my favourite places of escape. And of course there are always the undiscovered secret parts of Wales and Scotland just waiting across the borders of England.

One of the most memorable motoring holidays we ever had was up through the byways of England and into Scotland one warm springtime. Picnics under sturdy dry stone walls in the dales or by lochs in the foothills of the Highlands are not easily forgotten, and ending the day in the comfort of a small country hotel, with the fire lit, is my kind of restful change.

It comes as a surprise to some that there are many places where there is still a genuine warmth in the welcome, and that there are still villages and towns with character and characters. All you have to know is where to look. *Travellers' Britain* points the way. It encourages those of us who still cherish our own country to get to know it even better and to take our time about it, treasuring and savouring it as we go.

One final note of thanks to the author. On behalf of many of your readers and admirers, thank you for not revealing *all* the best-kept secrets, and there are still quite a lot of them, I assure you!

Preface

We were returning from four years as guests of Hitler's German government and flew low over Kent and Surrey – midget villages below, rolling light green hills, greener meadows and dark green woods, corn and hops, bright yellow mustard and dark green cabbages, off-white sheep and twin-coloured cows, all in small patchwork fields of eccentric shapes; through it all, winding, weaving, wandering, G. K. Chesterton's Rolling English Road.

The Canadian pilot from the Prairies next to me shook his head almost impatiently.

'It's got no *right* to be so goddamned green and smug!' he said.

You see Britain clearest from a low-flying, slow aircraft. You realize how gloriously unplanned our countryside looks, how it has evolved through men's lives over centuries and not been plotted on a drawing board. You see, above all, how compact the country is. That is what makes Britain such a glorious country to explore – slowly. There is so much to see in such short distances that the problem is what to miss out. Hurry past and you miss treasures by the score. Thatched roofs and Tudor beams, blackberries and dog roses, ancient oaks, hidden streams, cottage gardens, Norman churches, stately homes, museums of old cars, swords and old guns, aviaries of strange birds, woods of bluebells, smugglers' inns, pirates' estuaries, centuries-old gardens. Twenty-five miles is not too little to cover in a day. A hundred and fifty miles can be too much to enjoy the country. The land moves from mountains to fens, forests to wild moors to lush meadows, soft sand beaches to sharp deadly rocks and high cliffs, all in a day's drive.

Changes have come, of course, since I flew back in '45, but our countryside is far from ruined, even if our cities are not in good shape. Some villages have grown into miniature towns. Woods and meadows have been sacrificed in places for extra food production; many hedgerows have gone, opening wider horizons but driving many of the rarer birds and loveliest wild flowers from fields to country gardens and abandoned railway lines.

Motorways have come. Neither Napoleon nor Hitler could 'straighten out the crooked road an English drunken made'. But the Ministry of Transport has – by industrial demand.

But for motorways, there would have been no *Travellers' Britain* – only the world's longest traffic jam. Now our A-roads are more pleasant to drive on. Our B-roads are often surprisingly free of traffic for such a crowded country and often better than little local roads, on which passing can be a very tight squeeze indeed and every bend is a worry.

A pity that we are letting our road maintenance deteriorate so that some road edges look as if they were imported from Continental Europe; a false economy.

The drama, romance and humour of our heritage and history lure visitors from abroad. No country can compare with ours for the number of fascinating great houses, castles, manors, old farms open to the public visitor, with their treasures intact, and a smattering of knowledge of our people's past makes travelling around Britain ten times as absorbing.

On my recent travels I have been delighted with the improvement in small hotels, but particularly in food and cooking, despite the coming of the deep-freezer. Our cooking has improved beyond words, even if it is still quite different from that of the world's greatest cooks, the French and the dedicated Italians. Old myths die hard and you still hear Americans, of all people, sneering at our cooking. Trouble is, they will eat in London, and with a few exceptions you get far better cooking in small cities or little country hotels. We are still low on expensive pure-gourmet restaurants, perhaps, but you can eat very well at a reasonable price as easily in Britain as in any country except France or Belgium.

As with wines a few years ago, amateur snobbery and even pretentious nonsense are creeping into our appreciation of food. I can understand the *Michelin Guide to Great Britain* starring almost entirely restaurants with French cooking. More perplexing is to find French names for dishes offered in Somerset or in Lakeland. 'Medaillons de boeuf Glastonbury' or 'truite poché Derwentwater' is what floors me.

I love good sauces, but not with vermouth or pernod all the time. The New Cooking of Britain is apricots with everything. What happened to apples, redcurrants and cranberries? Yet we still have some of the greatest dishes in the world: steak and kidney pie, Cornish fish pie, British roast beef served with its natural juices and not murdered with a strong sauce, true Lancashire hot pot and, above all, fish and chips.

Let me be honest: I am not a professional cook or hotel keeper. I am a full-time professional customer, as I have been for 35 of my 62 years. When the Royal Automobile Club most kindly made me wine writer for their guides a few years back, they called me 'one of the world's greatest consumers'. So I am with food. I do envy sometimes those well-heeled people who can eat so often at the most expensive restaurants in Britain then write to the excellent *Good Food Guide* suggesting that a sauce was a little too bland or sharp. I have tried to keep down to earth in this book and suggest restaurants and hotels which are good value at any level, but particularly in the middle grade, with three-course meals around £6–7 and bed and breakfast around £10–12.

I have been delighted to find so many good small family-run hotels serving good meals – similar to Logis de France. Most are in the country, away from the coast, and in converted private houses. Like Logis, they can be short on private bathrooms to their bedrooms but do have charming décor, friendly service by the family and good cooking of fine fresh ingredients in which Britain abounds: local beef, trout, salmon, succulent lamb, and lovely vegetables, which they often grow themselves. Without our rainfall we should not have lamb which the French dare not let in to compete with their scrawny beasts, nor those vegetables which the little family-run hotels cook better than big restaurants with many mouths to feed.

Many of these new small-hotel owners are amateurs, often made redundant by industry. Not only their meals but their decorations and furnishings are refreshingly individual, with pretty bedrooms.

Our smaller hotel and inn bedrooms used to shock me. Downstairs there might be a comfortable lounge or a lovely old bar. Upstairs rooms were often freezing cells, smelling musty, with frayed carpets and seemingly furnished from a junk shop. They are better now but bedrooms without bathrooms should be considerably cheaper than most are. It certainly does not pay to travel alone. Single rooms are much more expensive per person than doubles. Basically, meals are much better value than beds in Britain, and I suggest that you look at your bedroom before accepting it.

Britain is a great country for short breaks. You can relax in the wilds or go around seeing a lot in a short time. Many hotels are now offering short bargain stays outside midsummer. I have marked many with the letters 'SB' (short breaks) in my hotel lists, but others may be offering them sooner or later, so if you fancy a hotel, ring or write and ask for latest offers. Usually you get cheap short breaks at weekends in towns where business travellers fill beds midweek; and in midweek in the country, where beds are often full at weekends.

The British Weekend Away, even in the middle of the week, is becoming again very much part of our way of holidaymaking. Some people prefer several of these breaks spread through the year to one longer holiday. Our weather has something to do with this. They will risk a rainy weekend but not a rainy fortnight!

We all know that most years our country is not for dedicated beachloungers and sunbathers. It is for travelling and exploring. There is nearly always something new and interesting to see under cover if it rains. Don't neglect the museums. Many of us were put off museums when young, but there are many which are interesting, unusual, even downright eccentric. It is a good sportsmen's country too, for players and spectators, and games like golf and tennis are much easier to find and cheaper than elsewhere. It is an excellent country for people interested in the lives of other people, past or present.

The routes have been chosen to meet up, so that you could go from North Scotland to Land's End or

Bournemouth on them – in a roundabout way! I have had to miss out some of my own favourite spots for continuity of travel. Parts of mid Devon, for instance, Cheshire, Isle of Wight. If I have missed your favourite, please forgive me. But distances are short enough to enable you to wander off the routes for a special visit.

And finally, the best motor touring advice I had when younger and faster was from Tom Wisdom, motoring journalist and road racing driver who had finished third at Le Mans and won the touring class of the Mille Miglia 1000 miles round Italy race:

'Don't be in such a hurry, old boy,' he would say. 'You'll get ulcers and miss half the best things in life.'

Then he would pull up for a glass of champagne – and let *me* drive on afterwards. A wise man, Tom Wisdom.

Arthur Eperon

Information about the book

Prices in this book are correct as far as possible up to November 1981, but are not guaranteed in any way.

Bed and breakfast prices are per person. The higher prices in many cases are for single rooms or one guest occupying a double room and these are often much higher than the cost per person of couples sharing.

All prices quoted include VAT but not necessarily service. Meal prices are for a three-course meal including VAT unless otherwise stated.

I have tried to keep symbols down to a minimum as they can be annoying. The following have been used:

FP –   fixed price meal, with or without choice in each course
card – meals priced by the dish (French à la carte)
BB –   bed and breakfast per person
DBB –   three-course dinner, bed and breakfast
SB –   special rates offered for short breaks, such as bargain weekends.

The cost of short breaks has not been given as these can vary according to time of year, time of week, etc.

Maps I have used for England and Wales are of a new series called Leisure Maps, based on Ordnance Survey, published in conjunction with the official area Tourist Boards. Apart from the usual information on roads, towns, etc. they mark the positions of many places of interest to travellers: castles, cathedrals, gardens, stately homes, museums, riding and trekking centres, sports centres.

Sixteen maps cover: 1 SE England; 2 Southern England; 3 Wessex; 4 Devon–Cornwall; 5 London; 6 East Anglia; 7 Thames–Chilterns; 8 Cotswolds–Wyedean; 9 South Wales; 10 English Shires; 11 Staffordshire–Shropshire; 12 North Wales; 13 Yorkshire–Humberside; 14 North West England; 15 North Pennines–Lakes; 16 Borders of England–Scotland – published by Estate Publications, 22 High St, Tenterden, Kent, and sold in bookshops.

Wales Tourist Board also publishes a good tourist map; for Scotland I used the Scottish Tourist Map published by Scottish Tourist Board; main tourist board addresses are: English Tourist Board, 4 Grosvenor Gardens, London SW1Y 0DU (tel 01 730 3400); Scottish Tourist Board, 23 Ravelston Terrace, Edinburgh EH4 3EU (tel 031 332 2433); Wales Tourist Board, Brunel House, 2 Fitzalan Rd, Cardiff (tel 0222 499909).

How to use the book

Each page is divided into three columns

The left-hand column gives you the road numbers to follow along the route, the places you will go through and towns or villages which are worth stopping at. The distances are given in parentheses.

The middle column recommends places to eat and stay at.

The right-hand column mentions points of historic, architectural or scenic interest about the area.

Route 1

Oxford – Cotswolds – West Country – Land's End – Dorset – Oxford

Oxford

Crowds, cars and car factories have not destroyed the great beauty and cultural heritage of Oxford. A city not only of Matthew Arnold's 'dreaming spires' and beautiful honey-coloured stone but of old trees and lush lawns. Its heart, around the university, holds as much of architectural and historic interest as anywhere in Britain outside London – packed into a square mile. You must park and walk. The newer Oxford is pleasant for shopping and sleeping, but 'town and gown' never mixed. Ever since the university started in 1249, students and townsfolk have been at odds even to the death; in the 14th century a bloody battle was fought in Merton College's Mod Quad.

Beneath its dreamy image Oxford remains a birthplace of studied rebellions. Even Harold Macmillan's Wind of Change in Africa was born not in Kenya or Nigeria or Westminster but in Balliol College, Oxford.

Few cities give greater rewards for time and study, and Oxford deserves both. If your stay is short, here are places worth visiting:

Magdalen College (most beautiful college, where great men from Cardinal Wolsey to Oscar Wilde studied; grounds to the river Cherwell); riverside Botanic Gardens opposite Magdalen; Broad Walk through riverside meadows; Pembroke College (window boxes and 17th-century quadrangle); Christ Church (largest college; superb quad, Tom Tower, designed by Wren, holding the bell Great Tom; splendid art gallery); Merton College (chapel windows with fine 13th- to 14th-century glass, oldest library in Britain); All Souls (memorial to English soldiers killed at Agincourt in 1415: 'that fought with us upon St Crispin's Day'; Wren was a Fellow of All Souls); Museum of History of Science (early and later scientific instruments, including astronomical); Ashmolean Museum (remarkable collection of paintings, sculptures, tapestries, watches, snuff boxes, musical instruments

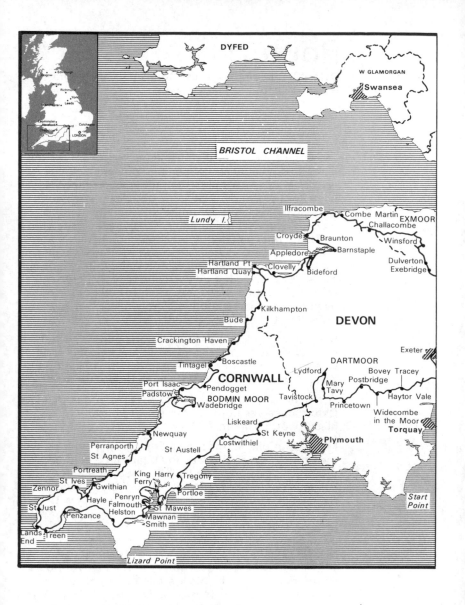

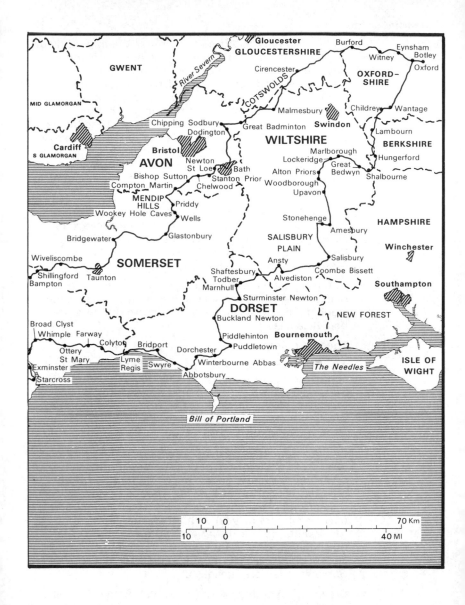

and jewels back to Alfred the Great); Wadham College
(lovely gardens); Blackwell's Bookshop; Sheldonian
Theatre (designed by Wren, used for degree
ceremonies and concerts); Bodleian Library (founded
1480, three million books include every new English
book published); New College (superb chapel); St
Edmunds Hall (last remaining medieval students' hall);
brass rubbing centre at University Church of St Mary
on the High (High Street); punts on the Cherwell from
beside Magdalen Bridge; Museum of British Telecom,
Speedwell St Telephone Exchange (by appointment,
tel 46601).

Remember, the university is for learning; too many
visitors could interrupt work, so visiting times vary
according to whether students are 'up' or 'down' –
there or not. Check with the Information Centre,
Aldgate Chambers (tel 48707).

Oxford has a wide range of accommodation and
restaurants; more vacancies in cheaper places when
students are away. Apply at the Information Centre for
bed vacancies.

These are useful:

Meals: Cherwell Boat House, Bardwell Rd (tel 52746):
converted boat house, quiet, beside river; set-menu
5-course meals 8 pm evenings, Sunday lunch £6.95.
Freshly cooked seasonal dishes from around Europe.
Wines: 100 French and German; £3.20–75. Buffet lunch
in marquee May–August.

La Sorbonne, Bleu-Blanc-Rouge and Casse Croute,
129–130 High St: three eating houses run by chef-
owner André Chavagnon. Sorbonne (tel 41320) offers
old French cooking at a price – meal around £12; Bleu-
Blanc-Rouge is cheaper – around £8–9; try jugged hare
(civet de lièvre) or veal with mushroom and cream
(blanquette de veau); Casse Croute is a room where
university folk meet for light lunch around £4 (try
classic onion tart). Sorbonne and Casse closed
Sundays, Bleu on Tuesdays.

Browns, 5 Woodstock Rd (tel 511995): cheerful, with
dangling plants, run by young team in conjunction with
cake shop next door. Open 11am–11pm. Lunch around
£3.50. Dinner £3.50–5.50. Reviving place for the foot-
weary. Try spaghetti with seafood sauce, salads, roast

ribs, steak and Guinness pie. Lurid-coloured cocktails or good-value wines (£3.25–4.95).

Nosebag, 6 St Michaels St (tel 721033): almost opposite Oxford Union; excellent value; meals £3–5. Try Nosebag salad (macaroni with diced meat, veg and fruit), goulash, moussaka. French wine £3.25.

Historic pubs: Turf Tavern, Bath Place, Hollywell (beneath New College Tower): 13th century; once a gambling hall; where Jude courted the barmaid in Hardy's novel *Jude the Obscure*. Four real ales. Bar meals – try casseroles (beef, rabbit in cider), fish pie. English fruit wines, including strawberry hock – 50p a glass.

Perch, Binsey Lane, Binsey (tel 40386): 12th-century thatched pub. Allen Bedford, ex-chef now publican, cooks superb bar meals up to £2.50. French wine £3.50 a litre.

Beds and food: Westwood Country Hotel, Hinksey Hill Top (tel 735408): owner is a chef, his wife a landscape gardener. Comfortable rooms, lovely three-acre garden. Two rooms and all doors designed for disabled. Dinner menus have variety of choice. Meals £6 (4 courses). BB £11–15. SB (winter).

Old Parsonage, 3 Banbury Rd (tel 54843): pretty, Cotswold stone, was hospital in 13th century; modern wing; chef James Chase trained under Sir Jeffery Crowther. Try roasts, trout, superb desserts. Dinner around £7, Sunday lunch £4.50 (roast beef). Wine from £4 a litre. BB £10–11.50.

Willow Reaches, 1 Wytham St (tel 43767): One mile city centre; quiet family hotel; SP dinner £4.50. Wines from £3. BB £10–11.50.

Parklands Hotel North, 100 Banbury Rd (tel 59860): comfortable, small, in same family for fifty years. Bar and dining room open to public. Bar meals, also restaurant dinners £3.50–6. Try local trout, venison, pork in cider. BB £10.50–17.50. SB (winter).

Earlmont Guest House, 322 Cowley Rd (tel 40236): BB only £6. The friendly O'Kanes offer 'real Irish helpings'.

Road past Oxford station to Botley, B4044 to Eynsham A40, then local road to Witney, Minster Lovell; on to A40 to Burford (19 m)

At Lew, A4095 (3 m from Witney), University Farm: guest house on 216-acre mixed farm; pretty bedrooms; oak beams; AA award winner. 4-course dinner £5.20; BB £7–12; DBB £14. Must book (tel Castle Bampton 850297).

At Asthall (just off A40 3 m before Burford), Maytime Inn (tel Burford 2068): huge bar, dining room; real ale; salads, charcoal grill, roasts; daily 'specials'; meals £5–8; try charcoal steak in garlic butter.

Burford, Corner House Hotel, High St (tel 3151): 15th-century beamed; grills and home cooking (try real steak and kidney pie); meals £4–6; BB £9.

Bay Tree (tel 3137): once home of Queen Elizabeth I's Baron of the Exchequer (his splendid tomb is in the church); same owners 46 years. Meals good choice and value FP lunch £3; dinner £5.50 and card. BB £12–17.50.

Lamb Inn, Sheep St (tel 3155): also 15th century; charming old furniture, flowers inside and out. English roasts, pies. FP lunch £4, dinner £5.50. French house wines £2.80. BB £13–15. DBB £18–20.

Inn for All Seasons, The Barringtons (tel Windrush 324): unusual and excellent; home cooking, warm bedrooms with own bathrooms; meals good value: buttery £3.50 (try omelettes); small candlelit dining room; FP dinner £6.50. BB £17 SB (good touring centre).

Witney has produced blankets for 1000 years; 13th-century centre with market square, spired church; 18th-century Blanket Hall for weighing blankets. Diversion of A40 has brought back calm.

At Cogges, on A4095, agricultural museum in ancient manor (settled 1086), restored as Edwardian farm with horse-drawn equipment.

Minster Lovell: lovely village of stone and thatch on river Windrush; remains of Lovell mansion with two legends – the 'Mistletoe Bough' story of the bride who, playing hide-and-seek, hid in a chest, was trapped and not found; one of the Lovells who supported Richard II hid in a vaulted room known only to one servant, who died suddenly. His master starved. His skeleton, at a table, was found 250 years later, his dog at his feet.

Burford – when horses pulled coaches, thirty a day clattered down the main street and it was known for inns serving huge meals: 'Burford bait'. Still rich in inns and cluttered with traffic. Pretty town with Tudor buildings. Tolsey Museum in old toll house. Tomb in church of Speaker Letnall, who defied Charles I's attempt to arrest Members in House of Commons (1642).

Cotswold Wildlife Park (A361 off A40, 2 m): leopards, monkeys, red pandas, pumas, penguins – many divided from visitors by ditches. Open daily.

A433 Cirencester
(15 m)

Crown, West Market Place (tel 3811): innkeeper ex-director Trust House Forte. Hot buffet £2; card around £4. BB £13.

La Ronde, 52 Ashcroft Rd (tel 4511): restaurant/guest house, ex-theatrical host; unassuming building; good food choice. Meals 4 course FP £5.85–7.50. BB £7.25–10.50.

Kings Head, Market Place (tel 3322): historic inn where first blood was drawn in the Civil War; not cheap but value; run by Michael Haigh Gannon, who worked at George V, Paris. FP lunch £5.65; FP dinner £7.40. Card £9. BB (own bath) £21–27.50. SB.

Stratton House, Gloucester Rd (tel 61761): lovely Jacobean/Georgian hotel, elegantly furnished, charming grounds, walled garden; old bedrooms spacious, modern rooms simpler. Try Cotswold lamb, Bibury trout, Gloucester sausage. FP lunch £5.50, FP dinner £7, card £5–10. Variety of wines from £3.90. BB £16.50–21.

Charming historic town, sometimes traffic-ridden. Roman town (Corinium AD 49) at junction of two Roman roads: Ermine Street and Fosse Way. Fine Roman antiquities dug up here, now in Corinium Museum, Park St. Superb silver in St John's Church. Abbey Estate (lawns, river, swan lake).

Cirencester Park is beautiful; 3000 acres freely open for walking and horse riding. Alexander Pope helped Earl of Bathurst lay out the estate. House not open. Polo ground.

On A433 at Kemble is Farm Museum.

At Bibury (on A433 from Burford), Arlington Mill: museum of antique farm machinery. Bibury trout farm (open March–October).

Barnsley (on A433) very attractive village with Norman church; William Morris called it 'most beautiful village in England.'

Near Ashton Keynes – 4 m SW Cirencester – is Cotswold Water Park; massive gravel-pit lakes; sailing, water-skiing, rowing, fishing, aquaplaning.

A429
Malmesbury
(11 m) B4040,
small road right
at Luckington to
Great Badminton
(9 m)

Old Bell, Abbey Row, Malmesbury (tel 2344): built on site of castle; medieval features, including spiral staircase. Host is classical scholar, chef Keith Joplin was head chef at the Old Ship, Brighton. Try Burgesses soup (chicken, asparagus, mushroom and prawns); good steak pudding. Lunch £5.50; dinner £7.50. House wine £4.50/litre (Argentinian). BB £14–23.50. DBB £19.50–22.

Apostle Spoon Restaurant, Market Cross, Malmesbury (tel 3129): in part of old abbey (13th century); meals £8–9. Wines from £4. Cellar bar with snacks. Shut Sunday evening.

Malmesbury, on a hill, was England's first borough in 880. In 1025 a monk of the abbey, Brother Oliver, tried to fly from the roof. He glided 200 yards, crashed and broke both legs. Remains of abbey now part of church. Pretty riverside walk from Flying Monk Hotel.

At Garsdon (2 m east) five of George Washington's ancestors buried in church. Abraham Lincoln's mother came from here. Great Badminton, a magnificent Palladian house, has belonged to the Dukes of Beaufort since built in the 17th century; contains fine paintings. Here the game Badminton was started in 18th century. Big stables; Badminton three-day event and trials held here in April. Open Wed pm June–Sept. (tel Badminton 202).

small road to B4040, across A46, on to A432 Chipping Sodbury, Old Sodbury small road to Dodington (8 m)

Chipping Sodbury: town hall has oak chest carved from solid trunk, weighs a ton. Market since Saxons.

Dodington House: striking neo-classical 18th-century house by James Wyatt, in 700-acre park laid out by

Capability Brown. Codrington family still own it. Little church open for brass-rubbing. Carriage rides round park, tropical fish centre, narrow-gauge railway, children's playground. Open weekends late April, daily end May–end August.

Just off A46, Dyrham Park: strange architectural mixture; French architect put a new front on a Tudor house. English architect built a back-to-back house on it Italian-style. Dutch furnishing and paintings. Some pieces belonged to Samuel Pepys. Fallow deer in park. National Trust. Park open all year (40p); house open most afternoons. April–September (£1.40), check times (Absom 2501).

Bath
on to A46 Bath
(10 m)

Bath is a gem of Europe still under-rated; plans are in hand to renew spa facilities. Superb elegance in streets and crescents of fine buildings in honey-coloured stone.

Hot springs gush quarter-million gallons of water daily at temperature of 49°C (120°F). Roman Great Bath still exists. Royal visitors went there for cures from early 1600s, but Bath was filthy and full of crooks. In 1703, Beau Nash, professional gambler and arbiter of extravagant fashion and manners, arrived from London, became Bath's master of ceremonies, setting standards of cleanliness, taste and manners, and inspired the Assembly and Pump Rooms. Ralph Allen, postmaster, improved transport and bought the stone quarries from which the lovely building stone came. Yorkshire architect John Wood gave Bath its Palladian style – after Palladio, the Italian who founded neo-classical architecture.

Try not to miss Royal Crescent; Pulteney Bridge, designed by Robert Adam with shops each side like Florence's Ponte-Vecchio; Lilliput Alley, where Sally

Bath
continued

Lunn sold her buns; costume museum, world's largest, in Assembly Rooms; carriage museum in Circus Mews; National Photography Centre and toy museum in Octagon; Holburne Museum, fine collection of silver, porcelain, glass and paintings by Stubbs, Reynolds, Gainsborough; Queen Square, Wood's first masterpiece, where Jane Austen and Wordsworth lived.

Claverton Manor: museum of American history, including eighteen rooms of early American furniture.

Prior Park; one of Britain's greatest Palladian houses, built by Wood for stone-quarry owner Ralph Allen. Now a Roman Catholic school; contents lack interest.

Hotels and restaurants
Bath has wide choice of hotels, guest houses and restaurants of every price, including some very good expensive places:

The Canary, 3 Queen St (tel 24846): pretty, delightful light lunch and snack café open daytime. Simon, son of owner Mary Davis, makes cakes and pastries; salads, light dishes 12 noon–2pm. Lunch £2–3. Wine.

Clarets Wine Bar, 4 Kingsmead Square (tel 66688): cellar with summer tables in Georgian square; imaginative bar meals; try potted crab, mushrooms; veg and cheese casserole; chicken Kiev; good desserts. Meals £3–8. Wines from £3.95. Closed Sunday evening.

Beaujolais, Chapel Row, Queen Square (tel 23417): owners Philippe Wall and Jean-Pierre Auge call it 'a little France in the heart of Bath'. But not, alas, with French prices. Informal and friendly, true look of a small bistro – I find it delightful; true onion soup, good fish and sauces. Meals around £10, but worth it. Shut Sundays, Bank Holidays.

Paragon Wine Bar, 1a The Paragon (tel 63141): really excellent snacks, fresh-made tarts, flans, pies. Shut Sunday, Monday.

Park Tavern, 3 Park Lane (tel 25174): outstanding bar dishes 45p–£2.75 except Sun. Real ales, wine.

Woods, 9 Alfred St (tel 314812): cheerful, currently fashionable; good soups, crudités (why can't we have raw veg more often in Britain?); some imaginative fairly simple dishes; inevitable cheesecake and syllabub. Good value. Lunch £3–5; dinner FP £4, card £6. Shut Sunday.

Old Mill, Toll Bridge Rd, Batheaston (tel 858476): on Avon river banks, with views, bright bedrooms; Italian chef-owner trained in France; try Cotswold lamb, venison; panzerotti alla Romana (ravioli with meat, chicken, mushroom sauce); FP meals good value. Lunch £5.25; dinner £7.50; card around £9. Wines £4.25 to £50 Château d'Yquem '61. BB £11–14. SB (winter/autumn).

Bath
continued

Pratt's Hotel, South Parade (tel 60441): in original John Wood house in famous cul-de-sac in city centre; greatly improved recently, snug, homely décor; FP dinner £5.45, plus extra for special dishes; try chicken Forestdale (breast in mushroom and garlic). Wine £3.25–22. BB £14.50–17; DBB £21. SB.

Royal York, George St (tel 61541): Queen Victoria stayed here before her coronation and her room is unchanged. Other bedrooms modernized; once a coaching inn. Spacious, dignified. Chef Terry McNeill once produced fifty recipes using brandy! Try his pork kebab or chicken with pineapple and sauerkraut. FP meals good value – lunch £4, dinner £5; card £8.50. Good-value wines from £4.

Villa Magdala, Henrietta Rd (tel 25836): well-run BB, only guest house in quiet area. BB £10–14.

At Hinton Charterhouse (3 m B3110), Homewood Park (tel Limpley Stoke 2643): pricey and very good 'restaurant with rooms'; opened recently by Stephen and Penny Ross (ex-Pobjoys, Bath); ten-acre park with riding stables next door. Superb unpretentious cooking; try starters smoked duckling, smoked trout mousse wrapped in smoked salmon, or Burgundian fish 'stew'; best English-type main courses (chicken, freshest fish, lamb, steak) with individual sauces or garnishes; do try pie of venison with chestnuts in port. Meals around £12 – good value. BB £17.50–25.

---

road west through Newton St Loe, Stanton Prior to join A368 to Chelwood, 2 miles on, take small road right to Chew Magna; B3114 past Chew Valley Lake to join A368 for ½ mile to Compton Martin, B3371, left on B3135 to Priddy; right on local road to Wookey Hall caves and Wells (27 m)

Miner's Arms, Priddy, (tel Priddy 217): once used by lead miners and drovers; now gastronomic restaurant with rooms. Own beer and

Chew Magna, fascinating village with streams spanned by old bridges, including fine 15th-century tun bridge. Outside is ale house where the church brewed and sold ale for parish funds – sensible. Now old inns – Pelican, Bear and Swan, and Queen's Arms – serve sustenance.

Chew Valley Lake: pleasant reservoir with fine trout fishing (boats for hire). The route takes you into Mendip Hills, with gorges and rocks, solitude. Here, sheltering from a storm, 18th-century parson Augustus Toplady wrote the hymn 'Rock of Ages'.

home-reared snails (served with Somerset cider sauce); good vegetables, meals around £9; Sunday lunch (roast) £4.50. BB (3 rooms only) £8. Lunch Suns only.

At Wells, Crown Hotel and Reed's restaurant, Market Place (tel 73457): historic inn, 1450. In 1695 Quaker William Penn arrested for preaching to large crowd from window; some four-poster beds; bar snacks £1–3; dinner £7–9; wines from £2.95; Saturday special 4 courses, wine, coffee, £18 for two. BB £13–16. SB.

Ancient Gate House, Sadler St (tel 72029): charming inn – one of England's oldest, in cathedral precincts, incorporates old city gate; fine old furnishings; carved four-poster beds; Italian owner and chef, English and Italian dishes: FP meals £6.50; wines: Valpolicella, Soave/£3.45 litre. BB £10–12.50. SB (Oct–end March).

Tor Guest House, Tor St (tel 72322): useful overnight, unlicensed; dinner £3.50; BB from £6.30.

At Shepton Mallet (A371 4 m), Bowlish House (tel 2022): worth a detour – very successful. Two fixed-price menus including wine; good imaginative cooking; ingredients bought fresh, locally, from trawler owner and dairy farm. Own wine business supplies thirty other restaurants. FP meals *for two* including wine £17–22. 19 wines at £2 a bottle! Fine, dearer list, plus many sweet dessert wines by glass. BB £22 *for two*: don't go alone!

Priddy, high and remote, prehistoric grave. In caves nearby remains found of bears, wolves, lemmings and Neolithic man.

Wookey Hole: caves bored by river Axe through limestone over 60,000 years. Boats to first three chambers. Explorers have reached another seventeen. Grand Cave floodlit, lighting gorgeous stalactites and stalagmites. Witch of Wookey massive stalagmite with local legend. The Hole was occupied by Iron Age people, nearby Hyena Cave by Stone Age hunters of mammoths, rhinos, lions and bears. Museum and Caves open daily.

Ebbor Gorge nearby has footpaths, picnic spots – a memorial to Winston Churchill.

I love Wells. It is two separate cities – modern outer part with too much traffic; inner peace around medieval 12th/14th-century cathedral. Interesting church with 400 statues of saints, angels and prophets on west front; Great Clock (1380 – one of oldest in Britain). At the hour, figures of four knights joust and one is unseated. Inside church, attractive inverted pillars built in 1338 when tower started to list. Superb chapter house with stone seats for the canons. Bishops Palace (fortified 1206), partly ruined. Swans in moat sometimes ring bell when hungry, as they have for centuries. Information Office in Town Hall open seven days a week in summer (tel 73026). Wells makes splendid Somerset cheese.

A39 Glastonbury (6 m)

Beckets Inn, Glastonbury (tel 32928): small Queen Anne inn, simple but splendid value; bar meals with good choice; dinner in restaurant or garden, 3 full courses £2–4. BB double rooms only £15 for two.

George and Pilgrims, (tel 31146): superb 15th-century inn with flagstone passage, genuine beams and choice of bedrooms – old and new. Good Anglo-French cooking; home-made bread. Hot or cold bar meals (good pâté); try egg baked in cheese, pigeon pie, fresh salmon; local farm cheese, butter; real ale; wine list includes English wines; meals £4–9. BB £15–17. Highly recommended.

Chalice Hill, Dod Lane (tel 31361): vegetarian and no wines served; I have not tried it; Georgian manor house with heated indoor pool (summer). Room for games and meditation called 'Sanctuary of Holy Grail'. Vegetarian dinner £5; BB £7–12.

A quiet market town steeped in our early history and legend of King Arthur. Only fragments remain of the abbey to which medieval pilgrims travelled. Here, Joseph of Arimathea came to convert the English; he leaned on his staff, it rooted and flowered – a symbol that he should set up a church. Holiest shrine in Britain until fire destroyed it in 1184. They say that he buried the Holy Grail at the foot of Glastonbury Tor (hill), and that Glastonbury, then amid marshy lakes, was the Isle of Avalon sought by King Arthur. Arthur was buried there after his final battle; and so was his Queen Guinevere, who had become Abbess of Amesbury. In 1191 monks of Glastonbury Abbey, guided by a vision, found their graves. They also say that Arthur only sleeps, and that, like Drake, he will arise when England needs him. So don't be too surprised if you meet him soon on Glastonbury Tor.

A39 Bridgwater (15 m)

Royal Clarence, Cornhill (tel 55196): old coaching inn; Czech chef; superb buffet – hot dishes in evening; salads and vegetables grown in hotel garden; also restaurant; meals around £6.50. BB £12–19.

At Holford, 10 m west on A39, Combe House (tel Holford 382): Danish owner-chef Richard Bjergfelt won Chef of the Year as graduate at Westminster College, then worked at Claridges, Browns Hotel and Director's Club; 4-course English dinner good

Quiet quay with modern shops on the river recalls days when Bridgwater was a rival port to Bristol. Small industrial town, but pleasant. Headquarters of Duke of Monmouth, possibly Charles II's son, who proclaimed himself King here in 1685 before losing the Battle of Sedgemoor to King James and his head at the Tower. House of Robert Blake, Cromwell's brilliant admiral, now a museum. (Blake St).

value at £5.50 (menu changes daily). 17th-century charming house, lovely views; five acres; riding stables nearby. BB £11–14. SB.

**A38, A361
Taunton (9 m)**

County Hotel, East St (tel 87651): nice Trust House Forte hotel; food good value in lovely dining room, rooms rather dear, but good. FP lunch £4.50, dinner £5; card £5.50–10. Bed £15.50–21 without breakfast; DBB £20.

Castle, Castle Green (tel 72671): a Prestige Hotel, nearest we have to Château Hotel de France. A formidable-looking pile, scene of historic dramas. Duke of Monmouth's officers besported themselves before the Battle of Sedgemoor; after, Judge Jeffreys held his 'Bloody Assize' there. Now peaceful with beautiful bedrooms, attractive garden, splendid wine cellar. Such delights cost money; but meals excellent value; £6.50–10; BB £20–53 (suite with lounge). SB.

In 1497 Perkin Warbeck seized Taunton and declared himself King Richard IV; the town was involved in bitter struggles of Civil War and Monmouth's Rebellion, when Judge Jeffreys sentenced 508 people to death. Now a lively commercial centre with fine old buildings. Norman castle contains good museum (historical, geological, dolls, birds, fishes).

Cider production: Sheppy's, Bradford on Tone (A38 3 m) has cider museum shop.

Telecommunications museum, North St, Taunton – telephones back to 1877.

West Somerset Railway, longest private railway in Britain, with steam and diesel railcars, runs Taunton, Watchet, Minehead.

**A361
Wiveliscombe,
Shillingford,
Bampton (20 m)**

Langley House, Langley Marsh, Wiveliscombe (tel 23318): Superb food in delightful atmosphere; McCullochs bought this country house in 1977. Comfortable bedrooms. Dinner FP 4-course £6.90; 5-course gourmet £9.78 (worth every penny); wines from French-bottled Bordeaux £4.75 to '67 Haut Brion £24.15. BB £12.36–15.80. Restaurant open daily March-Oct: Fri, Sat only Oct-March; hotel closed Oct-March. Gourmet weekends April, May, Sept, Oct.

Through vale of Taunton Dene. At Norton Fitzwarren (2 m from Taunton) is Taunton's big cider-making plant.

Bampton, market town on edge of Exmoor, has a stream running in conduit down its main street; it can attract traffic; sale of Exmoor ponies at end of October.

Bampton *continued*	At Bampton, Bark House, Oakford Green (B3222 toward Dulverton, left on A346) (tel Oakford 236): named because it was a tannery – dogs only by arrangement. Pleasant hotel; mostly grills with nice sauces and simpler dishes. Good soups, desserts. Meals £5–7. 40 bins wine from £3.45. BB £10–13.50. FP dinner £4.50 to residents. SB.	

B3222 Exebridge, B3223 Dulverton at crossroads (4 m) take local road right to Winsford (9 m)	At Dulverton, Carnarvon Arms Hotel (tel 23302): fishing centre, own salmon and trout water; clay pigeon shooting; heated pool. Comfortable; good bar snacks; good-value meals; FP £4.30 good choice; house wine £3.85; many under £6. BB £12.30–15. Three Acres Country House, Brushford, Dulverton (tel 23426): very comfortable, old style; good straight-forward cooking; FP dinner £6; BB £10. Rendezvous Restaurant, High St, Dulverton (tel 23613): Owner-chef Jean-François Prudon was trained in Lyon and Switzerland. His bistro with red-check tablecloths serves excellent English and French dishes; our 3-course lunch, including stuffed shoulder of lamb with three veg and coffee, was a bargain at £3.95. Dinner FP £7.20; card around £8, plus special dishes – lobster in garlic £9.95; frog legs £4.60; rich, beautiful sauces in tradition of Lyon. 29 wines. Closed Sun. Royal Oak, Winsford (tel	Dulverton: most attractive setting, in a ring of woods with rivers Barle and Exe flowing by. Charming tiny market place. Lorna Doone country. Southern gateway to Exmoor, rugged National Park stretching to the coast at Minehead and Coombe Martin. A land of heather-covered hills curving into valleys with rivers and streams, rich in trout, and salmon in lower reaches; here lives the last great herd of wild red deer in Britain. Hardy Exmoor ponies roam the hills and drink in the streams. Close, compact villages hide in the fold by the rivers, their white or grey stone houses often thatched. You will see a lot from your car, more if you park and walk for a while. At crossroad to Winsford, turn left (instead of right) to Tarr Steps. An ancient packhorse crossing of the river Barle, probably prehistoric. The massive stones are a mystery because they are not local and must have been brought here. Wimbleball Lake: reservoir

232): I went there first in 1948. Modernized since and posher – in different price grade. Beautiful thatched inn; chef admires fashionable *nouvelle cuisine*; I really prefer the old French sauces, but Ian Lawrence cooks very well. Dinner £8–12 – value, but pricey for a village inn. BB £14–18. Nov–March two nights DBB only. Trout fishing.

5 m from Dulverton and Winsford; brown and rainbow trout; fishing licence 75p a day from recreation area; boats for hire.

Winsford: lovely village round green on river Exe in beautiful country. Still has a ford. Ernest Bevin, trade union, Labour party and national wartime leader under Churchill, was born here; his mother was charlady at the Royal Oak.

---

through Winsford small road to join B3223 near Withypool, B3224 Exford Simonsbath (9 m)

At Withypool, Westerclose Country House (tel Exford 302): homely, quiet, superb views; English cooking, much home-grown produce; meals £6–7; wines £4.50–8. DBB £13–14.

Simonsbath House Hotel (tel Exford 259): one of the best reasonably priced hotels we have found in Britain. In a 1654 house, gracious living

Withypool is fishing centre – here R. D. Blackmoore wrote *Lorna Doone*. Fishing licences from Royal Oak Inn.

Exford: take B3224 east for 4 m, local road left to Dunkery Beacon (short walk to top); 1707 ft, highest point on Exmoor; fine views, even to Welsh coast.

Simonsbath: heart of Exmoor, best centre for

Simonsbath
continued

in elegant surroundings. Fine china, silver cutlery, sparkling crystal, bedrooms. Garden, squash court, river. Excellent cooking, using fresh food. Lunch at £5.50 could include local Taw salmon 'from river last night'; dinner £8.50, worth every penny. Fair wine list from £4.60/litre house wine. BB £14.50–23; DBB £21.50–30.

Emmetts Grange Farm (tel Exford 282): bargain. Don't go if slimming; farm-made butter, cream used in meals. Bring your own wine. Dinner £5.75, BB £7.

exploring. 1½ m north on B3223 road crosses infant river Exe.

Cloven Rocks (1 m east, south of B3223) is where in *Lorna Doone* Jan Ridd defeated robber Carver Doone, who sank into the bog.

B3358 Challacombe, right on B3226, A399 Combe Martin, Ilfracombe

At Parracombe, Woody Bay Hotel (tel Parracombe 264): lovely position in woods overlooking rocky cove; nice old house, recently renovated; some four-poster beds; FP dinner good value £6; also card £8–10; BB £14.50–15.50. SB.

At Combe Martin, Higher Leigh Manor (tel 2486): unconventional hotel; 16th-century house in fourteen acres with fine trees and gardens; model railway running through model towns; and Woolly Monkey Sanctuary – all open to public also. Home-cooked foods; BB £12.80–15.75; with 4-course dinner £14.80–17.75. SB (spring, autumn); shut mid Nov–mid March.

Saffron House, King St (tel 3521): quite a bargain; prettily furnished, good facilities. Heated pool; bar; varied, plentiful plain cooking. Dinner £3.50–4; eight wines under £3.10; BB

Parracombe: village of steep streets mentioned in Domesday Book. Medieval church one of the oldest not 'restored' by Victorians. Saved from destruction by John Ruskin. (1 m right off B3226 at Blackmoor Gate.)

Arlington Court (3 m left at Blackmoor Gate): National Trust house, 1822 in fine park grazed by Shetland ponies and Jacob sheep; house contains small furniture, model ships, shells, pewter, costumes. Carriage collection includes Queen Victoria's pony-drawn bath chair; grounds open each day; house Tues–Sun, April–end Oct.

Combe Martin: in a combe beside pretty bay, sheltered, mild climate; two dominating hills called Little and Great Hangman. Little sand-and-shingle beach; Pack of Cards Inn (17th-century folly).

£6–7.50; DBB £10–11.50. Optional children's meal 5pm. Shut Oct.

Langley Country Hotel, Langley Rd (tel Ilfracombe 62629): in big garden, oldest house in town – Elizabethan; two of Nelson's favourite officers owned it later; dinner £5 – 4 courses, good value. BB £7–12. Solarium.

Granville, Granville Rd (tel 62015): ugly Victorian fortress with magnificent coast views; very good value; full lunch, including roast £2.75; 4-course dinner £4.75; wines from £3; BB £8.50; DBB £12.50.

Ilfracombe: fishing village which started to be a resort by 1830; steep narrow roads lead down to its pleasant harbour; parks and gardens packed with flowers; Torrs Walk to west gives superb views. On Lantern Hill above pier a chapel burns a light for sailors as it has for 700 years. Caravan country inland.

B3231, crossing B3343, and on to Croyde

Little Beach Hotel, Woolacombe (tel 870398): Edwardian house with fine sea views. Run by ex-computer man and ex-BBC tv editor, who cooks well; try stuffed leg of lamb, Devonshire squab pie; dinner £6.25; house wines £3.50. DBB £14.30–19.30.

Putsborough Sands Hotel, 1 m N of Croyde (tel Croyde 890555): lovely sea views; family-run; computerized solarium for tanning, indoor pool; 4-course dinner with fair choice £6.90; BB £9.20–16. DBB £15–22. Shut end Sept–Easter.

Right on B3343 is Woolacombe, with 3 m of sand beach for swimming and surfing; sandy coves nearby. Much of the coast left to the National Trust by the Chichester family (Sir Francis Chichester's relations).

Croyde: sand and dunes; shallow water; surf. Gem museum with demonstrations of cutting and polishing stones found on Devon beaches.

B3231 Braunton, A361 Barnstaple (9 m)

At North Buckland, 2 m on A361 N of Braunton, Deneham Farm (tel Croyde 890297): working farm of 160 acres; DBB £11; SB.

Barnstaple, Lynwood House, Bishops Tawton Rd (tel 3695): pricey but very good; John and Ruth Roberts

Church dedicated to an Irish saint, Brannoc, contains interesting carvings including animals; dunes nearby are nature reserve.

Barnstaple: before the river Taw silted up, busy port; business was done at Queen Anne's Walk, impressive

Barnstaple continued	specialize in seafoods, mostly local; try pot of seafood thermidor; cold seafood platter; local salmon, trout, sole, skate; local game and steaks; I had superb large lobster – cost £9. Meals £9–12. Closed Sun; Sat lunch.	great colonnaded and carved building near river; covered pannier market, Butchers' Row (arcaded shops), parish church with 17th-century twisted spire; fine Long Bridge, sixteen arches, 13th century, widened. Highwayman Tom Faggus leapt over it (*Lorna Doone* again). Visits possible to pottery (red clay). Try Newport Pottery, Newport Rd.
A39 Bideford (9 m)	At Northam (A39), Yeoldon House (tel Bideford 4400): cordon bleu chef trained at Tante Marie, cooks well. Home-made fresh dishes; try pâtés, game. Dinner FP £7.95; £9 (5 courses). BB £8.50. SB (gourmet weekends Oct–May). The Mount, Northdown Rd: simple, cheap. BB £5.50–7; DBB £10.50. Riversford, Limers Lane (tel 4239): country house in three acres overlooking river; comfortable, friendly; solarium; English cooking; meals FP £6, card £7; DBB £14.75–17.70	Attractive, but summer traffic problems. Third port of Britain in 16th century when Bideford men crewed Grenville's *Revenge*, which fought fifteen Spanish ships for fifteen hours in 1591. Small craft still land at tree-lined quay from which narrow streets climb. Bridge with sixteen arches (all different widths) built 1460, widened recently. Burton Art Gallery (mostly modern); 17th-century Royal Hotel – where Charles Kingsley wrote novel *Westward Ho!* – has period ceiling.
A386 Appledore small roads to Abbotsham, join A39 at Fairy Cross, Horns Cross, Buck's Cross, B3237 to Clovelly (15 m)	Hoops Inn, Horns Cross (tel Horns Cross 222): 13th-century stone and thatch; superb inn, deservedly recommended by all guides especially US *Holiday* magazine, so book ahead. Antiques, beams, old fireplaces; one four-poster. Fine cooking. Torridge river salmon, fish from the bay. Meals FP £6 (good value), card £9; wines £3.65–20, Bardolino £3.85. BB £7.15 (winter), £15+ (midsummer). SB 1 Oct–31 May.	Appledore: charming old shipbuilding centre between rivers Taw and Torridge, revived by recent covered dock. *Golden Hind* replica built here in 1969. Narrow street, old fishermen's houses; lobster pots and nets on quayside. Maritime museum. Clovelly: stepped streets tumble sharply to the sea down cliffside; donkeys still carry goods as cars cannot enter tiny stone-walled harbour; unique – and crowded July, August.

Foxdown Manor, Horns Cross (small road left off A39) (tel 325): secluded country house in lovely grounds 1 m from sea: fine cooking. Dinner 6 courses FP £8; wines from ten countries; house wine £2.90. Swimming pool, sauna. BB £9–16, DBB £14.28. Shut mid Nov–mid March.

At Buckland Brewer, 2 m Horns Cross, Coach and Horses (tel Horns Cross 395): 13th-century, thatched coaching inn; resident ghost; cheap bar meals; restaurant card £6.50. BB £7–8.50.

At Clovelly, New Inn (tel 303): famous pub; good bar snacks; restaurant meals FP £3.25 or lobster, sole in season (closed lunch outside season); wines from £2.95; real ale. BB £8.50–9.50.

Red Lion, beside harbour (tel 237): meals around £4. BB £8.50.

Charles Kingsley's father was rector. Iron Age fort with twenty-acre earthworks just inland. Said to have been home of a family of cannibals who ate 1000 people, mostly pickled. They were burned alive.

---

local roads to Hartland Point, Stoke, Hartland Quay to A39 by Hartland Forest, Kirkhampton, Bude

Hartland Quay Hotel (tel Hartland 371): Atlantic views, swimming pool; reasonable prices: meals £4–5; BB £8.50. Shut mid Nov–mid March.

Meddon (just off A39 by Hartland Forest), Meddon Court (tel Morwenstow 439): old stone farmhouse. BB £6.50; DBB £9.50.

At Bude, Strand Hotel (tel Bude 3222): attractively set by river; many bedrooms have sea views, all have baths. Trust House Forte; lunch card £3–6; dinner FP £4.95; card £9.

Hotel Penarvor, Crooklete Beach (tel 2036): beside surf sand beach; cheerful, light,

Hartland Point cliffs drop sheer to the sea; sometimes Lundy Isle is visible. Quay built by company including Drake and Raleigh, now enjoyed by geologists and rock-hounds exploring among rows of jagged rocks; sand at low tide. Good fishing.

Just south, Morwenstow, Cornwall's northernmost parish, was once base for wreckers luring ships with false lights on to rocks to plunder them; in churchyard is figurehead of *Caledonia*, wrecked in 1843, drowning forty men. Vicar here was poet R. S. Hawker 1803–75 ('and shall Trelawney die?

Bude
continued

comfortable. Meals average £6.50. BB £8.60–10.80. DBB £12–15. SB (except July, Aug).

At Marhamchurch, A39 S, Bullers' Arms, (tel Widemouth Bay 277): fine old pub with good extension; long list of bar meals, plus restaurant (eves, Sun lunch); dinner from £6; BB £7.50–10. Dance every Sat; jazz fans – Chris Barber and Acker Bilk annual visitors.

here's 20,000 Cornishmen shall know the reason why'). He invented Harvest Festival.

Bude: golden sands flanked by spectacular cliffs have lured holidaymakers, including surfers. Part of old canal used for boating.

Twin town Stratton, with steep streets, more attractive. Here lived 7 ft 4 in giant who fought for Royalists at nearby Stamford Hill in 1643.

---

local coast road by Widemouth Bay, Crackington Haven, on to B3263 to Boscastle, Tintagel (15 m)

At Boscastle, Bottreaux House (tel 231): value; good service, imaginative dishes on card. Comfortable bedrooms. Meals FP £5.25; card £7–8; try pork fillets in sherry sauce with spiced oranges, or local lobster; wines from £3. BB £9.50–11. SB (3 or 5 nights).

St Christopher's Country House (tel Boscastle 412): friendly young couple offer very good value meals; try local salmon trout with lemon and herb stuffing; beef with walnuts and celery; peaches stuffed with ham. Dinner FP £4.50. No bar (pub opposite); wines from £3.40. BB £7.50–10. Open March–Nov.

At Treknow, 1 m S Tintagel, Atlantic View Hotel (tel Tintagel 221): away from crowds; superb clifftop sea view; steps to beach; heated pool. Enthusiastic young couple run hotel; exceptional value, especially spring breaks. Dinner 4 courses + coffee FP £6. Wines £3.50–12.50. BB £8–14. Baby listening. Open 1 March–31 Oct, Christmas. SB (except July, Aug).

After Bude's beaches, a curve of cliffs to Tintagel, with stark walls dropping to jagged rocks below. Spectacular, and awesome when Atlantic rollers are fierce. Between high cliffs the sea enters Boscastle harbour in a dog leg around stone jetty where once ships loaded slate from quarries; 100-ton vessels were pulled in by rowing boats and horses ashore; 'Devil's bellows' – name for sound of the sea rushing through a blowhole in cliff in a cloud of white spray an hour before low tide. Boscastle stands up the cliffs – a dramatic spot. Once had eighteen inns; now only three.

Thomas Hardy, as architect working on nearby church, married the vicar's sister-in-law – his snobbish first wife who tried to get *Jude the Obscure* banned as obscene. Turner painted the harbour – inevitably in a storm. Witchcraft museum.

Tintagel: steeped in romance of King Arthur, its ruined castle, almost severed from the mainland by the sea, looks magnificently

At Trenale, 1 m off B3263, Trebrea Lodge (tel Tintagel 410): superb old country house; lovely views; chintzy bedrooms; good English cooking; dinner FP £4.60; 4 house wines £4/litre; BB £11.50. DBB £12.90; good value.

Trebarwith Strand Hotel (tel Tintagel 326): almost on beach; run by four young people. Good cooking, local food: mussels, dabs, Cornish rarebit. Meals SP £5.75; card £6.50; house wine £3.60/litre, several under £4. BB £9.50–10.60. Also cheap House on the Strand restaurant for snacks, or meals around £3.50.

Mill House Inn, Trebarwith (tel Tintagel 200): attractive inn, converted cornmill; cosy bedrooms; children banned under 7 years. Local seafood and shellfish; meat and veg from local farms. Meals: card £7.15. House wine £1.95/½ litre; Muscadet £4.05; '70 Richebourg £37.95. BB £9.20–12.19. No single rooms.

mysterious in Atlantic sunsets. Prince Charles, as Duke of Cornwall, owns the castle. Alas, 12th-century date of castle clashes with legend. I prefer the legend. Modern Hall of Chivalry nicer inside than tourist exterior promises; impressive stained glass and interior colour. Tintagel gets crowded. Old Post Office is in tiny old manor house.

Bossiney, a separate place, once had Francis Drake as its MP. Nice sand beach; puffins live on Lye Rock.

Trebarwith Strand, S of Tintagel: fine sands used for surfing (lifeguards in season). Old Delabole slate quarry – 1½ m round, 500 ft deep; see hand-splitting of slate and museum of geology and history.

B3263 Slaughter Bridge, B3314 to just past Pendoggett, right to Port Isaac. Small road to Trelights, Port Quin, back to B3314 to Polzeath, Trebetherick, Wadebridge (24 m)

Port Gaverne Hotel, near Port Isaac (tel Port Isaac 244): old inn well kept. Owner Fred Rose is American, chef Ian Brodey (weighs 20 stone) is Cornish cooks splendidly, making full use of local seafood and cream. Try crab in cheese sauce, local smoked mackerel, crab soup; lobster; chicken breasts in cream, sherry, pimento. Dinner FP £6.50; card around £10; fair wine list £3.50 up; BB £11.50–16.50; SB (except summer).

Port Isaac: 'postcard' Cornish fishing village; strict parking control has saved it from ruin; still a working village; mostly crab and lobster caught, kept in harbour pounds; area is lovely April, May, June with wild flowers in hedgerows and roads uncluttered. One narrow alley called Squeezy-Belly Alley. I failed the test.

Port Quin: picturesque deserted village, until recently. Men out fishing

Port Isaac
continued

Treselda, 14 Tintagel Terrace, Port Isaac (tel 477): simple guest house, sea views, good value; people return annually; children and dogs welcome; English cooking; FP menu £4; BB £6.

Harbour Café, Port Isaac (tel 272): historic building, using old ship's timbers; for sale when we last called; real local dishes, try Cornish fish pie. Wines: snacks. FP menu £4.50.

Wheelhouse, Harbour Port Isaac (tel 226): old, very attractive; platter lunches – single dish £1.50–2.90; dinner: card £7–9.

were lost in a storm at end of last century, women and children then driven out by poverty; now houses being renovated – but still ghostly.

Wadebridge: pleasant market town with 320 ft bridge over river Camel; 15th-century, said to rest on bales of wool to hold against river mud.

A39, A389
Padstow B3276
Bedruthan Steps,
Newquay (20 m)

At Padstow, Treglos Hotel, Constantine Bay (tel Padstow 520727): traditional English hotel; grounds overlooking bay; good chef (Paul Becker); try braised duckling with figs, onions brandy; frog legs in lobster sauce, mushrooms; scampi in puff pastry; sole in lobster sauce with prawns; meals 7-course FP £7.25, card from £8. BB £14.50–21. DBB £18–24. Central heating, log fires, charming heated indoor swimming pool opening on to lawns.

Newquay has hotels, guest houses, restaurants of all sizes, types and prices. Many will book only by the week in summer; overnight accommodation depends on available beds; so consult the Information Centre, Cliff Rd (tel 4558/2119/2716/2822).

At Pentire, nr Newquay; Corisande Manor, Riverside Ave (tel Newquay 4557): turreted headland hotel with direct access to Gannel

Padstow: old town with another attractive harbour on river Camel; labyrinth of crooked sloping streets. 16th-century Raleigh Court on quay is where Sir Walter held court. 13th- to 15th-century church. Prideaux Place (medieval and Tudor, with towers). Harbour silted up after local man accidentally shot a mermaid with an arrow. Tropical bird gardens. At Bedruthan Steps, cliffs look down to sand and rocks which were stepping stones for a local giant; steps closed – too dangerous.

St Mawgan (4 m N of Newquay); village in wooded valley; retreat from midsummer resort crowds; fine carvings in church; early Christian cross in churchyard from days when Romans fled from Britain (5th century) and Celtic saints invaded Cornwall.

sands; family run; meals good value; owner-chef David Painter cooks well and traditionally. Full bar lunches with choice; dinner FP £5.25 (4 courses); house wine £2.50. BB £7–9.50; DBB £10.75–14. Solarium. SB except midsummer. Shut Oct–end April.

Newquay: happy, attractive resort crowded midsummer; ten beaches of firm yellow sand. Towan is most sheltered; some used for international surfing. Take care if bathing on these. White stone Huers' Tower, like Algarve cottage, used as lookout for pilchard shoals until they mysteriously disappeared. Trenance gardens has a Zoo.

Trerice, Elizabethan manor (1572) built for Arundel family; fine ceilings and fireplaces; open April–end Oct; 11am–5.30pm.

A3075 right to Cubert, small road to Perranporth (6 m)

Cubert: Wesley preached here, in probably oldest chapel in Cornwall; now a licensed restaurant.

Perranporth: 3 m of sand (surfing) and dunes; caravans; St Piran built a church in 6th century, sand covered it, then covered a new one nearby. Dug out in 1835, it contained three beheaded skeletons. Hang gliding, sand yachting. Boating lake.

B3285 St Agnes, B3277, then right to Mount Hawke, Mawla, follow signposts on to B3300 to Portreath (14 m)

Portreath: little old port with gently sloping deep sands; rock pools each side; cave with pool at low tide; Tolgus tin mill with tin mining museum.

4 m inland by B3300, Gwennap Pit: natural amphitheatre where Wesley preached, 1762; services still held here.

B3301 Gwithian,
Hayle, A30, then
soon right to
Lelant, St Ives
(14 m)

Steep road with Alpine-like
bends along National Trust
clifftops. Beach coves below
where Atlantic seals live.

Hayle: superb estuary sands;
Bird Paradise devoted to
exotic birds including
endangered species;
children's zoo, 10am–dusk.
Local pub 'Jolly Parrot'. 2 m,
Lelant model village.

At St Ives, Karenza Hotel,
Headland Rd, Carbis Bay (tel
Penzance 795294): lovely
views on to sand beach and
along coast; superb clifftop
gardens; swimming pool;
railway nearby. Very good
value; 4-course dinner with
coffee and fair choice of
courses FP £5. BB £9.50–
14.50; DBB £14–18. Shut mid
Oct–early March.

Trecarrell Hotel, Carthew
Terrace (tel St Ives 795707):
pleasant hotel overlooking
bay; bright décor; good
value. 4-course dinner £4.25,
card £1–3 extra; house wine
bottled in France £2.85. BB
£7–14.50; DBB £8.50–16.60.

Garrack Hotel (tel St Ives
6199): tricky to find, so ask;
fine family-run hotel; son
Michael trained at Claridges;
chef Graham Jones ex-Ecu
de France, London. FP dinner
(4-course) £6 is a bargain;
card £8–10; special shellfish
menu. Wines: some under
£4; policy; 'better the wine,
better the bargain'. BB £8–
15.50, SB (spring, autumn).
Shut mid Oct–Easter.

Glan Mor, Trewidden Rd (tel
794182): useful for
overnights; BB £5.50.

St Ives: sculptress Barbara
Hepworth and painter Ben
Nicholson opened Penwith
Gallery here 1949. Now there
is a Hepworth museum, and
visiting amateurs try their
hand at sketching or
painting. Whistler and Sickert
first made it an art colony,
and a glance at the cobbled
streets and old cottages will
tell you why. Alas, tight
packed with people in late
July and August.

Perkin Warbeck landed here
in 1497, was proclaimed
Richard IV, marched on
London and got as far as
Taunton. Museum of
cinematography.——

B3306 Zennor,
St Just (15 m)

Bosweddon House, Cape Cornwall, St Just (tel Penzance 788733): friendly, comfortable, homely, but no children under 7; dinner FP £5. BB £7–8. DBB £11.50–12.65. Shut Nov–Feb.

Zennor: on bench in chapel a mermaid is carved; she heard a chorister sing and lured him into the sea. He can still be heard singing to her under the waves. Wayside Folk Museum of crafts and archaeology.

1 m N St Just, Pendeen: tin mining museum.

3 m N St Just, Chun Castle: Iron Age hill fort and stone burial chambers (500 BC or much earlier).

St Just: westernmost town in Britain; impressive coast scenery; antiquities; medieval amphitheatre.

A30 Land's End
(5 m)

At Sennen Cove, down narrow road from Sennen, Old Success Inn (tel Sennen 232): happy memories of my well-squandered youth. Road's-width from sands; 17th-century fisherman's pub remodelled into hotel but still used by fishermen (Charlie's Bar). Dinner FP £6.90. Good bar snacks. BB £9.20–11.00. Shut two weeks end Oct.

Sennen, westernmost English village. Land's End, commercialized and rather tawdry; turn your back and look out to sea to Longships Lighthouse.

B3315
Mousehole,
Newlyn,
Penzance (11 m)

Cairn Dhu, Raginnis Hill, Mousehole (tel 233): highly praised; old English recipes (pork and apple pie); bedrooms with sea views, 4-course meals FP £6.50; card £7. BB £9–17. SB (low season).

Smugglers, Newlyn Harbour (tel Penzance 4207): ancient inn, sea views most rooms; good cold buffets; dinner choice extensive (try pork in cream and Marsala wine); card £5–8. BB £9–11.

At Penzance, Admiral Benbow, Chapel St (tel 4207): artist and deep-sea diver Roland Morris has brought up from shipwrecks around Scilly Rock treasures now spread around the world's museums. He found the treasures of Admiral Cloudesley Shovel's flagship *Association*, laden with Spanish loot. He bought the derelict inn, Admiral Benbow, old smuggling headquarters, during Napoleonic Wars, and renovated it as a pub-restaurant and museum of relics. So fish and décor both caught locally. Splendid seafood. Wines from £3.25 with interesting 'bin ends' – not smuggled. Dinner FP £8; buffet bar lunch. Resident ghost called Arabella.

Enzo, Newbridge (tel Penzance 3777): chef-owner Vicenzo Mauro from Capri was trained in Italy, Switzerland and Claridges (London). Makes his own pasta – superb; cooks local scallops in tasty sauce of cream, apple, artichoke, mushroom. Meals £6–7.50; fair wine.

Porthcurno: pleasant spot with low-tide sands round to Logan Rock; in 1824 sailors pushed it into cleft; public outcry caused them to replace it at officers' expense; 'logan' comes from 'log' (to rock); this one doesn't.

Minack Open Air Theatre on clifftop; started in '30s by girl in her garden; backcloth of sea; take cushion and warm coat. Dripping shipwrecked sailors once appeared over clifftop during performance of *The Tempest*.

Mousehole (pronounced Mowzell): superb scene but crowded high summer; colour-washed, granite houses round harbour still draped with fishing nets.

Newlyn: fishing port, old houses up steep hill; artists found it ten years ago (Laura Knight, Frank Bramley, Munnings – see works in Passmore Edwards Museum).

Penzance: pleasant port; superb gardens, 2 m NW – Trenwainton, sea views, shrubs, flowers which grow nowhere else in Britain. Age of Steam Museum – woods, lawns, lakes; rail relics, models, steam train rides, boating lake.

Lovely sweep of bay with St Michael's Mount, island said to have been part of King Arthur's lost land of Lyonesse (now has 11th-century monastery; 15th-century fort). Climate very mild; tropical plants in seafront Morrab Gardens; statue to local lad Sir

Trevaylor, Cuival, Penzance (tel 2882): Georgian granite house in 10-acre garden; sea views. Co-chef was head of sixth form college. Veg from large kitchen gardens, local fish, cream; varied cooking. Dinner £5.50; house wines £2.50. BB £8.50–11.50.

Dunedin, Alexandra Rd, Penzance (tel 2652): simple Victorian family hotel; English cooking; value; dinner FP £3.50. BB £6–7.15. DBB £9–11.

Humphrey Davy, inventor of miners' safety lamp. Egyptian House in Chapel St is a Regency whimsy. Museum of Nautical Art. Port for steamers and British Airways helicopters to Isles of Scilly – superb isles with semi-tropical shrubs, beaches, gripping history of shipwrecks and smuggling; narcissi and daffodils often in bloom by Christmas; exported in millions. Everyone should visit Scilly once at least. Also reached by plane from Newquay.

A30 Marazion, A394, B3280 to Belubbus, Townshend, right on local road Godolphin Cross, on to B3302 Helston (16 m)

Goldithney (B3280): World of Entertainment mechanical music museum. Godolphin House: parts 15th/16th century; owned for 200 years by family who made fortune out of tin mining. Open June, July, Thurs 2–5pm; August–Sept, Tues–Thurs.

Helston: much publicized Furry Dance (Fair Dance) takes place only on 8 May. Interesting museum. In Coinagehall St is cottage of Bob Fitzsimmons, boxer, who in 1897 won world heavyweight championship by knocking out 'Gentleman Jim' Corbett of the US.

5 m S at Poldhu, Marconi's assistant broadcast first transatlantic radio message to Marconi in St John's, Newfoundland (1901). News of *Titanic* disaster first heard here. The Loe, 2 m SW, one of lakes where King Arthur's sword Excalibur was cast.

3 m N Poldark Mining Museum.

A3083 past Culdrose naval airfield, small lanes marked left to Gweek, Porth Navas, Mawnan Smith, past Penjerrick Gardens to Falmouth (12 m)

At Mawnan Smith, Meudon Hotel (tel Mawnan Smith 250541): Harry Pilgrim and family run a Prestige Hotel – independent, privately run but chosen as a special place for the Prestige booklet: higgledy-piggledy (old manor with modern extensions), country-house décor, tranquil, superb hanging gardens, possibly originally by Capability Brown, improved over last 35 years by present gardener Joseph Hojek. I love this hotel. Finest English cooking, especially local seafoods (lobster, oysters); not cheap but splendid value. Dinner £8; BB £10–16. SB (spring, autumn).

Left 1 m on A3083, Aero Park, Pemboa: hovercraft, old warplane controls, spy radios, log book of Dambuster Guy Gibson VC, brought up in nearby Porthleven.

Gweek: seal sanctuary. Feeding times 11am, 4.30pm.

4 m S Gweek on B3283, UHF station Goonhilly Downs: important satellite communication station; made history with first space satellite picture transmissions with US (1962).

Porth Navas: secretive creeks, shaded lanes; try Prince Charles' oysters – millions bred here; they belong to the Prince as Duke of Cornwall.

Glendurgan Gardens, nr Mawnan Smith: lovely semi-tropical shrubs, walled and water gardens; pines, laurel maze (temporarily closed for repairs 1981). Open March–end Oct, Mon, Weds, Fri 10.30–4.30pm.

Penjerrick Gardens, Budock: subtropical plants, spectacular in spring; open Weds, Sun, pm.

At Falmouth, Somerdale, Sea View Rd (tel 312566): well-run hotel in converted, extended house; good bedrooms; baby listening; plain English cooking, high standard; 5-course FP dinner £5.20; card £5–9. BB £10–13. SB, including golf and bowling breaks.

Green Bank Hotel (tel 312440): overlooking harbour, where packet captains met; ships' models and prints of old times;

Falmouth: delightful resort and port; huge attractive harbour where sailing ships used to call to find out where to go next ('Falmouth for Orders'). They jammed the wide estuary (Garrick Roads). 17th/19th-century fast packet boats sailed to the whole Empire with mail, so local paper *Falmouth Packet* scooped the world with news of Battle of Trafalgar; Falmouth still has fishing fleet: shark fishing for visitors; sailing. Excellent

recently renovated; nice bedrooms; comfortable. Same chef for eighteen years. Lunch FP £3; dinner £7.50 (4 courses, coffee). BB £15.50–22. SB (Oct–May).

Telford, 47 Melvill Rd (tel 314581): ordinary guest house, clean, simple, cheap; meals £2.50 (value); BB £5–5.75; DBB £7–8.25. Unlicensed.

beaches below cliffs; flowers and lawns. Henry VIII built Pendennis Castle and St Mawes opposite to defend harbour entrance. Magnificent views from castle tower. Last castle to fall to Cromwell, it sheltered Charles I's Queen Henrietta. Falmouth originally a village called Pennycomequick (Pen-Y-Cum-Cuic – 'head of creek'). Built up by Killigrew family who built Lizard Lighthouse and lived on piracy. One headed a Royal Commission into piracy while his wife ran a pirate fleet! Then they turned to smuggling and took tin to France. Attractive boat trips up Helford river.

A39 to outskirts of Penryhn, right to Flushing, local roads to Mylor Bridge small road to A39 at Perranarworthal (9 m)

Flushing: village opposite Falmouth where sea captains used to live. Houses were scene of balls and parties. Attractive but parking limited.

Mylor harbour was training centre for Royal Navy boy entrants. Now fine little yacht centre with repair facilities. Attractive holiday flatlets.

---

on A39, small road right at Devore signposted Trelissick Gardens and King Harry Ferry (cross on ferry) B3289 St Just, St Mawes (10 m)

Idle Rocks, St Mawes (tel St Mawes 771): I declare a sentimental interest over forty years. Since the Powell family took over, it has returned to former glory. Though overlooking busy quay, was first British hotel made a Relais du Silence by the French (peace, calm, tranquillity). Fine lunch bar snacks, especially seafood. Dinner FP 4 courses £7.50; card £8.50. Straightforward cooking. House wines Italian

Trelissick Gardens: National Trust; fine exotic and subtropical plants; 100 types of hydrangea; lovely camellias; views down river Fal; open Easter–Oct.

Queues for King Harry Ferry in midsummer but route round river Fal via Truro takes time in summer too. St Just in Roseland – tiny village by creek; 13th-century church; great variety plants, shrubs, trees. Very pretty. Pedants say Roseland means

St Mawes
continued

£2.35; nice French £3.25. BB £14–18; DBB £20–24. (some rooms in annexe).

Braganza, Grove Hill (tel St Mawes 270281): lovely old house with nice bedrooms; BB £7.50–9.50; dinner by request, only £5.

'heathland', from Cornish word 'rhos', but I prefer the legend that Henry VIII, here with Anne Boleyn, christened it when he saw the wild roses from his bedroom window.

St Mawes: fashionable, beautiful. Old fishing port with narrow, steep streets and a Mediterranean look to its harbour. Henry VIII built the castle towering over it. Sailing and fishing in sea or long inlet; crowded midsummer but protected position makes it a splendid hideaway, warm even in winter.

back along A3078, then local road to Portscatho, local road to Trewithian, A3078 for 2 m local road to Veryan, Portloe, local roads to Tregony B3287, A390 St Austell (16 m)

Rosevine, across bay from Portscatho (tel Portscatho 230); comfortable, lovely garden overlooking bay; quite pricey but worth it. Chef produces fine sauces; dinner FP 4 courses £8; BB £15–20.

Place Manor, St Anthony (tel Portscatho 447); delightful manor house in same family since 1600, run more like a country house party. Lawns run to sea wall with dinghy parking. Very quiet. Children welcome; DBB £13–16.

Portscatho: fine old fishing village, recently found by tourists but not yet taken over. Pleasant harbour; quiet hamlets nearby; walk along shore to superb Pendower Beach. Good sailing.

Veryan: lovely village; 2 m inland from bay. Regency thatched round houses were built so that the devil could find no corner to hide; they are still there.

Portloe: delightful fishing hamlet hidden in a tiny cove;

Carne Beach, Veryan (tel 279): super hotel, superbly situated just above safe bathing beach; swimming pool overlooks beach. Old house tastefully extended. Owners were butchers near Smithfield and specialize in fine quality meat and shellfish. Good value; dinner FP 4 courses £8.50. BB £11–22. DBB £17–29.

Luggar, Portloe (tel Veryan 322): 17th-century inn good bar lunches; dinner FP 4 courses £7.50; Sun lunch £4.50. BB £14–18; DBB £20–24. Shut Nov–mid Feb.

Tregony House, 15 Fore St (tel Tregony 671): partly 17th century; good value; dinner FP 4 courses £5.50; BB £7.50–8; DBB £11.50–12.

Porth Avallen Hotel, Sea Rd, Carlyon Bay, St Austell (tel Par 2802): a winner. Elegant house; fine gardens. Two menus: FP £5.75, 4 courses, excellent value; gastronomic FP £9.20, 5 courses, with splendid starters; wines Rioja £3 to high quality bin ends. BB £12–22. SB. Shut Christmas.

cosy and usually warm in winter.

3 m along coast past Portholland is Caerhays Castle (private): Gothic building used in TV film of Daphne du Maurier's *Rebecca*; seen from road.

St Austell: working white-china-clay mining town; exported not only for china but various chemical processes. Quaker Meeting House (1829). John Hoge, inventor of the fire engine, born in St Austell. Carthew (2 m N) open air clay mining museum.

A390 Lostwithiel, small roads to Herodsfoot, St Keyne, B3254 Liskeard (17 m)

At Lostwithiel, Royal Oak, Duke St (tel Bodmin 872 552): 13th-century inn, once an ale house used by Fowey river smugglers. Secret passage said to have been used by the Black Prince when at Restormel Castle; oak beams, friendly service; home-made steak and kidney, ragout of venison, chicken casserole; good bar menu, meal from £3; restaurant from £6.50; wines from £3. BB £8–10; DBB £12.65–15.

Lostwithiel was capital of Cornwall in 13th century; pleasant market town; 15th-century bridge; river Fowey; in Civil War, Cromwell's Roundheads held a service in the 13th-century church, with a horse representing King Charles. Masonic Hall was the Exchequer where tin was weighed and taxed.

1 m N: Restormel Castle, 13th-century romantic ruin; remains include gate, keep, great hall, kitchens.

| Lostwithiel, St Keyne *continued* | Pelyn Barn Farm, Pelyn Cross, Lostwithiel (tel Bodmin 872 451): BB £7–8; snacks.

At St Keyne, Liskeard, Old Rectory (tel Liskeard 42617): old, pleasant, friendly, quiet, nice garden; dinner FP 4-course, little choice but freshly cooked £5.75 (£4.60 if staying overnight); BB £11.50–15.50. Shut Nov, Dec. | St Keyne: Paul Corin Musical Museum; interesting organs (Old Mill 2 m S). Also the well believed to have healing qualities in old times.

Liskeard: market town with fine old houses; crowded midsummer.

St Cleer (B3254 2 m N): Tremar Potteries make stone tableware.

Dobwalls (2 m W): miniature railway, steam and diesel, carries passengers through countryside. |
| A390 Tavistock (18 m) | At St Mellion (2 m S Callington), St Mellion Golf and Country Club: golfers' paradise; pricey but remarkable; started in 1974 by two golfing farmers; championship course, superb clubhouse; luxury modern hotel; also heated pool, sauna, solarium, squash, badminton: salmon fishing; imaginative cooking by Patrick Gray – try his own scallops. Beef Wellington; deep fried mushrooms and Stilton; dinner FP £6.75; also special dishes; BB £14–23. SB (all year).

At Horrabridge (A386 S of Tavistock), Overcombe Hotel (tel Yelverton 3501): comfortable; home cooking; dinner 5 courses £5.25; wines £3.38–9. BB £8.75–9.75; SB (winter – explore 'Dartmoor weekends'). | Tavistock was the estate of a Benedictine abbey until Henry VIII dissolved the monasteries and the Dukes of Bedford got their hands on it. Drake's statue is in Plymouth Road – he was born here in 1542. Partly built of green volcanic stone, Tavistock is attractive. Edge of Dartmoor.

Dartmoor's 350 square miles of National Park privately owned; public access to most areas, beware of bogs, especially in winter. Most bogs have light green spagnum moss growing; peat bogs are broken by fissures – usually wet but dry in fine summers. Barren summits, heather-clad moors; waterways gentle in summer, torrential in winter; pretty villages, isolated farms; ruggedly beautiful in summer, cruel in winter when mists can be all-enshrouding, blizzards and snow can block all roads. You must not drive more than fifteen yards from a public road. Nature reserves for rare plants and wildlife. |

The ponies belong to local farmers. Feeding attracts them to roads: dangerous for them. Fallow deer roam the East Moor.

small road to Brent Tor and Lydford

Moorland Hall, Mary Tavy (tel Mary Tavy 466): two generations family-run hotel in Victorian house; peace, tranquillity; 4 acres, with children's play area, tree house, paddling pool. Menu changed daily; local rainbow trout delicious; dinner FP £5.50 good value 4 courses; wines from £2.95 include '74 Barolo red £4.75, genuine '70 Chianti £4.25; BB £7.50–11.50; DBB £11.50–15.50. Children really welcome.

A386 S to Mary Tavy 2 m on take small road right to B3357, turn left small road on right marked to Princetown, left on B3212 to Two Bridges (20 m)

Dowerland Farm (tel Mary Tavy 345): home cooking; dinner from £3; BB £5–6; DBB £8.

Peter Tavy Inn, just off A386: real ale and what hosts call 'real food' – no refined products; brown unrefined rice, sugar, flour, even brown pasta (which I hate). Nothing tinned, packaged, dehydrated or frozen. I have not eaten here; friends find the limited menu good. Cheap.

Cherrybrook, Two Bridges (tel Tavistock 88260): comfortable; own veg, hens; meat, cream, cider from nearby farms. English cooking. Dinner FP 4 courses £4.50; wines include twenty under £3. BB £8.50.

Brent Tor, 1130 ft of volcanic rock, has 12th-century church on top built by Tavistock monks.

Lydford Gorge is truly spectacular: 100 ft waterfall and Devil's Cauldron below. Remains of Lydford Castle built 1195 to imprison those who broke forest and mining laws.

A run across heart of Dartmoor. Princetown, largest town on the moor, bleak, 1400 ft up, includes Dartmoor Prison, built to cage French prisoners in Napoleonic Wars. Town is centre for exploring prehistoric remains, but grey and depressing. Prison was built to save Frenchmen from terrible conditions of Plymouth prison ships, but 1000 died there. In 1812 American prisoners were put there; 200 died. Closed in 1816 as unfit to be used; reopened 1850 and still used. The church has a window given by widows of US prisoners of war.

B3212
Postbridge
small road to
Widecombe in
the Moor,
Haytor Vale,
Bovey Tracey
(14 m)

Lydgate House, Postbridge (tel 88209): above river, with trout fishing in grounds; real old English teas, with Devon cream. Traditional Devon food – halibut in cider; tipsy baked rabbit; cider baked pork; lunch £3.50; dinner from £4.25. DB £8.50; DBB £11.80–12.65.

At Poundsgate (3 m S Widecombe), Leusdon Lodge (tel Poundsgate 304): kind to families; fine Devon cooking; dinner FP £8.30; residents' dinner FP £4.75. BB £9.20. SB.

Rock Inn, Haytor Vale (tel Haytor 205): old inn; family run; meals good value. Home-made bar dishes; dinner £4.95. BB £7.50–8.50.

At Bovey Tracey, Coombe Cross Hotel (tel. 832476): a charming, peaceful hotel. Nice bedrooms; fine garden. English-style meals, good value if simple. Buffet full lunch £2.50; dinner £5.50. BB £11–13; DBB £16.50–18.75. Shut Christmas–mid Feb.

Willmead Farm, Slade Cross, 500 yards off A382 near Lustleigh (tel Lustleigh 214): beautiful 14th-century thatched farmhouse; log fires; minstrels' gallery; comfortable beds. Dinner 4 courses £6 (bring your own wine); BB £9. Do phone.

Edgemoor Hotel, Bovey Tracey (tel 832466): cheerful, four Morleys run it with a country house party atmosphere. Fine grounds; fine cooking; ex-chef at the Dorchester. Dinner 4 courses FP £6.60; card £7–8. BB £13–15. SB (mid Oct–mid May).

Postbridge:- 13th-century Clapper bridge across river Dart – three big stone slabs on pillars.

Widecombe, made famous by Uncle Tom Cobleigh song, has its fair on second Tues in September; photogenic village in a high fold; 14th-century church of St Pancras called Cathedral of the Moor; NW is Hameldown Beacon and Bronze Age barrows. Further N at Grimspound is Bronze Age stone compound used by shepherds, Dr Watson's hiding place in Sherlock Holmes's case *The Hound of the Baskervilles*.

Bovey Tracey's 14th-century church, with lavishly carved pulpit, is on the site of one built by Sir William de Tracey to atone for his part in killing Thomas à Becket in 1170. In Civil War, Royalists, caught gaming by Cromwell's Roundheads, threw the stake money out of the window to gain time. But Cromwell won the battle.

small roads to
Chudleigh,
across A380 on
to B3381 to
Starcross (11 m)

Chudleigh, Ugbrooke House:
medieval largely rebuilt by
Robert Adam 1763 for
Clifford family. Lord Clifford
lives there. Chapel in Italian
style. Half house open
afternoons 23 May–30 Sept,
except Fri, Sat. Also gardens.

Chudleigh Rock: scrambling
paths. Starcross area known
for wildfowl. Old warehouse
here was pump house of
Exeter–Plymouth railway –
Brunel's great failure. Air
was sucked from cylinders
between rails to pull trains
by vacuum. It worked but
rats ate airtight seals!
Abandoned 1848.

A379 Topsham,
small road left to
Exminster A379
Exeter
(10 m)

At Kennford, nr Exeter,
Fairwinds Hotel (tel Exeter
832911): modern, well fitted,
bright and cheerful, good
overnight to keep out of city.
Fresh food, unexciting, but
fair value meals: £4.20–5.75;
wine from £2.95. BB £11.50–
15. SB (weekends).

In Exeter, the usual wide
choice of all types of
accommodation in a city; HQ
West Country Tourist Board,
37 Southernhay East, Exeter
(tel Exeter 76351).

Powderham Castle (right off
A379): seat of Courtenays
(Earls of Devon) since 14th
century, additions until 19th
century. Name means 'Short
Nose'. Main branch of family
liquidated by Henry VIII; they
got earldom back in 18th
century. House once stood
on an island; land round
drained. Well worth seeing.
Open mid May–end Sept
2–6pm except Fri, Sat.

Topsham: sail lofts converted
into charming Dutch gabled
houses; built 1700 with
Dutch bricks brought by
merchantmen as ballast.

Exeter: a city cursed by
hurrying motorists in
midsummer, for the
motorway ends around here
and even the double-track
A30 cannot cope. But a
delightful and underrated
city. Norman cathedral (1133)
has grown into a lovely
building over centuries; but

Exeter *continued*		the river Exe makes the atmosphere of Exeter. Fine buildings: tall shops and houses; Mol's Coffee House, where the great Elizabethan sea dogs – Drake, Frobisher, Hawkins, Raleigh and Gilbert – drank. Tudor house in West St half timbered; 14th-century Guildhall. The university has given the city a new life and purpose.
B3212 Broad Clyst (5 m)		N of Broad Clyst, Killerton House (National Trust): Georgian house, former home of the Aclands, now houses a superb collection of period costumes; nice hillside garden; April–Oct.
small road to Whimple, across A30, B3174 Ottery St Mary (8 m)	Lodge, 17 Silver St, Ottery St Mary (tel 2356): ex-jet pilot and airline girl, who have lived in Far East, run good restaurant with odd pricing – menus are for two people with wine: £18 and £23. Long wine lists, nine house wines. Shut Sun dinner, Mon. Kings Arms, Ottery St Mary (tel 2879): coaching inn (1756); bar meals, dinner around £6. BB £9.90.	Ottery St Mary: pleasant town in lovely country; 14th-century church modelled on Exeter Cathedral. Cadhay House's 18th-century front hides attractive and interesting Tudor house; worth seeing; open Sun, Mon, spring, summer, also Wed, Thurs, mid July–mid Aug, 2–6pm. Poet Coleridge born in the vicarage.
B3174 to Farway Country Park small roads to Colyton		Farway Country Park: 70 acres of country and woodland; riding; survival park for rare breeds – sheep, pigs, goats and cattle; also deer, ponies, badgers. Colyton: little market town of thatched roofs and narrow lanes; riverside walk; At Musbury, A358, Ashe House: home of Churchill's ancestors.

From Axmouth eastwards is Downlands Cliff nature reserve: 5 m coastal strip; nightingales nest with other rare birds; lizards sunbathe; 400 species of wild flowers. Landslide chasm. Pathway, can be treacherous.

A3052 Lyme Regis (18 m)

Bay Hotel (tel 4059): 15 yd from sands; get a front bedroom; comfortable. English cooking; own lock-up garage 2 mins walk. Bar lunches; meals £5–6; wines from £3. BB £12.50–15; DBB £16–19.

Mariners, Silver St, A3070 (tel 2753): book early – a winner. 17th-century coaching inn used by Beatrix Potter in *Tale of Little Pig Robinson*; spectacular views of Dorset coast from garden containing 326-year-old tulip tree; comfortable bedrooms; good cooking; superb fish; dinner FP 4 courses £7.75 good choice; card also; BB £12.50–16.50; DBB £18–22; SB (spring, Oct). Shut Nov–Mar.

Kerbrook, Pound Rd, Lyme Regis (tel 2596): pretty 18th-century thatched house with nice garden; owners experienced in hotel keeping, sea views from some bedrooms; home cooking; dinner £3.95; litre wine £3.19; BB £7.50–9. Good value. SB. Shut Nov–Feb.

At Uplyme, Amherst Farm (tel Lyme Regis 2773): delightful, but you may have trouble booking less than three nights. 40 acres; trout fishing in 7 pools from river Lynn; woods; old farmhouse; good cooking of

Lyme Regis is delightful old port and small resort, but crowded July, August. Nestles between cliffs, backed by hills; long sand beach, harbour protected by huge wall, the Cob, used by Edward I to sail against France and by the Duke of Monmouth in 1685 in his rebellion against James II; narrow steep high street and bridge restrict parking; main park ½ m up hill. Jane Austen loved it; wrote *Persuasion* here; good sailing, fishing boats, especially for lobster and crab.

Charmouth, 3 m E Lyme:– sand and shingle beach flanked by cliffs and famous for fossils (21 ft ichthyosaurus found in 1811 – Barney Hansford's fossil museum open); Charles II hidden in Queen's Arms Hotel after defeat at Worcester; planned to escape to France but wife of captain who was to sail him locked her husband in a room without his trousers; Charles fled just as a blacksmith recognized the foreign shoes on his horse. Catherine of Aragon rested at the same inn on her way to marry Henry VIII.

Lyme Regis *continued*	superb ingredients – trout, wild duck, crayfish, Jacob breed lambs, own farm produce includes greenhouse aubergines, melons. Dinner £4.60. (£4 to residents); BB £7–9. At Charmouth, Queen's Armes (tel Charmouth 60339): one of Britain's oldest inns, originally a pilgrims' hostel; dinner from £6.50; also card; bar lunches; BB £11.50–14; open May–Oct.	
A35 Bridport (10 m)	At Chideock, picturesque village on A35, Chideock House (tel 242): 15th-century beams, old fireplaces; HQ Roundhead army against Royalists in 1645. Snack bar; restaurant; dinner 2 SP £7 and £9. BB £9–14. New grill room. Thatch Cottage (tel Chideock 473): attractive, cheap; dinner £4.50–5.50 – residents or appointment; BB £6–6.50.	Bridport, one of the world's biggest producers of netting; originally produced rope for ships and hangmen ('Bridport Dagger' was a hangman's noose); streets made wide for 'rope walk' – place to twist and dry rope twine. Georgian town hall. West Bay, now yachtsman's harbour, was 18th-century cargo port.
B3157 Swyre, Abbotsbury, local roads to Winterbourne Abbas on A35 Dorchester (14 m)	At Dorchester, Greenwood Tree, 51 Icen Way, High East St (tel 68500): 3-course lunch £2 or under; carafe wine £2.20; meringues menu, all at 55p; Open 9–5.30pm; King's Arms, High East St (tel 65353): comfortable, warm, nice atmosphere; tasty Dorset dishes – devilled crab, lamb pie, pork in cream, cider. Lunch £6, dinner £7.50. House wine £3. BB £14–18.	At Burton Bradstock starts the Chesil Bank, massive bank of shingle between sea and land; runs to Portland (16 m); from Abbotsbury it goes through water, leaving a long lake of brackish water – the Fleet. Swimming is dangerous but beachcombers have found treasures washed up. Abbotsbury: village of thatched cottages, a mile from the sea, beneath a 14th-century chapel atop of hill. Huge tithe barn of 11th-century Benedictine abbey whose monks started the swannery for food. In May, 1000 swans now nest in the

swannery on the Fleet. Rich subtropical gardens, open April–Sept;

Worth stopping in Dorchester, an interesting town: Old Crown Court, High West St, where Tolpuddle Martyrs were tried and deported in 1834 for forming a Friendly Society of Agricultural Workers. Public opinion forced their 'pardon' in 1836. In the Antelope Hotel is a room where Judge Jeffreys held his 'Bloody Assize' after Monmouth's Rebellion, sentencing 282 men to death; many heads were kept on the church rails as a warning. Jeffreys' ghost haunts his lodging in High West St. Military museum, Bridport Rd, includes Hitler's desk taken from Berlin Chancellery. Dorset County Museum, High West St, has Thomas Hardy memorabilia.

A35 Puddletown, small roads west to join B3143 to Piddlehinton, Buckland Newton, King's Stag

At Piddletrenthide, B3143, Poachers (tel 358): 15th-century inn. Order a scotch and Piddle water – Bill Pearson bottles water from the river. Imaginative meals – try North Sea salad; pork with sauce of calvados, apricots, raisins, cream. FP 4 course £6–7; BB £11.50–14. Good value.

New Inn, 14 Long St (tel Cerne Abbas 274): small country inn serving good bar meals, including Cerne Valley trout. Meals up to £6; fair wine selection. BB £8.50.

At West Stour, 2 m N Todber on A30, Ship Inn (tel East Stour 640); renovated inn. Home-grown veg, local meat; good English cooking; dinner FP 4 course £5.50. BB £8.50. Value.

Higher Bockingham (3 m A35): Thomas Hardy born here in 1840 and later came back to write *Far from the Madding Crowd* and *Under the Greenwood Tree*. Now thatched cottage is National Trust; ten minutes' walk through woods from car park; interior seen by appointment (tel. Dorchester 2366);

At Tolpuddle, just past Puddletown, sycamore under which six farmworkers met to fight starvation wages (see Dorchester): Martyrs' Tree.

Cerne Abbas: remains of Benedictine abbey. Carved on chalk hillside N is a club-wielding giant, 180 ft high. Maybe a fertility symbol, maybe the Roman demigod Hercules.

At A3030, turn right on A357 to Sturminster Newton; B3092 to Marnhull, Todber, small road right to Shaftesbury (32 m)

Shaftesbury, Royal Chase Roundabout (tel Shaftesbury 3355): charming smaller hotel; a monastery until 1922; comfortable bedrooms, mostly with own bathrooms. Informal restaurant called Country Kitchen. English, especially Dorset dishes. Dinner card £6.50–8; bar lunches and snacks; five real ales; local North Wooton wine. BB £13.75–21. Tipping discouraged. SB (good value);

Grosvenor Hotel, The Commons (tel 2282): fine hotel with lovely old courtyard. Now Trust House Forte. In *Jude the Obscure* Hardy called it 'The Duke's Arms in the Market Place'. Meals very good value. Lunch: £3.25–4.25, or single course if you wish; card for lunch or dinner: £6.50–8.50 (fresh local produce). Dorset jugged venison; Priddy Oggie (pork fillet, stuffed cheese, parsley, baked in puff pastry). Rooms £14–20 per person without breakfast; SB (weekends).

Sturminster Newton: approach over 15th-century bridge – triangular marketplace and pleasant streets; many houses bow-windowed, or thatched. Hardy wrote *Return of the Native* in greystone mansion Riverside on outskirts. Market day Mondays.

Shaftesbury: grew up around a nunnery endowed by Alfred the Great, it stands on the edge of a 700 ft pleateau so has superb views over Blackmore Vale, with many roads running down to it (Gold Hill, a steep cobbled street). Interesting variety of houses, many of green sandstone. In 18th-century Grosvenor Hotel is a beautiful sideboard carved in 1862 from a solid block of oak and showing scenes from 'Ballad of Chevy Chase' – one of the many historic Border punch-ups with the Percys (Hotspur) playing for England and the Douglases (Black Douglas) playing for Scotland.

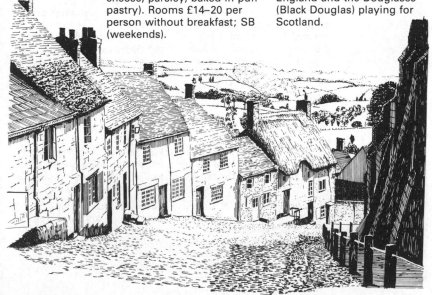

A30 Ansty, small road south to Alvediston, Broad Chalke, Coombe Bissett A354 Salisbury (20 m)

At Salisbury, Mayor Ivie, 2 Ivy St (tel 3949): old restaurant named after 17th-century local hero; old English cooking, including recipes from 1390 manuscripts by cooks of King Richard II. Try Gaelic beef, creamed haddie, civet of venison, home-made ices; dinner FP £5; card £7. House Bordeaux £3.50; four English wines; last order 11pm, licensed till 2am.

Provençal French Restaurant, 14 Ox Row, Market Place (tel 28923): English run but genuine French cooking. Try feuilleté of devilled crab; real cream brûlée; lunch FP £5; dinner card £12–13 includes wine; three house wines £4.50/litre (import own Loire Blanc de Blancs). Shut Sun; Sat lunch.

Cathedral Hotel, Milford St (tel 20144): comfortable, central; rooms £8–10.50 per person. breakfast extra; no other meals; pub attached – bar meals.

Chough Hotel, Blue Boar Row (tel 22042): home-made bar meals; 2-course £2.50. BB £7–7.50.

Salisbury cathedral: delicate, almost feminine, one of Europe's loveliest buildings. Started 1220, finished 1280, was built before the rest of the city; not hemmed in although you cannot see it as clearly as John Constable did when he painted it from the Bishops' Palace. Cathedral's superb spire was added 1334. Inside, columns of Purbeck stone give dramatic effect; still built into the tower and used for repair work is the original huge windlass to pull up stone; two men can work it; also oldest working clock in the world – wrought iron, built 1386, it has no face or hands but tells the time by chiming hours. In the close are 13th-century Bishops' Palace, 18th-century Mompesson House; has superb decorations; baroque plaster and panelling; collection of 18th-century glasses (National Trust). Open April–Oct pm (except Thurs, Fri). 15th-century ornate Poultry Cross where poultry sold. Only foundations remain of Old Sarum, forerunner of Salisbury and original Roman fortress. Old Sarum was most notorious Rotten Borough, abolished by the 1832 Reform Act; ten electors returned two MPs to Parliament. One was William Pitt the Elder (1708–78) who became Prime Minister.

A360 to A303 Stonehenge A344 Amesbury A345 to just past Uphaven (17 m)	Stonehenge: Bronze Age; the stones look awesome at sunset. Outer ditch 1800 BC. Later bluestones brought from Pembroke on rafts across Bristol Channel. Dragged over logs to Salisbury Plain. Amesbury: set in bend of river Avon; five-arched Palladian-style bridge; abbey on site of priory to which Queen Guinevere retired after King Arthur's death (Thomas Malory's *Morte D'Arthur*). Just outside is Woodhenge, Neolithic earthwork older than Stonehenge.
local road left off A345 to Woodborough, Alton Priors, Lockeridge, Marlborough (11 m)	After Alton Barnes, Pewsey Downs Nature Reserve: many scarce chalk-loving plants and butterflies. White horse cut into milk hill around 1812. Marlborough: handsome town; fine broad High Street, partly arcaded; Georgian buildings. Also alleys of old timbered cottages; enclosed bridge to Marlborough College – public school, 1843.
A4, then right into Savernake Forest, along Grand Avenue left at T-junction, then right to Great Bedwyn, Shalbourne, A338 Hungerford A419 Chilton Foliat then small road to right, under M4, left on B4001 to Lambourn (21 m)	Savernake Forest: old royal hunting forest; superb trees, deer, rare birds, wild flowers. Grand Avenue, 4 m long, almost arcaded by trees. At Crofton you can see 19th-century beam-engine still working: pumps 11 tons of water a minute from reservoir into Kennet and Avon Canal. Lambourn Downs are racehorse training country; see horses exercised in open country. Seven Barrows (burial mounds) 2 m N.

| B4001 Childrey
B4507 Wantage
(30 m) | At Wantage, Bear, Market Sq (tel 66366): fine old inn; bedrooms rather pricey but all have TV, telephone, radio; also teamaker (more interesting in bedrooms). Lunch FP £5.95: dinner FP £9.95 (3 courses plus water ice, coffee); also card; bar snacks and meals. Wine bar. BB £14.25–19.50. | 17th/18th-century buildings; narrow streets and passages; one leading from Newbury St has cobbles made from sheep bones. Church of St Peter and Paul has tombs of Fitzwaryn family; Dick Whittington married into it. King Alfred the Great was born here AD 849; statue in marketplace. |

A338 to Botley
Oxford
(20 m)

Route 2

**South East and South
(through Canterbury, Brighton, Bournemouth and
Winchester)**

Orpington A224,
A21, A2028
Dunton Green,
just into
Sevenoaks (7 m)

Al Mattarone, 7 Tubs Hill
Parade, Sevenoaks (nr
station) (tel 54385): Italian
cooking; excellent fettuccine,
25 Italian wines; meals
£6.50–8 (FP lunch £2.80).
Shut Sun.

Through Sevenoaks, Knole:
superb house in lovely park
with herb and landscape
gardens and deer; house
started 1456, enlarged by
Henry VIII in 1540s; Sackville
family owned and altered it,
from when Elizabeth I gave it
to courtier poet Thomas
Sackville in 1603 until they
gave it to the National Trust.
Family still live there;
magnificent furniture. Closed
Dec–end March and Mon,
Tues.

A25 Sundridge;
at crossroads
small road left
Ide Hill; right on
to B2042 Four
Elms (5 m)

Ide Hill, Emmett's Gardens
(NT): rare trees, gardens,
terrace with views. Open
Weds to 5pm, April–Oct.

Four Elms (2½ m right on
B269, right on B2026),
Chartwell: not pretty but
home of Winston Churchill
from 1924 until he died; fine
views; mementoes. Open
March–Nov pm, also some
mornings. Park with studio
containing his paintings.
Open Mar–end Nov (except
Mon, Fri).

left along B2027 for 1 m, right on small road to Hever small road in 'Horseshoe' to Chiddingstone (6 m) small road B2027 to Chiddingstone Causeway; B2176 Penshurst; B2188 to Fordcombe (6 m)

Castle, Chiddingstone (tel Penshurst 870247): first reference in 1420; run excellently for seventeen years by Joseph and Nigel Lucas (Nigel ex-Mayfair and Claridges); fine bar snacks; excellent meals – not cheap but good value; menu varies every two weeks to include fresh seasonal food. Lunch FP £4.25 & £5.75; 4-course dinner £12.50; wines £4 (French) to £64.

Leicester Arms, Penshurst (tel Penshurst 870551): useful touring base; Italian chef-innkeeper; meals £3.50–9. Restaurant closed Sun evening, all Mon; BB £13–16; SB.

Spotted Dog, Smarts Hill (tel Penshurst 870253) (2nd right on B2176 from Penshurst, then left): ½ m diversion to find charming clapboard inn where, aged fourteen, I bought my first 'round'; cosy in winter; summer terrace with superb views; bar meals £3.50; restaurant meals FP £5.50; card £8–9; ambitious cooking. Try deep-fried mushrooms stuffed with seafood, served with cheese sauce; don't be put off by names of dishes ('Utter Bliss') or apricot sauce on pork in middle of Kent apple country; wines include local Penshurst white and Leoville Barton '73. BB £15 (3 single rooms).

Hever Castle: built 1380; 15th-16th-century home of Bullen (Boleyn) family; Anne Boleyn (wife of Henry VIII, mother of Queen Elizabeth I) born here; became farmhouse until bought in 1909 by US millionaire William Waldorf Astor; outstanding panelling; good tapestries. Italian garden, big lake. Open end Mar-end Sept (Tues, Wed, Fri, Sun).

Chiddingstone Castle: dull castle-like house with treasures inside, Egyptian and Oriental: mementoes of Stuart kings. Open end Mar–end Oct (pm Tues–Fri; all day Sat, Sun).

Chiddingstone: Tudor village owned by Streatfield family 450 years; now National Trust. Shop, church, school, pub, cottages.

Penshurst Place: built 1340; soldier, statesman and poet Sir Philip Sidney born here 1554; his family have lived here for 400 years; the present owner, Viscount de L'Isle, who won VC at Anzio, is a descendant. Magnificent Great Hall (1340) with good paintings and minstrels' gallery; toy collection; open 1 April–end Sept (pm daily except Mon). Entrance through tiny Leicester Square, named after Elizabeth's Earl of Leicester. Lovely village near meeting of rivers Eden and Medway.

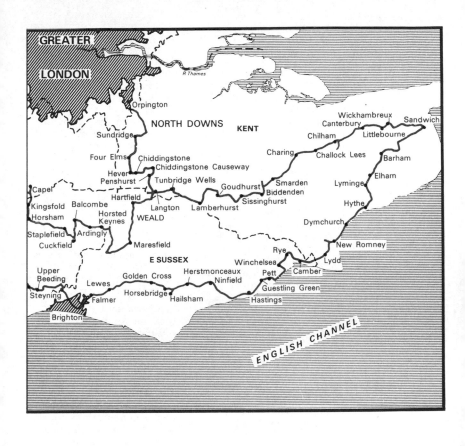

B2188 to A264
through Langton
to Tunbridge
Wells (4 m)
B2169 Bells Yew
Green,
Lamberhurst
(7 m)

Royal Wells, Mount Ephraim (tel T. Wells 23414): owner Geoffrey Sloan and two sons (his chefs) make regular expeditions to France. They go in the hotel's bus – 1909 Commer. Much of the cooking is British and good; try jugged hare and haddock mousse; FP meals £5.75 & £9.75 (5 courses); card; good wine list, few cheaper wines; BB £11–14; all rooms baths, TV.

Russell Hotel, 80 London Rd (tel 44833): nice ordinary hotel with good French-born, French-trained chef. Dinner £5 (good value); house wine £3/litre; 30 other wines. BB £10.50–11.50.

A Marianne, 30 London Rd (tel 24277): has some superb dishes; try quenelles of blue trout and chevreuil en croute (venison in red wine sauce in puff pastry). Good value but service amateur on my two visits. Lunch £5.50; dinner £6.50; card £8–10. FP residents' menu £5.50 including wine. BB £9–11. Shut Sat lunch, Sun.

Don Pepe, 3 Cumberland Walk (tel 40754): José Gonzalez serves Spanish, French and English dishes. FP lunch £3; dinner card £5–10; good Rioja wines.

Bruins, 5 London Rd (tel 35757): restaurant plus popular bar with real ale. Simple dishes cooked well; meals £4–7.

Horse and Groom, Lamberhurst (tel 890302): genuine old inn, good cooking, fine value, meals £7–9.

Tunbridge Wells: rival to Bath as Regency spa, when Beau Nash presided here; still elegant, with Septimus Burton houses; lovely Pantiles, 18th-century shopping walk shaded by limes, looks little changed. Pretty county cricket ground; large common rising to sandstone outcrop High Rocks; further outcrop of rocks at Eridge (5 m) form Bowles Mountaineering and Outdoor Pursuits centre for dry-slope skiing, climbing, canoeing, fishing. Tunbridge Wells Assembly Hall has wide range of entertainment from classical concerts to pop, jazz, famous comedians, actors and actresses.

Lamberhurst: before coal took the iron and arms businesses to Birmingham, this was an arms-making town, using charcoal from huge Wealden oaks. Smugglers thrived, too; 16th-century Owl House used as smugglers' lookout, with owl's hoot as danger signal. Now, Lamberhurst produces apples, lambs and wine.

Scotney Castle (1½ m A21): ruins of 14th-century moated castle in landscaped gardens.

Bewl Bridge reservoir (entrance 5 m): sailing, fishing and canoeing.

A21, right on to
B2162
Horsmonden
(5 m)

Gun Inn, Horsmonden (tel Brenchley 2673): magnificent meat cooked over applewood in huge inglenook; spit roast beef, some of the best I have tasted, Wed, Sat; pork, Fri; barbecued steak, Tues, Thurs. Dinner £7; excellent bar snacks; lunch dish of day; good wine list; farmers' bar with old farm implements.

At Brenchley, 1½ m, Rose and Crown: fine old pub in beautiful village; try cheese and prawn envelopes, jugged hare, duck in game sauce. Bar lunches (daily special dishes); dinner FP £7.95; also card; wines reasonable.

Horsmonden: area rich in hops, apples and old houses – Tudor timbered and Kentish clapboard. In Gun Inn opposite big trees on village green ('Heath') 17th-century gunmaker John Browne (a Scot) designed guns with impartiality for Charles I and Cromwell, the British and enemy Dutch navies. Woodland walk to Furnace Pond which once powered the bellows for iron furnaces. Smugglers, highwaymen and sheep stealers were hanged on the Heath, hence Gibbet Lane.

On B2162 just before village, Sprivers: old house (NT) where garden ornament artist Michael Dibben works. Garden open Wed pm, April–end Sept.

keep Gun on
right to take
local road to
Goudhurst (4 m)

Star and Eagle, Goudhurst (tel 211512): splendid centre for discovering this lovely area; good chef; many local variations of recipes; first class buffet bistro separate from restaurant. Main meals around £8. Real old English inn. Nice old bedrooms. Service variable. BB £10–14.

Goudhurst: lovely hillside village, with pond at bottom of street lined with Tudor houses; 13th-15th-century church; medieval Star and Eagle Inn, once joined by tunnel to church, was base of notorious smuggling gangs, including 18th-century Hawkhurst Gang. Spyways, smugglers' sentry house with windows covering main street both ways, still stands.

Pattyndenne Manor: fine Wealden manor. 15th-century; well worth seeing.

On B2079 1 m S of Goudhurst, Bedgebury Pinetum: pine forest with walks, shrubs, ponds started by Kew Gardens when London fumes destroyed Kew's pines.

A262 to Peacock Inn, right along B2085 2 m, then left on narrow road to Cranbrook (4 m)	Peacock: old inn run with natural friendliness and near-eccentricity by racehorse owner; drinking garden where goats may receive you. Good bar snacks.	Cranbrook: tiny town with white clapboard houses and windmill.

Willesley Hotel (tel Cranbrook 713555): looks a bit dull from outside but good chef produces some fine generous dishes; fish dishes particularly tempting; pleasant garden with drinking terrace; lunch FP £4.50 (fine value); dinner card around £8.45. Rooms comfortable but a little pricey, £16.50–24. Peaceful.

Windmill Inn (tel Cranbrook 713119): edge of town, on high bank, so ask where it is; very nice inn with bar-restaurant; good value around £4–6.

A262 Sissinghurst, Three Chimneys, Biddenden, A274, B2077 Smarden, Pluckley, Charing (16 m)

Ye Maydes Restaurant, Biddenden (tel 291360): delightful dishes; try selection of fish pâté; house salad melon and avocado with prawns in pink mayonnaise; lamb casserole; FP lunch £4.80; dinner £8–10 card.

Three Chimneys, Biddenden (tel 291472): most attractive, very popular, well-run pub; outstanding bar meals around £4–5 or individual dishes; fair wine choice, several real ales; convivial; can be crowded.

Chequers, Smarden (tel 217): genuine local with small restaurant; small selection of good, fresh cooked dishes; fair wine choice; meals £5–6; good bar snacks; BB £7.50.

Sissinghurst Castle was once an Elizabethan manor. Vita Sackville West made one of the finest gardens in Britain from surrounding wilderness in '30s; left it to National Trust. Open daily 1 April–mid Oct from midday. Fine herb garden.

Biddenden: Tudor weavers' cottages; sign depicts Maids – 11th-century Siamese twins – who left annual dole for the poor.

Pluckley: most haunted village in Britain, with thirteen ghosts, including a white lady, a red lady, a pipe-smoking gypsy lady and a brick worker.

Charing is on the Pilgrims Way followed by pilgrims to the shrine of Thomas à Becket in Canterbury Cathedral. Remains of palace where Archbishop Cranmer lived. Views.

A252 Challock
Lees Chilham
(8 m)

At Chilham, 1 m on A28 Ashford Rd, Pope Street Farmhouse (tel Chilham 226): 15th-century farmhouse on land given to Archbishop of Canterbury by King of Mercia in AD 900. Beams, inglenooks, but also h & c in bedrooms: buffet supper £3; BB £6–7.

Cona Guest House, Shottenden nr Chilham (tel 405): run by a Texan and family *for* families. BB £7.50; dinner £5.

At Chartham Hatch, Howfield Manor (tel Chartham 495): Augustinian priory of 1181, modernized in 17th century, bathrooms added to bedrooms later; attractive, restful, friendly; good cooking but dinner around £8, for residents only; good value wines. BB £11.50–15.

Chilham: photogenic hilltop village with superb square flanked by timbered black-and-white Tudor houses and impressive gates to Chilham Castle (1616); in the gardens, laid out by Capability Brown, is a Norman castle keep on Roman foundations and a squadron of eagles and falcons which happily obey their falconer; a Battle of Britain RAF museum in the house.

A28 Canterbury
(6 m)

The Romans found a British tribe at a crossing of the river Stour and built a Roman town. In AD 603 Augustine, first Archbishop, consecrated a cathedral on the site of an old British church where he had baptised King Ethelbert of Kent; in 1070 Lanfranc, friend of William the Conqueror, started the present long grey building which is Mother Church of all Anglicans, has grown through centuries and survived fires, wars, desecration by Puritans and bombing by Germans. Archbishop Thomas à Becket was murdered here in 1170 by knights who had heard King Henry II, in a rage, ask: 'Who will deliver me from this turbulent priest?' Rome, trying to get the English royal family to tow the papal line, made Becket a martyr-saint and pilgrimages to his tomb continued until Henry VIII denounced Becket for 'treason, contumacy and rebellion'. Pilgrims had taken the Pilgrim's Way from Winchester for nearly 400 years and left behind one of the greatest literary classics, Chaucer's *Canterbury Tales*, written around 1388. 13th-century stained glass windows show scenes from Christ's miracles and suggested miracles of Becket – beautiful, known as the Poor Man's Bible to pilgrims who could not read. Do see tomb of the Black Prince: modern windows by Hungarian artist Erwin Bossanyi; large Norman crypt, Trinity Chapel and lovely 12th-century choir.

Canterbury is a lively city but much of its past remains still: 13th-century city walls; 14th-century West Gate shut even to pilgrims at dusk to keep out robber bands and now containing an arms museum; Kings School, which has produced many great Englishmen from the playwright Christopher Marlowe, commemorated in Canterbury's excellent Marlowe Theatre, to David Gower, current cricket hero. From Tyler Hill (named for Wat Tyler, hero of the Peasant Revolt of 1381), the University of Kent (1961) looks down on the 2000-year-old city.

Hotels and restaurants
House of Agnes Hotel, 71 St Dunstan's St (tel 65077): splendid value; 400 years old, supposed house of Agnes Wickfield, beautiful heroine of Dickens' *David Copperfield*. The Frosts, both chefs, made it a private hotel employing a Swiss-trained chef; fresh local meat, fish and vegetables; grills and roasts; lunch FP £3.50; dinner £3.95 plus card. Full central heating. BB £7.50–12.

Falstaff, St Dunstan's St (tel 62138): famous old inn beside West Gate; oak beams; comfortable bedrooms with teamakers; English dishes (steak and kidney pudding, roast beef, lamb, pork); meal £4–6; wine prices reasonable from French house wine £3, Chablis '78 £6.45, Fleurie '78 £6.30. BB £11–14.

County, High St (tel 66266): lovely old inn modernized without spoiling it; traditional English lunch £4.95; dinner £6.95 or card; quick service meals in coffee shop; BB £18.50–27, private bath, TV, teamaker; SB.

Cathedral Gate Hotel, 37 Burgate (tel 64381): 'hospice' in the Middle Ages for pilgrims; became in 1620 one of Britain's first tea and coffee houses; charming old building alongside cathedral gate; simple English cooking; typical meal (soup, roast beef, veg, apple pie) £3.70; BB £10.50–12.

Pilgrims Guest House, 18 The Friars (tel 64531): useful overnight, good value; BB £6–8.50.

A257 Littlebourne, local road left to Wickhambreux, Ickham rejoin A257 just before Wingham A257 Sandwich (15 m)

Duke William, Ickham: good buffet, carvery and snacks; reasonable.

At Wingham, Red Lion (tel 217): built 1286; pricey meals for pub but I have known it thirty years and satisfied regulars return; dinner £8–10 card; BB £8.50.

At Sandwich, 16th-century Tea House, 9 Cattle Market (tel 612392): splendid value; FP lunch weekdays £2.70 – 3-course, plenty of choice, eg roast leg of lamb, plaice, steak pie; weekends £3.50 (roast beef); evening card from £3.50; 32 wines include British white £2.40/bottle; Spanish £3.20/litre; Biddenden white £3.90.

Fleur de Lis Hotel, Delf St (tel 611131): host formerly managed Playboy Club, specializes in seafood; buffet meals £2.50; card around £6; bedrooms pleasantly furnished with antiques. BB £8–10.

Little-known area of small farming villages.

Wickhambreux, round triangular green, most attractive; old houses; weatherboard mill on Lesser Stour river; 14th-century church with art nouveau and 13th-century stained glass.

Sandwich: an original Cinque Port – élite ports given privileges in return for providing ships for defence of England. The river Stour silted up and now Sandwich is a delightful backwater 2 m from sea; lovely medieval buildings; town gate from 1384; gate house built by Henry VIII; timbered Guildhall (1579); small craft in the river; pretty, but traffic bottleneck on fine summer days or when golf championships held at Royal Sandwich Course (British Open 1981). Sandwich Bay (toll road) has huge sands backed by three golf courses; James Bond played here in *Goldfinger*.

local roads SW from Sandwich to Chillenden, Barfreston, then crossing A2 to Barham (10 m) B2065 Elham, Lyminge, Newington, Hythe (11 m)

At Bridge (N of Barham), Duck Inn, Pett Level (tel Bridge 830354): gastronomic cooking in country pub; John Laing uses vintage Bentley to collect from Boulogne market items Kent cannot supply; meals £10.

Doll's House, Elham Valley Rd, Barham (tel 241); comfortable, value; English roasts; lunch FP £3.50; dinner FP £6 (4-course); card £6.50.

Lower Arpinge Farmhouse, Arpinge (remote, 3½ m from Hythe near Ethinghill) (tel Folkestone 78102): worth hunting out; Jane Mathew lived eighteen years in Canada and USA, mixes English and American country dishes; bargain value BB £6; DBB £9.50.

Hythe Stade Court Hotel, West Parade (tel Folkestone 68263): odd looking, most comfortable; known for good local fish; indoor heated pool, squash, tennis, putting, golf (at sister luxury Hotel Imperial) included in price; meals FP £6.50; card; BB £13–19; DBB 2 nights £32–35. SB; solarium, sauna.

Barfreston Church, built 1080, elaborately carved inside and out, with weird heads and faces, animals playing musical instruments, birds and leaves; South door shows Christ with Becket.

Barham: village of red-roofed houses in twisty streets; Barham House (Queen Anne period) has grandiose brick doorway in garden wall by Sir Edwin Lutyens.

Hythe: another Cinque Port; charming 18th-century houses in narrow streets; Martello towers and a dreamy tree-lined canal behind the beach built to defend England against Napoleon's threatened invasion.
Saltwood Castle, ruined by earthquake in 16th century, was overnight stop for Becket's killers. Norman church crypt has a macabre mystery find of 2000 human skulls and 8000 thigh bones – different from any found in Britain except at Spitalfields; Hythe people were 3 inches shorter than average.

A259
Dymchurch,
New Romney,
(Littlestone).
B2075 Lydd,
Camber, Rye
(20 m)

At Dymchurch, Chantry, Sycamore Gardens (tel 3137): pleasant little family hotel run by ex-oilman and schoolteacher wife; dinner FP £4.60; card £8. BB £9.20. Shut Nov, Jan.

At Rye, Flushing Inn (restaurant), Market St (tel 3292): in historic building with barrel-vaulted Norman stone cellars from 13th century; wall painting from around 1550 discovered 1905, owned by Mann family for 22 years; superb dishes; delicious local fish, interesting ices, excellent cheese board; lunch £5–6; dinner £7.40–9.80 French wines, 40 Italian, German, English. Bordeaux Sauvignon £4.80. Immaculate service. Gastronomic occasions in autumn, winter.

Saltings Hotel, Captain's Table Restaurant, Hilders Cliff (tel Rye 3838): cheaper but excellent chef. Terry Platini, worked at Savoy, and fourteen years at Wheeler's, London's great fish restaurant, as executive chef. Try his locally caught plaice, sole, English roast meat; lunch £3.75; dinner FP £5.25; card £7.50. Bedrooms centrally heated: BB £10–14; DBB £15–17.50.

At Peasmarsh (2 m A268), Flackley Ash Hotel (tel Peasmarsh 381): comfortable Georgian house; all bedrooms with bath. Own trawler at Rye catches fish for restaurant – excellent; try also veal in ginger wine. Dinner FP, £5.95; card £7 (restaurant closed Mon, Tues, except for residents; also

Smallest public railway in the world (Romney, Hythe and Dymchurch) runs fourteen miles Hythe–Dungeness Point (Easter–Oct) using scale model steam locos. Built 1927 by gloriously eccentric Count Zborowski who raced original 'Chitty Chitty Bang Bang' car with Zeppelin airship engine.

Dymchurch lies behind grass-covered sea wall dating from Romans. Martello tower restored, with cannon on rotating platform.

New Romney: Cinque Port once at mouth of river Rother until storm changed its course; Romney Marsh, now drained pastureland for sheep; once haunt of smugglers who terrorized Kent and Sussex far inland with murder, robbery, rape and protection rackets; smuggled wool to France, brought back lace, salt (heavily taxed) but mostly, in Kipling's words, 'brandy for the parson, baccy for the clerk', hurrying it to the Weald on pack ponies. Pitched battles were fought with excisemen.

Safe swimming at Lydd as currents run parallel to beach; sand below shingle bank. Near Dungeness Point and nuclear power station is 12,000 acre seabird reserve and observatory – 200 species spotted. (Permission to visit from Royal Society for the Protection of Birds, The Lodge, Sandy, Bedfordshire.)

Camber: one of England's finest stretches of safe sands

Camber, Rye
continued

Weds, Thurs in winter); BB £15–18.50; DBB £20–22; SB. Trout and sea fishing.

Mermaid Inn, Mermaid St (tel 3065): one of Britain's finest old inns, splendidly run by Gregory family since 1959; good value; serves Sussex beef, Romney Marsh lamb, Rye Bay sole and plaice; local veg; all cooked, not surprisingly in Rye, in English, not French manner; succulent. Lunch £5.25; dinner FP (4-course) £6.50; card £8; house wine Bordeaux, red or white, plus exclusive shipments around £4 (not smuggled). BB £15–19. SB.

Playden Oasts (1 m B2082), (tel 3502): pleasantly surprised by this little restaurant in converted oast house; dinner £5.50–8; cottage-style bedrooms with simple comfortable furniture; BB £11.50–13; DBB £17.75. SB (Oct–May – good value).

Monastery Hotel, High St (tel 07973): early 19th-century house on medieval monastery site; useful overnight; local ghosts (monk and his lover buried alive) not been seen lately; good English cooking: try saddle of Romney lamb; dinner card around £8 (shut Tues June–Nov; check Nov–June); BB £8–9.50. Good SB (winter). Monastery garden includes original chapel wall.

Little Saltcote, 22 Military Rd (tel 3210): well-known innkeepers, the McKenzies from Winchelsea, retired to run quiet, comfortable guest house. BB £6–7.

and dunes; golf course; village looks like temporary wartime development; sand now held by grass planting.

Rye is beautiful, but park and walk, despite hills; streets narrow, cobbled, many steep; you enter by a 14th-century gate and most buildings are nearly as old. Once an important port, now on two rivers, two miles from receding sea; fishing and pleasure boats moored at riverside quays. Rye had a near-private war with the French for centuries. Town was burned down by a French raid in 1377 so Portmen – Cinque Port sailors – immediately sacked Boulogne. Still arguing with Boulogne over fish. Smuggling reached peak in mid 18th century when notorious Hawkhurst Gang used Mermaid Inn (see opposite), sat boozing and smoking pipes with loaded pistols on tables beside them. No magistrate dared interfere – and they got quick service, too. The Mermaid was burned down by French but cellar remains; rebuilt 1420. A smugglers' stairway is hidden behind a bookcase in Dr Syn's Bedchamber, named after fictional parson-smuggler from Russell Thorndyke's novel *Dr Syn*. Inn was rehabilitated in 1945 by a Canadian who had been billeted there in the war. Delightful Lamb House, Mermaid St (NT), was home of American author Henry James from 1897–1916. Open Wed–Sat pm, Apr–Oct.

A259
Winchelsea,
small coast road
via Cliff End,
Pett, Guestling
Green
A259 Hastings
(14 m)

At Winchelsea, Strand House (tel 276): 14th-century lovely house; double rooms; dinner by order £5; BB £6.50–7.50.

At Pett, Crossways, Pett Level Rd, Fairlight (tel Pett 2356): good value; all fresh food; lunch £2.40; dinner £3.50–5.50. BB £6.

Fairlight Lodge, Fairlight Rd, Hastings (tel Pett 2104): old smugglers' house in seven acres; comfortable; DBB £11.

At Hastings, Judges, 51 High St: bakery-restaurant; remarkable value; fresh roast joint daily, local fish, chicken, pies, meals £2.75; Bordeaux wine £3.20.

Beauport Park (3 m on Battle Rd, A2100) (tel 51222): delightful country house hotel in 33-acre gardens, woods; pool, tennis, riding stables; owner catches fish for hotel. Excellent cooking, friendly welcome. Lunch FP £4.50; dinner FP £6; card average £7.50. House wine £4. BB £14–19; DBB £19. SB.

Winchelsea: pleasant little old town once a Cinque Port, now 2 m from sea where beach is hidden by high wall to protect pastures of Pett from flooding; town was first in Britain town-planned (by Edward I) but little was built. Three gates of original wall stand.

Hastings: a little run-down, but old town is fine – narrow streets, timbered houses to fishing harbour where fish still landed and sold on beach; tall old wooden huts for drying nets; fishermen's museum contains old sailing lugger; lift up cliff to ruins of 13th-century castle. 243 ft long Hastings Embroidery, made in 1966 to mark 900th anniversary of Norman invasion; inspired by Bayeux tapestry, shows 81 scenes from British history (in Town Hall). Battle between William and Harold took place 6 m north, at Battle.

A259, A2036,
A269 Ninfield
A271
Herstmonceux

At Ninfield, Moor Hall Hotel (tel 892330): elegant house in charming landscaped gardens, built by a maharajah who left it when his daughter was drowned in lake; nice bedrooms; quiet; cooking pleasant but oddly cosmopolitan (English, Kurdish, French, Spanish); meals FP £5.25; card £8.50; BB £13–16.

Sundial Restaurant, Herstmonceux (tel 2217): Guiseppe Bertoli, Venetian, has a lightness of touch and can cook anything including

Herstmonceux Castle is a fortified 15th-century house, moated and romantic; lady owner's chamber placed so she could keep an eye on the kitchen. Royal Observatory moved away from here. Old church opposite castle entrance has crusaders' tombs. Trugs (garden baskets made from curved bands of willow) still hand-made in Herstmonceux.

Herstmonceux
continued

sauces. Try anything! Lunch FP £6 (bargain); Sun lunch £7.50; dinner FP £8.50; card around £10. 200 wines. Shut Sun eve, Mon, most Jan, mid Aug–early Sept.

Cleavers Lyng, Church Road (towards castle) (tel 3131): old cottage hotel, pretty, quiet; fresh home cooking, lovely pies (turkey, steak, rabbit, ham), good value; meals £3.50; card. French-bottled wine £3.80/litre. Sussex wine £3.65. BB £8.50; DBB £11 (bargain). Shut Jan.

White Friars, Boreham Street (on A271) (tel Herstmonceux 2355): good Italian chef. FP meals English-style, card English and Italian. Lunch FP £4.25; dinner FP £4.95; card £8. BB £14–17.

A271 Hailsham, Horsebridge, A22 Golden Cross, B2124 Ringmer B2192 Lewes (15 m)

At Lewes, White Hart (tel 3794): Thomas Paine, author of *Rights of Man*, ran a political debating club here (1761), later called it 'the cradle of American Independence'. Protestants were imprisoned in wine cellars before being burned at the stake by Queen Mary (1555–7). In 1929 British Foreign Secretary Arthur Henderson met Soviet envoy here and agreed to resume diplomatic relations with Russia – sometimes called White Hart Treaty. Tory Stanley Baldwin sneered at him for surrendering to Soviets 'at a hotel where bitter beer is sold'. Still sells it – Harvey's real ale. Known for food, too: ribs of beef, saddle of lamb, free range turkey. Meals: card £5–7. 60 wines £3.70–14. BB £11–19.

Michelham Priory 2 m S Hailsham off A22: 13th-century Augustinian priory with Tudor additions (1599); early musical instruments; old farm crafts and wagons (open mid April–mid Oct).

1 m S Ringmer, Glyndebourne Opera House, added to Tudor manor by John Christie 1934.

2 m on is Glynde Place (16th-century) open Wed, Thurs pm, mid May–mid Oct.

3 m N Ringmer: Bentley Wild Fowl Gardens open mid Mar–end Sept.

Lewes: 1000 years of history packed into narrow streets; 16th-century Barbican now archaeological museum. Southover Grange (Elizabethan), Keere St: home of 17th-century diarist John

Pelham Arms and Sussex Kitchen, High Street (tel 6149): 1624, known for Pelham pie (steak and kidney); meals £5.50, card.

Evelyn – gardens open. Anne of Cleves' House, Southover High St (part of Anne's divorce settlement with Henry VIII). Museum includes children's toys – open weekdays except Jan, also Sun April–Oct.

Firle Place (4 m A27): 18th century but incorporates Tudor House; includes items from America of General Thomas Gage, British Commander at outbreak of War of Independence. Gage family have lived here since 15th century; one was constable of the Tower of London when Princess Elizabeth (later Queen Elizabeth I) was prisoner there. Fine pictures.

A27 Falmer,
Brighton (8 m)

The fishing and farming village of Brighthelmstone. In 1750 Dr Richard Russell of Lewes moved there to extol beneficial effects of sea air, bathing and drinking sea water. The Prince of Wales (later Regent, then George IV) sampled the cure and the Prince decided to move there and commute to Whitehall on horseback. He could keep his secret wife Mrs Fitzherbert in 'Brighton'. Henry Holland, then John Nash, built for him the Royal Pavilion, an extravaganza, with eastern touches of onion-shaped dome, pinnacles and minarets. Elegant squares and crescents of superb houses – Royal Crescent, Regency Square – one of Europe's most elegant resorts. The Prince Regent's rich if overpowering furnishings remain in the Pavilion; rooms in Chinese and Egyptian style, interesting kitchen with pillars like palm trees; music room, magnificent dining room. Open daily. The Dome, once the Prince's riding school, puts on classical and pop concerts. The narrow twisting lanes, lined with fishermen's cottages, now rich in antique shops and restaurants. Hotels, restaurants and guest houses line the three-mile promenade above gardens and beach; swimming pools, children's pools and entertainment. New marina luring more yachtsmen, London shows at two theatres, pop concerts, discos, dancing, racecourse, good restaurants – among top European resorts.

Hotels and restaurants
Granville Hotel and Trogs Restaurant, 125 King's Rd (tel 26722): I could not believe it; among shabby and ordinary bow-fronted houses on the seafront is this freshly painted guest house with Grecian double bath in one bedroom – blend of new décor, older furnishings; FP 3-course dinner, plus a cocktail, crudités (raw veg) with garlic dip, and coffee £7.95; fine dishes like Zesty trout with onions, lemon, peppers and herbs, Stilton and onion soup, pork cassoulet. Super calorific sweets. Chenin blanc house wine £3.64; another £3. Audrey Simpson and David were lecturers at London School of Economics. SB. BB £12–18.

French Connection, 11 Little East St (tel 24454): expensive, worth every penny. Rich spicy dishes, with old English touches, like Cumberland sauce, which includes port, with lamb and port in the steak and

kidney pie. I love the cooking, especially best end of lamb, boned, Provence herbs and garlic, baked in puff pastry (garre d'agneau Beaumanière). Meal £10–15.

Le Grangousier, 15 Western St (tel 772005): back to France, with all-French staff; name means vaguely 'The Great Swallow or Guzzle'; like a 4-star Relais Routiers; you sit at a long table, served first crudités; big basket of various sausages, then large pâté to help yourself; next course – choice of three dishes (with us, roast pork, steak or trout) with chips and veg; help-yourself choice of sweets. Brie cheese. Cost £6.45 lunch or dinner including half-bottle of wine. Shut Sun.

Pump House, 46 Market St (tel 26864): one of the oldest buildings in Brighton. Seawater once pumped up here for curative baths. 3-course steak meal £4.25; lunch £4.50; dinner £4.70–7. French menu, 3-course with aperitif, ½-bottle of goodish wine, coffee – £7.75.

local roads NW to West Blatchington, Devil's Dyke, Poynings, left to Fulking, Edburton, left down A2037 to Upper Beeding and Steyning (10 m)

At Poynings, Au Petit Normand (tel 346): Christian cooks and washes up; his wife Wendy serves – just like my home. Norman dishes include duck with pears; dinner (Tues–Sat) £7–9.

At Bramber, Old Tollgate (tel 813362): lunch FP £4.75; carvery £6.75; dinner (Fri, Sat) FP £6.50 inc wine; carvery £9.50 inc wine.

The Devil dug his dyke to flood churches of Sussex but he mistook a candle for dawn and thought it was knocking-off time.

Bramber: House of Pipes contains 25,000 smoking implements from 150 countries spanning 1500 years. National Butterfly Museum, Tudor House 'St Mary's': one million.

Steyning: Nice town of gabled old houses.

A283 skirting Wiston Park to Washington (4 m)

Washington: Not DC nor State but Saxon settlement of the 'sons of Wassa'. Known for its beer praised by Hilaire Belloc in his 'West Sussex Drinking Song'.

A24 Findon A280 High Salvation A27 Arundel

At Arundel, Norfolk Arms (tel 882101): supreme 18th-century coaching inn; elegant décor; try local game and trout; lunch FP £3.85; dinner FP £5.85, plus special items (excellent value). BB £13–19.50. SB.

Black Rabbit (tel 882828): charming pub beside river; bistro menu on blackboard – game pie, 26 oz T-bone steak (£5.80), Surf and Turf (fillet steak and lobster), prawn and pepper soup; plus homelier dishes. Meals £5–9. Buttery only Sun evening, Mon.

Arundel Castle, built 11th century: many additions, and excellent restoration; owned by Dukes of Norfolk for 500 years. Pictures, furniture, armour, china, tapestries. Splendid tombs in Fitzalan Chapel (1380); superb view from 12th-century keep. State robes and family miniatures especially interesting. 1200-acre park freely open to walkers. Castle open pm April–end Oct (not Sat). Museum of Curiosities (stuffed animals and birds in tableaux) in High Street. River Arun runs through town centre, Wildfowl Trust Centre (1 m) Swanbourne Lake: ponds, weedbeds, observation hides; birds include blackneck swans, diving and sea ducks. Open daily.

A27, then local road past Fontwell Park back on to A27 at Boxgrove Chichester (8 m)

At Chichester, Jason's Bistro, Cooper St, off South St (tel 783158): home cooking by Yorkshire chef; good soups, fish, game; meals: card lunch £3.50; dinner £7.

At Lavant (3 m on A286), Hunters' Lodge (tel Chichester 527329): produce from 2-acre garden used for English dishes (some Victorian, Edwardian): meals FP £6; card £8. BB £9.50.

Ye Olde Farmhouse, Holdens Farm, Bracklesham Lane, Bracklesham Bay (A286 from Chichester, B2198 near static caravan site). 18th-century house, inglenook, log fires in winter, warm welcome from Pat Humphreys and her American husband. Delightful cooking; pear salad with tarragon cream sauce and walnuts; sardine, lemon and fresh cream pâté; cubed pork in cider and apple sauce. Lunch FP £3.95; dinner FP (Mon–Fri) £5.95; card from £5. BB £7.50–9.50. SB including gourmet weekends.

At West Itchenor, Chichester Harbour, Ship (tel Birdham 512284): host is Cdr Derek Woods DSC – Americas Cup challenger '58. Fine buffet £3.20–6.90. BB £11.

Chichester: already tribal settlement when Romans used it in AD 43 as base camp; a city by AD 200. Cathedral started in 1091, high nave, graceful spire 277 ft; altar tapestry by John Piper (1966); pennant of *Gipsy Moth IV*, boat Sir Francis Chichester sailed solo round world (1966–7). Elaborate Market Cross (1511) in pedestrian shopping area. Park and walk. Festival Theatre (1962) modern, hexagonal, apron stage, very well equipped. Festival Theatre season (1 May–mid Sept): classics and contemporary plays, top actors and actresses. Military Police Museum, Rousillon Barracks.

Chichester Harbour S: 50 m shoreline, 17 m navigable channel; yachtsman's delight; yacht basin.

Bosham: between tidal creeks, picturesque but muddy; here King Canute proved to his courtiers that he could not command the tide. Saxon church rests on Roman base. Featured in Caen's Bayeayx tapestry with King Harold setting off for France. Now filled with yachting enthusiasts.

A27 towards Arundel at roundabout take small road left signposted Goodwood pass entrance to Goodwood Park House, racecourse; small road down to Charlton A286 Singleton (6 m)

At Goodwood, Richmond Arms (tel Chichester 557737): pretty, comfortable; good local game; meals FP £5.30; card £14.25–21. DBB (weekends) £17.50, good value.

At Charlton, Woodstock House (tel Singleton 666): super village hideaway; simple, comfortable, friendly; good walking base; home cooking. I love it. Dinner 4-course FP, little choice £6; good house wine £4. BB £10–13; DBB (2 days) £13.50–17. Shut Dec, Jan.

Goodwood House: seat of Duke of Richmond, designed by Wyatt 1790 round earlier house; 18th-century Gobelins tapestries, Sèvres china; paintings by Van Dyck, Stubbs, Romney, Canaletto; fine furnishings, super stables, gardens. Open May–mid Oct Sun, Mon. Also Tues–Thurs in August.

Goodwood Racecourse: long views, classic races; stand on the Trundle, Iron Age hill fort, for good view.

Singleton: Weald Open Air Museum – rescued old buildings (medieval farmhouse; smithy; charcoal burners' camp; treadmill, market hall, wheelwrights).

Chilsdown Vineyard, Singleton: 20,000 vines, tanks for 60,000 bottles; open May–end Sept.

A286 West Dean local road sharp right, on to B2141 Chilgrove, South Harting, Petersfield (9 m)

At Petersfield, Punch and Judy (tel 2214): simple lunch spot in handsome building (1613); roasts, puddings, grills; lunch card £4.75; single dishes; licensed.

West Dean Gardens: 30 acres, informal, 1748 horse-chestnut, (huge spread); 300 ft pergola; greenhouses (peaches); Museum of Gardening – old tools, lawnmowers from 1850, some pony-drawn.

South Harting, Uppark: house built 1690 for Lord Tankerville; Emma Hart, later Lady Hamilton and Nelson's mistress, lived here and danced on the dining table.

Little road north to Steep, follow signposts round Wheatham Hill to Hawkley and Empshott on to B3006 near Selborne Common Selborne, Chawton A31 to New Alresford Winchester (10 m)

At Winchester, Mr Pitkins, 4 Jewry St (tel Winchester 69630); from a derelict building Mr Anthony Pitkin has made a good old-style wine bar and eating house, with good traditional dishes, from roasts and steak pie to beef in claret; 3-course meals: lunch £5.50; dinner (tourist until 9pm £5.95); 4-course dinner £7.50; bar food. 100 wines £3.25–38.50 (Latour '66).

Wykeham Arms, 75 Kingsgate St (tel 3834): useful central inn for snacks, meals (casseroles, pies, puddings, pâtés) and exploring. Meals £4–5.50. BB £8–10. SB restaurant shut Sun ev, Mon.

Old Chesil Rectory, Chesil St (tel 3177): built 1450; Italian and English dishes; some very good – charcoal grilled Test Valley trout, Italian veal dishes, excellent home-made ravioli. Not cheap, average meal £9–10.

Southgate Hotel, 14 Southgate St (tel 51243): founded 1715, designed by Christopher Wren five years after he had finished St Paul's. Comfortable, TV in bedrooms, very good value. Meals: lunch £4.50; dinner £5.50. BB £11.38.

Rambling road of hills and trees, with nice views, worth detour. Gilbert White, pioneer naturalist (1720–93), was curate of Farringdon, near Selborne, wrote *The Natural History and Antiquities of Selborne* (1789). His house, The Wakes, is a museum, devoted to him and Antarctic explorer Captain Oates, 'an English Gentleman'.

Chawton: tiny village where Jane Austen lived (1809–17) and wrote *Emma, Mansfield Park* and *Pride and Prejudice.* Now a museum with personal belongings. She died in Winchester, was buried in the cathedral.

Winchester: city of beauty and, alas, too much traffic. King Alfred made this old Roman city capital of Saxon England in 9th century and it stayed so for 200 years. The 556 ft long cathedral started in 1079, was finished 1404. In Middle Ages, St Swithin's shrine was visited by pilgrims before continuing to Becket's shrine in Canterbury. St Swithin died in 862 asking to be buried in the churchyard where rain would fall on him. When in 971 his remains were reburied in the church, he made it rain for 40 days; so even now if it rains on his day 15 July we get 40 day's rain – as all cricketers know. Treasures include memorial window to 'Compleat Angler' Izaak Walton, a black marble Norman font, seven elaborately carved chancery chapels for special masses,

Winchester
continued

medieval wall paintings, stained glass, splendid tombs with bones of ancient kings, including Canute; in the library, 13th-century Bible and 10th-century History by Bede. City is rich in architecture from 13th century to Georgian. Two original city gates survive. Westgate is a museum; Kingsgate has medieval church over it. City mill (1774) spanning river is a Youth Hostel.

Winchester College, founded 1382, is one of the oldest public schools in Britain. Its motto is 'Manners Makyth Man' but in Latin is written in classrooms 'Learn, Leave or Be Licked'.

A3090 Standon, small road right to Braishfield, Timsbury, S to Abbotswood Romsey (11 m)

Old Manor, 21 Palmerston St, Romsey (tel 517353): attractive 1540 house; owner-chef Mauro Bregoli cooks some excellent dishes. Not cheap, but good value. Imaginative starters: marinated fresh salmon slices in piquant sauce; slices of roast beef marinated in milk, with tunny fish mayonnaise (delicious); snails; frog legs in white wine. Main courses include quail with grape and port sauce; local lamb marinated in herbs, garlic, then grilled. Meals: card around £12. Wines from £3.95 Italian to mouthwatering items – Richeborg '66 at £24.50, Talbot '62 claret £21.50. Lunch bar snacks more earthbound – home-made Lasagne. £1.15; local trout £1.55; New Forest venison £1.95; roast beef salad £1.95. Shut Sun eve, Mon.

Romsey – river Test is one of England's best trout and salmon rivers. Market town built round abbey founded 10th century, sold when Henry VIII dissolved monastries; 12th-century church remains. Broadlands House: two great Englishmen have lived here – Lord Palmerston, brilliant Foreign Minister in Victorian reign who achieved friendship with the French after centuries of wars and was called by the Germans 'the devil's son'; and Earl Mountbatten, uncle of Prince Philip, wartime naval hero, Viceroy of India, murdered by Irish Republican terrorists recently. Georgian. The Queen and Prince Philip spent part of their honeymoon there in 1947 as did the Prince of Wales and Lady Diana Spencer in 1981. Open Apr–Sept Tues–Sat, also Mon, Aug–Sept.

A31 Calmore, small road left, then soon right again to Bartley, near Cadnam small road south to join A337 to Lyndhurst (10 m)

Lyndhurst Park Hotel (tel 2824): I like it; 30s millionaire look from outside, friendly within; lively children around pool and lawns, attractive Mums dressing up at night, handsome Dads to warn me off. Landscape swimming pool, golf driving net; comfort, service; traditional menus with surprises. Large choice on each course. Dinner £6.45 and £7.85. French house wine £3.25. BB £16. SB – good value; Riding holidays.

Green Dragon, near Cadnam: thatched pub, nice people; home-cooked bar snacks with dish of day; home-made soup 50p. Pam Harvey Richards third-generation publican. BB around £8. Log fires, real ale garden.

New Forest: 90,000-acre forest, wildlife preserve for 900 years, first as Royal Hunt where a commoner could be blinded for disturbing a deer; now protected by Verderers' Court mounted guards called Agisters. 2,000 horses roam, donkeys, deer, badgers, otters, rare birds, rare wild flowers. Riding country; many stables. Verderers' Court, started 1388, meets in 17th-century Queen's House, Lyndhurst, to arrange care of forest. Stirrup hanging over fireplace was used once to measure size of forest dogs. If a dog could not pass through it, he was a 'danger to game' (deer). Beautiful coloured windows by William Morris in the church.

B3056 Beaulieu, B3055 Brockenhurst (12 m)

At Brockenhurst, Rose and Crown (tel 2225): small 17th-century coaching inn with cottage garden; pleasant bedrooms; Italian owner-chef; excellent pasta, especially my favourite – tortellini; fish soup, jugged hare, venison casserole; buffet lunch; dinner: card £4.50–7. BB £10–11. SB winter.

Palace House, home of Lord Montagu of Beaulieu. Heaven to engineers, enthusiasts and historians. Pick your favourite and dream; model railway, rides in early buses, fine gardens. Open 10 am to 5–6.30pm daily.

2½ m Buckler's Hard: pretty inlet village turned into ship-building centre in 18th century to use New Forest oaks. Built thirty ships for Nelson, including his favourite *Agamemnon*. Maritime museum in New Inn, including charts of Sir Francis Chicester who started from here.

local forest road to Burley, left to Bransgore, left at crossroads (signposted Lymington) in 2 m turn left, then right across A35; in 1 m Chewton Glen (15 m)

At New Milton, Chewton Glen (tel Highcliffe 5341): expensive, tasteful, relaxed luxury – one of my favourite hotels in the world. Superb gardens, big pool. Young French chef shows skill equal to most in Europe. FP lunch £8. Meals around £15 (card); superb wine list from Provence at £4.25 to Lafite Rothschild '52 at £90. BB £28–55 (suite) without breakfast. SB winter.

A337, Christchurch B3059, A35 Bournemouth (7 m)

At Bournemouth – hotels and restaurants of all shapes, sizes and most prices – Crust, Bus Station Arcade (tel 2143): well above average; fresh vegetables cooked to order, fresh shellfish, fish, game; meals £8–10 with wine; 100 extra wines, including '61–'66 bargain vintages.

Opus One, Southbourne Grove (tel 421240): experienced English couple run international restaurant, Georgian style, recommended by all experts. Lunch up to £3.50. Dinner FP £5.50. Card £8.

Bournemouth: forget the bathchair image; the last one is in the museum. Bournemouth is a genuine all-year resort for entertainment. Big clean sands, mild climate, 2000 acres parks and gardens; theatres with top shows, symphony concerts. Sports facilities – golf, tennis (championship courts), riding, water skiing, sailing, fishing. Lures droves of Continental visitors. English language schools entice students from worldwide, livening up the resort.

A3049, right on to A348, left on A341 until just past Canford School left on small road to A349 turn right past Yaffle Hill Gardens, over river Stour into Wimborne Minster (10 m)

Merley Bird Garden, before Wimborne: 100 species of tropical birds in outdoor avaries. Thomas Hardy lived in Wimborne, wrote a poem about its 'jack-o-clock' on West Tower with a grenadier striking quarter hours with a hammer. 16th-century Priest's House, High St museum with fine horse brasses.

B3078 for nearly 4 m, small road left to Witchampton small road N Moor Crichel, Wimborne St Giles; right out of village take B3078 left to Fordingbridge

At Redlynch, 2 m off A338 to right, Langley Wood (tel Earldoms 348): attractive quiet country house restaurant with three double rooms. Nice meals; card £9–10. BB £9. Shut Sun.

A338 Salisbury (28 m)

Salisbury – see Route 1.

A343 Over Wallop, Middle Wallop, small road to Nether Wallop, on to A30 left to Stockbridge Sutton Scotney; local road Stoke Charity, Micheldever to A33 right on A33 for 2½m, left on small road to Northington, right on B3046 to Old Alresford

At Middle Wallop, Fifehead Manor (tel Wallop 565): partly 11th century, once a nunnery closed because of frivolous behaviour of nuns; then home of Earl Godwin and his wife Lady Godiva. Owner-chef Margaret Leigh-Taylor has all-woman staff (not *too* frivolous), Try trout from river Test in garden herbs. Meals card £7.50 plus; bar snacks. Variety of wines. BB £16.50–20.

Wallops: three delightful villages by a stream, with framed thatched cottages. Worth dallying.

Old Alresford: Admiral Rodney, victor over French at Cape St Vincent in 1780, buried here in church.

---

local road left to Bighton, Meadstead, Alton B3004 Lindford B3002 Hindhead (60 m)

Hindhead: superb scenic views from 850 ft hill. In Saxon days area was covered in a huge forest; the word 'fold' means 'clearing in the forest'.

local roads to Haselmere B2131, left on to A283 Chiddingford A283 for under 1 m, then right to Hambledon (10 m)

At Haslemere, Lythe Hill Hotel, Petworth Rd (tel 51251): in 14-acre park on hill, with fine views, are twin hotels: Auberge de France – 14th-century half-timbered yeoman's farmhouse, now with superb French restaurant and romantic bedrooms; also efficient modern hotel, international restaurant ('Entente Cordiale') specializing in roast beef and Yorkshire 'popovers' (puddings)! English-style cooking good; French auberge cooking delightful. 'Entente' lunch FP £4.75; dinner FP £6.75; also card. 'Auberge' meals card around £10. BB £16–27 (some full suites).

Fourteen, Petworth Rd (tel 52625): nice restaurant, food cooked to order; lunch (Tues–Fri) FP £2.45 (bargain); dinner FP £6.50; card £11. Long, good wine list. Shut Sun, one week Aug.

At Chiddingfold, Crown (tel Wormley 2255): a gem; lovely half-timbered inn, best bar snacks I know, gastronomic dinners; chef from Imperial (Torquay) and Switzerland. Bar snacks hot and cold include Greek, Italian, Swedish dishes. Family Bistro (8am–10pm) dishes £1.45–4.75; try real Greek moussaka, classic coq au vin, Danish fish dishes. 4-course gastronomic meals; lunch (Tues–Sat) £9.90; dinner, Sun lunch £12.90. BB £16.50–22, private baths.

Haslemere: famous for craftsmanship until Industrial Revolution – leather, wood, glass, iron. Now Dolmetsch family make lutes, harpsichord and other early instruments and give recitals. Pleasant tidy town among woods and hills.

Chiddingfold: beautiful village with green, duck pond and 13th-century inn, Crown (see opposite), originally guest house for monk pilgrims on way to Canterbury. Edward VI boy-king, stayed there 400 years ago while retinue camped on village green. Villagers made windows for Westminster Abbey, St George's Windsor; early glass in 13th-century village church.

Hambledon: pioneer village of cricket, in 1777 Hambledon defeated All England; village blacksmiths carried sign: 'Pitch a Wicket and Play at Cricket with any Man in the Land'. Opposite original pitch on Broadhalfpenny Down is Bat and Ball Inn, where all true Englishmen stop for a pint of beer. Vineyard on nearby Windmill Hill produces good wine.

small road north to Hydestite, Busbridge, Godalming, A3100 Guildford (8 m)

At Godalming, Mead Hotel, 65 Meadrow (tel 21800): neat, pleasantly furnished little hotel praised by BBC viewers. Home cooking. Licensed. Dinner £4; snacks, buffet. BB £10–12.

At Guildford, Quinns, Guildford Rd (tel 60422): ex-actor Michael Quinn runs pleasant, useful hotel; weekly film show for residents; dinner £7.50; BB £9.50–12.50.

Rowley's Wine Bar, Tunsgate, 124 High St (tel 63277): 16th-century building; family run; rightly proud of game pie, own pâtés; meals £4.50–6; import own French house wine £3.30; 30 others.

Godalming: narrow streets, half-timbered houses, Russia's Peter the Great stayed at King's Arms in 1689; Tsar and Prussian King met for dinner in 1816. Winkworth Arboretum, 3 m SE, hillside of rare trees with lake and views.

Guildford: old county and market town, now city; buildings range from keep of Henry II castle to new modern-Gothic cathedral, recent University of Surrey. Pleasant place. Guildhall, 17th-century façade on Tudor building; 1683 clock; attractive waterway winds through locks beside mills and pubs; pleasure craft.

Clandon Park (3 m E): Palladian house (1733), splendid rooms, fine 18th-century furniture; don't miss it. Open Apr–mid Oct, pm, not Mon.

A246 Newlands Corner, local road to Shere, A25 Gomshall, Abinger Hammer B2126 Holmbury St Mary, Ockley to A24 at Capel right on A24 Horsham (18 m)

At Gomshall, Black Horse (tel Shere 2242): rumoured Gladstone held cabinet meeting here in 1880; certainly wrote emergency dispatches about Montenegro! Home-made English dishes. Dinner £7; bar lunches; BB £13.80.

At Horsham, King's Head (tel 3126): good cooking. Meals FP £4.70; card £9. BB £13–22. SB (weekends).

At Lower Beeding, 3 m SE Horsham, Cisswood House (tel Lower Beeding 216): first-class restaurant in house built by then owner of

Newlands Corner: grand viewpoint down wooded slopes to other counties.

Shere: attractive village with stream through centre. 12th-century church with medieval glass.

Abinger Hammer: smiths' hammers long since silenced, but a model blacksmith still hammers on bell on the village clock.

Horsham: 13th-century iron town; building stones still quarried, but mostly market town for cattle and farm produce. No longer can you buy a wife as in mid 1800s (price around 30 shillings – £1.50).

Horsham
continued

Harrods, now owned by internationally known chef and family. Almost immaculate cooking; meals around £10 card; good wines; rare white Burgundy. Shut lunch Sat, Sun, Mon, Tues; Sun, Mon eves.

A281 to edge of Horsham, small road left through St Leonards Forest across A279, under A23 to Slaugham and Staplefield right on B2114, B2115 to Cuckfield (10 m) B2036, small road left to Balcombe; right in Balcombe across valley to Ardingly (signposted) 1 m S on B2028, turn left to Horsted Keynes

St Leonards Forest: deep wooded valleys; heather and gorse on hills.

Ardingly, Wakehurst Place Gardens: exotic shrubs, plants, trees, pretty watercourses linking lakes and ponds; run by Royal Botanic Gardens, Kew. Open daily.

Horsted Keynes, Sheffield Park: Bluebell Railway, joy to all romantics, closed by British Rail 1958, bought by preservation society, staff include amateur enthusiasts; steam locomotives back to 1872, original coaches; stations have old ads; used for films. Runs through woodlands thick with bluebells early summer.

---

right on small road S to T-junction, left until A275, right alongside Sheffield Park to North Common Nature Reserve left on A272 Maresfield (21 m)

Sheffield Park: garden and house separately owned. Garden (NT) lovely through the year. 77 acres and five lakes laid out by Capability Brown in 18th century. Magnificent. Closed mid Nov–end Mar, and Mon. House 18th-century Gothic. Open May–Oct, Mon, Wed, Thur, Sun.

A22 left, B2026
Duddleswell and
Hartfield
right B2110 to
Withyam,
Groombridge,
Langton Green
Tunbridge Wells
(14 m)

Just after turn on to B2026
on left is the Enchanted Place
of A. A. Milne's story of
Winnie the Pooh. Take
second left along B2026 (tiny
road) then quickly right to
find, unmarked, Pooh Bridge
where the bear played Pooh
Sticks – and if this is Double
Dutch to you, read *Winnie
the Pooh*!

Route 3

Oxford – Wye Valley – Forest of Dean – Hereford – Malverns – Stratford – South Midlands – Oxford

Oxford A34
Woodstock (8 m)

Oxford – see Route 1.

At Woodstock, Bear (tel 811): part of England's tradition – first licensed 1232, old when much of old Oxford was new; no one remotely connected with Oxford would deny knowing it. Charmingly decorated; cooking to fit such taste; lunch FP £3.20 and £7.10; dinner FP £7.45 and £8.95. 100 wines, known for superb ports; BB £22.50–36.50.

Luis Restaurant, 19 High St: Luis Castro came from Coruna in north Spain, where Sir John Moore fought his last battle against Napoleon and the people are still violently independent; taught Spanish and French cuisine; now combines dishes of both with English cooking; good value; lunch FP £3; dinner FP £5.80; card £8.50.

Modern building should not have been allowed to destroy Woodstock's 18th-century elegance, but some is left.

Blenheim Palace: gift from the nation to our greatest general, John Churchill, Duke of Marlborough, for four great victories over the French, especially over French and Bavarians at Blenheim, 1704. Vanbrugh began the building, fell out with the formidable Duchess; it was finished by his partner Hawksmoor. The nation's gratitude fell short by £50,000 (a lot of money then) which the Duke had to pay himself. Superb in its park setting, with lake, designed by Capability Brown in 1760. Wonderful water garden. Enormous hall, lovely dining room and library; room where Sir Winston Churchill, grandson of 7th Duke, was born in 1874. Open end Mar–end Oct; park all year.

B4437 Charlbury, B4026 Chipping Norton (10 m) B4450 Churchill, right on small road to Kingham, Bledington, B4450 again to Stow-on-the-Wold (8 m)

Chadlington House Hotel (1½ m left off B4026) (tel Chadlington 437): real country house hotel, remote, in own grounds, lovely views. Family run. Everything home-made including bread. Meals FP £6.50 (extra for steak); house wine £3.25; others reasonable. BB £8–12.50.

At Kingham, Langston Arms (tel 319): once Squire Langston's hunting lodge; big stables contain collection of horse-drawn carriages, used for films and taking hotel guests on local trips. Tasty home cooking. Lunch FP £4.50; dinner FP £5.50; card also. BB £11.15; DBB £15–16.50; SB, good value.

At Stow-on-the-Wold, White Hart, The Square (tel 30674): old inn with rumpy floors, low doorways, serving old English pub grub, from steak and kidney and shepherd's pies to 18th-century lampie and Elizabethan fidget pie of ham, apples and onions, enormous Gloucester sausage; chef-owner Maurice Bird was trained at Broadway's Lygon Arms. Pub meals £3–4, lunch or dinner; restaurant card £4–7. DBB £16–18. SB.

Rafters, Park St (tel Stow 30200): good cooking, mostly straightforward but good specialities (saddle of hare in puff pastry, scallop mousse). Lunch weekdays FP £4.95; Sun FP £7.25; lunch and dinner card £8–11. Shut Sun eve, Mon.

Charlbury: canoeing on river Evenlode. Wychwood Forest: 1500 acres have survived of huge Royal hunting ground from Henry I's time. Nature reserve; many deer.

18th-century Ditchley Park (2 m NE): once owned by family of Robert E. Lee, Confederate general in American Civil War; now Anglo-American conference centre.

Chipping Norton: 'chipping' means 'cheapening' – a market. 700 ft high, at road junctions; busy; Victorian tweed mill; parish church has fine brasses; White Hart Inn has much original 18th-century furniture. Rollright Stones (3 m N), Bronze Age circle erected 1800–550 BC.

Stow-on-the-Wold: 'where the wind blows cold' – old saying refers to exposed position on hill between two rivers. Once most prosperous wool town in England. Medieval cross in square, old houses; Cromwell imprisoned 1000 Royalists in 12th-century church after a battle.

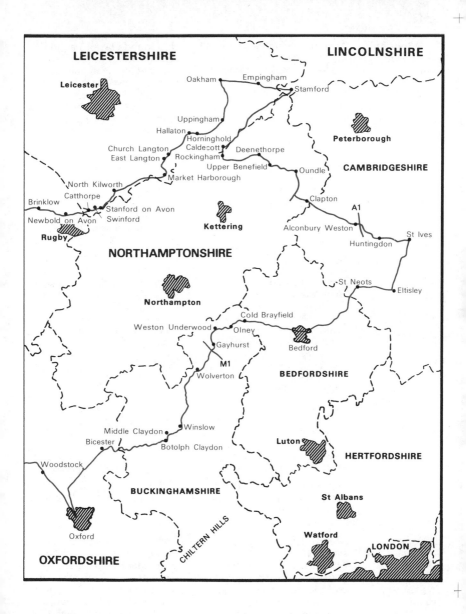

A429 Bourton-on-the-Water (3 m)

At Upper Slaughter, Lords of Manor Hotel (tel Bourton-on-the-Water 20243): home of Witts family for 200 years; hotel since 1972; Francis Witts (rector 1808–54) wrote *Diary of a Cotswold Parson* (pub 1978). Run by members of family; delightfully furnished, lovely gardens. Simple cooking, fresh local food. Also bar dishes. Lunch FP £4.55 (£5.50 Sun); dinner card around £8. BB £17–28. SB Nov–late March; horse riding.

The Manor, Lower Slaughter (tel Bourton 20456): sorry, another pricey manor house, granted by James I to George Whitmore in 1608. A modern touch – heated indoor swimming pool; grounds with tennis, badminton, squash, trout river, woodlands, lovely garden. Dinner £11; BB with bath £20–25. SB (3-day DBB £26.50 per day).

At Bourton-on-the-Water, Brookside (tel 20371): 17th-century manor overlooking river and village green; pleasant; local trout. Meals FP £5. BB £10.50–13.

Old New Inn (tel 20467): in same family for fifty years. Dinner £6.50; BB £12.50.

Upper and Lower Slaughter (off A429 to right): outstanding even among many lovely villages in rich, honey-coloured Cotswold stone; river Eye runs through both; many lovely old houses, few new ones. Upper Slaughter manor house built by Slaughter family, when they took over manor from Abbé of Fecamp in 1539, on top of older house. They emigrated mid 18th-century to America. Terraced garden. Open Fri pm, 1 May–30 Sept.

Bourton-on-the-Water: almost too beautiful, attracts summer crowds. River Windrush meanders through it under low stone bridges; riverside path takes you to quiet spots with willows dipping into water.

In gardens of Old New Inn is a one-ninth scale model of village, with every detail. Birdland, in grounds of Tudor manor, has vivid parrots and macaws flying around, penguins in glass-sided pool, flamingos, toucans and hummingbirds in aviaries. In 18th-century corn mill is motor museum.

B4068, left on A436, miss A40, turn right on A435 to Cheltenham (15 m)

At Hazleton (2 m left off A436), Windrush House (tel Northleach 364): modern house, comfortable; good cooking: tarragon chicken, jugged Cotswold hare, delicious pigeons in wine with celery and walnuts – all fresh veg; dinner £5–6.50; bring own wine; BB £7–8. Closed Jan.

Cheltenham: Regency spa, elegant terrace on tree-lined promenade; music, art, sport (county cricket, steeplechase course); waters still drunk in Pittville Pump Room which has lovely grounds with tree-flanked lakes; also at town hall. Original medicinal springs found in 18th century, developed by retired

Cotswold Hotel, 17 Portland St (tel Cheltenham 23998): good pub for bar lunches, snacks; dish of day; often fresh salmon.

Malvern View Hotel, Cleeve Hill (2 m NE) (tel Bishops Cleeve 2017): almost immaculate cooking by owner-chef; good choice; well-kept rooms. Dinner £9.50; remarkable wine list a joy to read, from £5 to £175 for double magnum Mouton Rothschild '70. BB £14–17.

Mister Tsang, 63 Winchcombe St (tel Cheltenham 38727): true Cantonese cooking; Willie Tsang grew up in family restaurant in Hong Kong, 25 years in restaurants Singapore, Malaysia; then Paris, London. Specializes in seafood; meals around £4; wine; shut Sun, Mon lunch.

pirate; George III made it fashionable in 1788, but biggest boost came in 1816 when Duke of Wellington, fresh from Waterloo victory over Napoleon, took waters for a liver disorder. Alkaline waters contain magnesium, sodium bicarbonate, sulphate.

Music festival, started 1944, includes new works of British composers. Gustav Holst (1874–1934, British despite Swedish name) born at 4 Clarence Road, now a museum, composed *The Planets* orchestral suite.

Staverton airport (4 m W) contains museum of Second World War British planes.

B4070 Birdlip, small road right Bentham A417 Gloucester (8 m)

Peebys, 10 Worcester St, Gloucester (tel 25636): useful little bistro-style restaurant with English cooking; local salmon, trout. Lunch (omelettes to steak) £2–3; good dinner menu; try Gloucester smokie starter (hot crab creamed in double Gloucester cheese); marinated mushroom salad; baked, boned trout stuffed with apples; chicken breast stuffed with ham and nuts; good home-made sweets; dinner FP £7.95 includes coffee, liqueur. Shut Sun.

Tasters, 22 London Rd (tel 417556): stockbroker and wallpaper-designer wife run true bistro for quick-service, good little meals; try lamb terrine, Smoky Joe (smoked haddock in wine, cream) as starters; main course cider-baked gammon to moussaka; dish of day; £2.50–4; fair wine choice; 'bottomless' coffee 35p. Shut Sun eve.

Gloucester: Roman fort of Glevum, became retirement centre for demobilized Roman legionaires. Glorious cathedral; Normans built it as abbey church 1089; medieval craftsmen beautified it in 13th century; superb tower added 15th century. Magnificent 14th-century cloisters; stained-glass window 72x38 ft, second biggest in Britian (biggest at York), memorial to those who died at Battle of Crécy in 1346 when Black Prince defeated French. Interesting tomb of Edward II, murdered at Berkeley Castle 1327. Bishop Hooper's Lodging in Westgate St is timber-framed house in which Protestant bishop spent last night before martyrdom by Catholics (1555 burned at stake). Gloucester now commercial city, canal built 1827 connects it with Bristol Channel.

A48 Westbury on Severn, Newnham, small road right to Cinderford (12 m)

At Cinderford, White Hart, St Whites Rd (tel Dean 23139): bistro meal £5; restaurant £8. BB £7.

Westbury: unique 17th-century Dutch-style water gardens of former Westbury Court; long derelict, now restored.

Newnham: attractive little town on edge of Forest of Dean, views across Severn estuary to Cotswolds.

B4226 through Forest of Dean, Coleford, B4228 Ross on Wye (18 m)

At Coleford (2 m S), Wyndham Arms, Clearwell (tel Dean 33666): famous for hors d'oeuvre; fresh salmon in season; remarkable lunch (main dish often roast lamb, beef or trout) FP £3.15; lunch or dinner card around £10. 5 house wines £3.75. BB £7–8. All good value.

At Ross on Wye, Brookfield House, Over Ross (tel Ross 2188): lovely Queen Anne house (1704) with Georgian additions; turned into hotel by the Bakers who have made a good job of it. Dinner FP £5.50; house wines £3.25; BB £9.25–10.75. Shut mid Nov–end Jan. SB summer/winter.

Pengethley Hotel (4 m along A49 Hereford road) (tel Harewood End 211): pricey but much to offer; elegant Georgian house, lovely garden, beautiful views; bedrooms vary but all with bathroom, colour TV. Family rooms; coach house ground-floor rooms suit disabled. English country house cooking; garden produce, Hereford beef, Wye salmon. Fine kitchens, very experienced chef. Lunch FP £5.50; dinner FP £9.50, plus card; 200 wines; BB £24–37; SB.

Forest of Dean: 27,000 acres, 22,000 covered with 20 million trees, mostly oak, beech, also birch, ash, conifers, holly. Hills with fast flowing streams in valleys. Beautiful drives and walks; was remote until Severn Bridge (1966) made access easy from Bristol. People of forest, called Foresters, have ancient privileges for coalmining (enormous coalfield beneath forest), cutting stone, grazing sheep. Foxes, badgers still abound; kestrels, owls, sparrowhawks, snipe, herons, ring dove. Speech House: 17th-century courtroom for settling disputes between Foresters and iron founders of forest; now hotel dining room.

At Goodrich, road left over river Wye leads to Yat Rock with magnificent views over Symonds Yat, gorgeous horseshoe sweep of river with 4 m loop returning to within 400 yd of original course; canoeing.

Goodrich Castle: superb ruins overlooking river Wye; 12th-century home of Talbot family; held out against Welsh raiders but destroyed by Cromwell in Civil War.

Ross: modest town with big market; good touring centre for magnificent countryside.

small road N from Ross to Brampton Abbots, Hole in Wall, How Caple, Fawley Cross, King's Caple, Fownhope join B4224 Hereford (16 m)

At Carey, by King's Caple, Cottage of Content (tel Carey 242): good value, specializes in game dishes; bistro meal £6; barn restaurant (Thur, Fri, Sat only) £9; bedrooms in farm opposite, BB £10.

At Fownhope, Bowens Farmhouse (tel 430): third derelict farmhouse which Amy Williams has turned into super farm guest house; 17th-century beams, inglenook; nice garden; Amy's famous English cooking; pork in cider, chicken in cream and sherry, beef in red wine, super home-made soups; Dinner £4.90; wines £3–4.75; BB £8–9; DBB £13.75.

At Hereford, Green Dragon, Broad St (tel 2506): lovely 18th-century front hides older coaching inn; world famous Italian chef Pietro Chirizzi. English dishes very good, Italian beautiful; try home-made pastas. Lunch FP £4.75 (children under 14 half price); dinner FP £6.50. BB £15–22.75, all with bathroom. SB.

Saxty's, 33 Widemarsh St (tel 57872): King Edward VII would be at home with mahogany counters, marble tops and music; joint owners admit to eccentricity; Peter Saxty Hill, estate agent, chairman Hereford United FC; Peter Williamson, horticulturalist, world traveller 'seeking ideas'. Lunchtime, home-cooked wine-bar fare, menu around £4; evening same plus restaurant menu, around £7.50. French house wines £2.90.

Fownhope's most famous son was prizefighter Tom Spring (b Tom Winter at Rudge End, 1795). All England champion 1823–4, fighting bare-knuckle, he had a fight of 77 rounds lasting 2 hrs 29 mins. A round then lasted until someone was knocked down. Early Norman church has fine 12th-century carving of Virgin and Child.

Hereford: David Garrick, actor, born here; so was Nell Gwynne (plaque in Gwynne St). Once defence centre for English against Welsh; now market centre for superb farming country, known for rich red soil, white-faced cattle, apples, cider, hops, salmon. River Wye flows under 15th-century arched bridge. Pink sandstone cathedral, partly 12th century, one of England's finest; contains map of world drawn around 1300; oldest chair in England. Chained library has 1500 books back to 9th-century Anglo Saxon gospels in Latin. Churchill Gardens Museum, Aylestone Hill, has costume collection 1750–1930, with suitable furniture. Bulmer's: world's biggest cider factory, has railway centre, home of famous loco *King George V* and other relics; engine in steam some days, open weekends Apr–Sept.

| A438 Ledbury (15 m) | Applejack Bistro, 44 The Homend (tel Ledbury 2481): owned by Bob Evans, racing motorist, Le Mans; good cooking for simple place; meals £5–7.50; Italian house wine £3.95. Shut Sun, Mon.

Hope End, just N Ledbury (tel Ledbury 3613): Barrett of Wimpole Street built exotic eastern-style house up the hill; father of Elizabeth Barrett, who lived 23 happy years here; later eloped with poet Robert Browning. House gone, but stables now little country house hotel; walled garden; home-grown produce. Dinner 5-course FP £10; DBB £26–28. | Ledbury: seven historic inns; market supported on chestnut pillars; half-timbered houses; charming little town. Narrow Church Lane unchanged since Tudor days; battle fought in main street between Cromwell's soldiers and mounted Cavaliers led by ostentatious Prince Rupert of the Rhine; for once, Royalists won. Hops grow around here. |

| A449 Little Malvern, Malvern Wells, Great Malvern (8 m) | Holdfast Cottage Hotel, Welland (½ m little Malvern) (tel Hanley Swan 288): in charming garden, surrounded by farmland; popular, so phone ahead. Excellent dishes, old English; try trout pie, parsnip and apple soup, hot spiced apple and sultana pie. Dinner 4-course FP £7, very good value; BB £11–12.50.

Walmer Lodge, 49 Abbey Road (tel Malvern 4139): uninspiring house, simple bedrooms, but Maurice Bunton's cooking is superb; ex-chef London Ritz; many awards: French and English dishes. Dinner card around £8; good Burgundies, Rioja and Portuguese Dao wines; BB £9.20–10.35. | Malvern Hills, 9 m long, have six townships along them. Great Malvern, a spa where you can still take the waters (Holy Well, Malvern Wells). Interesting Victorian town on hillsides where under old common rights sheep are allowed to graze on grass beside avenue. Expensive to run them down. Town put on George Bernard Shaw's plays when others would not and Shaw Theatre Festival now revived. Elgar the composer lived at Malvern Wells. Jenny Lind, 'Swedish Nightingale', lived at Wynds Point, buried here. Fine 15th-century priory church, stained-glass monk's stalls. Morgan sportscars still hand-made here. Most attractive surrounding scenery. |

Malvern Wells *continued*	Cottage in the Wood, Malvern Wells (tel Malvern 3487): expensive but worth it. Delightful house, 7-acre garden, spectacular views; each room individually furnished with flair; Michael Ross owns one of the best hotels in Britain. Lunch FP £5.75, £11.75; dinner FP £9.75, £11.75; house wine £4.50/litre; BB (bathroom, teamaker, TV) £18–24. SB winter.	
small roads S Hanley Swan, B4209 Hanley Castle, Upton on Severn (17 m)	Cromwell's, Church St (tel 2447): craft shop and bistro in timbered old house; interesting dishes; lunch £3–4; dinner £8–9; house wine £3.25. Shut Sun, Mon eve. Swan (tel 2601): on riverside; bar snacks; bistro lunch from £1.25; dinner about £10 with wine. White Lion, High St (tel 2551): historic inn, English cooking; meals £7–8; wine Nicolas £4.85/litre to Latour '67 £35. BB £11.25–18.	Upton: until 1900 an important port on inland waterways; now new marina has awakened it; packed with small craft in summer; little streets and old inns full of people. Market; Georgian and older houses. Civil War battle here just before final Battle of Worcester. 300 Royalist troops defeated in churchyard by 18 Roundheads who had crossed broken bridge silently at dawn. River trips on boat with bar.
A4104 Pershore (7 m)	Angel, 9 High St (tel Pershore 2046): old posting inn, imaginative dishes; old English salamagundy, sole in cider and cream, duck in Yorkshire sauce. Dinner FP £6; card £8–9. 80 wines. BB £12–17.50. SB winter.	Market town; Georgian houses, still surrounded by many plum orchards despite EEC agricultural policy. 14th-century six-arched bridge over river Avon.
B4082 then small road to Wyre Piddle, Lower Moor, to A435 Evesham (8 m)	Wyre Piddle, Avonside Hotel (tel Pershore 2654): on river bank with lawns to water, swimming pool on terrace; elegantly furnished, outstanding little hotel. Dinner FP £5.75; card £7.75. BB £9–16. Evesham Hotel, Coopers Lane (tel 6344): Jenkinson	Set in loop of river Avon, waterside park, sailing, canoeing. Passage from marketplace, under Abbot Reginald's Gateway (1135) leads to remains of abbey (AD 708). Obelisk on green in memory of Simon de Montfort, father of English Parliament, killed fighting

family run historic, pretty, efficient and eccentric hotel. Built 1540, called Mansion House, sold 1735 to a dissenter; John Wesley stayed often, preached under elm tree; became hotel in 1906. Cedar of Lebanon planted in 1809 is hotel emblem. Complete new menu weekly, so 1000 different dishes served each year. Very good cooking. Wines from 20 countries, not France or Germany. House wine from Chile £4. Includes Great Wall Dry White from China: 'Mongolian winds give it a crispness not found in Muscadet – light, pleasant, revolutionary' says wine list. Outstanding lunchtime buffet £4.15; carvery lunch £7.15; dinner card £10. BB £19.50–25. SB.

Prince Edward (later Edward I) in 1265. Elegant town, many Georgian houses; surrounded by apple blossom in spring.

Bretforton, 3 m E: a gem; whole village charming except car park on green. Fleece Inn, 14th-century oak beamed, with witch marks on stone floor to keep out evil spirits; antiques worthy of museum include 48-set piece of Stuart pewter I covet for my collection. Inn was in same family from 14th century to 1977, when last owner left it to National Trust. 13th-century church, fine carvings, linked to Manor House by avenue of yews.

---

small road Badsey, Willersey A44 to Broadway (6 m)

At Broadway, good spots for light meals are:

Gallery, North St: former 15th-century coachouse run by ex-racing driver Geddes Yeates; menu includes taramasalata; charcoal grilled steaks. Around £4. Wine.

Goblets Wine Bar, High St: snacks to curried chicken; dishes 75p–£2.50; house wine £4.

Cotswold Rest, The Green: run by same family since 1939; English cooking; long varied menu; home-made ice cream; £1.70–£4. Wine £4.

Hotels: Milestone, 122 High St (tel 853432): friendly, homely; roasts (nice duck); local fruit, veg. Lunch FP £4.50; dinner FP £6.50; card £8. Wines £3 (Bordeaux) to

Broadway: beautiful, commercially exploited; called 'Painted Lady of the Cotswolds'. Pretty houses, flowers, produces some of the world's best modern furniture. Industry started by Gordon Russell in 1904 to mend antique furniture for Lygon Arms Hotel; products since exported round world from Baghdad Palace, cathedrals to Beverly Hills homes. Broadway gets crowded midsummer.

Broadway Hill (1024 ft) is country park (nature trail); topped by tower, 18th-century fake castle built as 'folly' by Earl of Coventry. 12th-century church; Fish Inn (18th-century) has sundial on it – built as summer house. Snowshill Manor, past country park: 15th-century,

Broadway
continued

£11.20 (Gevrey Chambertin).
BB £12–17.

Lygon Arms (tel 852255):
magnificent 14th/16th-century
buidling, magnificently
furnished with antiques; old
beams, panelling, log fires,
fine china, glass, pretty
garden, in heart of beautiful
Broadway. Chef renowned
for 'nouvelle' cooking. Could
have become a clip joint but
for genius of one of Europe's
best hoteliers, managing
director Douglas Barrington,
here when I came first in
1946. Lunch FP £6.50; dinner
FP £11.50; good wine list
from £4.50. Rooms beautiful
but expensive; BB from £29.
DBB 2 days £70. SB winter.

given to National Trust 1952
by eccentric collector; rooms
full of old musical
instruments, early bicycles,
guns, tools, Japanese
Samurai armour and
weapons. Open May–Sept
Wed–Sun; Apr, Oct Sat and
Sun.

small road signposted Dovers Hill, then Chipping Campden (3 m)	Noel Arms (tel Evesham 840317): nostalgic memories of postwar weekends; 600 years old; now bathrooms to most bedrooms; one four-poster bed dated 1651. Lunch from £4.50; dinner from £7: BB £11.70–16.	14th-century wool town; Woolstaplers Hall now museum of photographic and medical equipment; fine market hall; NE lovely gardens of Hidcote Manor (open April–31 Oct, except Tues, Fri), and Kiftsgate Court (lovely views, open April–30 Sept, Sun, Wed, Thur). Chipping Campden runs own Olympic Games, started 17th century, including shin-kicking contest (professional fouls?).
small road Aston Subedge, right on A46 Mickleton, local road to left just outside village to Long Marston, Welford on Avon, right to Stratford Upon Avon (13 m)	At Ilmington, 3 m W Mickleton, Howard Arms (tel Ilmington 226): owner chef Robin Shepherd trained Paris Cordon Bleu school and London Hilton; dinner £6–7; Open Tues–Sat eve, Sun lunch.	Welford: village of thatched timber-framed cottages in loop on Avon; narrow bridge: village green with chestnut tree and old striped maypole; lychgate to church; three inns; a proper English village.
Stratford Upon Avon	Somehow it retains its identity as a mellow market town, despite daytime crowds. William Shakespeare was born in Henley Street in 1564; his timbered birthplace was bought in 1847 for the Shakespeare Trust for £3000; more than 500,000 visit it each year; a lovely old house. He probably went to Stratford Grammar School in Church Street – 250 years old when Edward VI refounded it in 1553. In 1582 he married Anne Hathaway, farmer's daughter of Shottery, 2 m away; you can visit the thatched cottage there. He returned to buy New Place, corner of Chapel Street, died there in 1616; it was later demolished. He is buried in Holy Trinity Church by the river; a bust, quill in hand, is set among gravestones. His greatest memorial is the Royal Shakespeare Theatre where the Royal Shakespeare Company play. Its Picture Gallery and Museum houses costumes of the greatest actors and actresses, back to Irving, Garrick, Ellen Terry, Sarah Siddons, and paintings by Reynolds, Romney and others.	

Stratford
Upon Avon
continued

Harvard House, 16th-century, in High Street, was home of Katherine Rogers, who married Robert Harvard. Their son, on leaving Cambridge University, emigrated to the US and founded Harvard University.

Stratford Motor Museum, Shakespeare St, has superb vintage cars; also old petrol pumps and 1920s garage.

River Avon, with riverside walks, is lovely here; boat trips April–Oct.

Hotels and restaurants
Arden Hotel, Waterside (tel 294949): good, medium prices; in garden opposite theatre, overlooking river; known for fresh roasts, big cold buffet, home-made puddings; most bedrooms with bathrooms. Lunch around £4; dinner FP £5.50; card £7.50, (good value); house wine £3.40; many others around £4.15. BB £13–21. DBB £20.

Ashburton House, 27 Evesham Place (tel 292444): pre-theatre dinners from 6pm (pre-order) £6.60; 5-course dinner £10. Salmon and trout fishing. BB £8.80.

Stratford House, Sheep St (100 yd from theatre) (tel 68288); high quality bed and breakfast hotel; beautifully furnished. Drinks cupboard; book ahead – very popular. BB £15.50–24.50; also family room for 4 with bathroom. BB £13.50 each person.

Marianne, 3 Greenhill St (tel 293563): French cooking by French owner and chef. Very good value. Lunch FP £3 (or dish of day £1.50); dinner £5–10. Shut Sun.

At Shottery, 2 m, Thatch, Cottage Lane (tel Stratford 293122): tourist nosh restaurant; quick lunch, snack lunch; salad lunch; cream tea; pre-theatre 3-course supper; 3-course lunch with roast; 3 courses under £5. Wine. Pleasant; thatched roof; outside tables.

Billesley Manor, 4 m A422 (tel Billesley 763737): pricey, but away from Stratford crowds. Superb manor house, age unknown but Shakespeare used the library; sumptuously and tastefully furnished; pretty bedrooms, all with bathrooms; Shakespeare suite rumoured to be where he wrote *As You Like It*. It has priesthole and gold-plated taps in bathroom. Beautiful cooking, outstanding sauces and vegetables. Dinner FP £10; card £12. BB £20–27.50. SB weekends.

A46 Warwick follow signposts right to Leamington Spa (10 m)

Zaranoffs, 16 Market Place (tel 42708): pleasantly eccentric; better phone – popular; Josej Zaranoff is Russian-Latvian refugee, ex-wrestler, boxer, film 'heavy'. Vicky is English, ex-boarding school art teacher. They buy what looks good at several markets; only frozen foods used are frog legs, from India. Cooking truly cosmopolitan, very good, with large helpings; everything lavish. We liked it all. People tend to eat late. They import wines from around world. Lunch FP £3; card £5; dinner card £7–10. Wines from £2.80 (drinkable Minervois, and – to me undrinkable – Retsina).

Tudor House Inn, West St (tel 45447): built 1472, pub with many ales and lagers; good hot, cold snacks; steak pie; jacket potatoes with choice 15 fillings; lasagne, sausage pie. Also restaurant around £7. Rooms – and ghost, who heads for Stratford leaving door open and not paying his bill.

Warwick is a medieval walled city on banks of the Avon, with fine old timbered houses; you must park and walk to see it. The castle, with formidable walls and turrets, rises above river. See it best from across the river. Built in 14th century on site of another of William the Conqueror's time, it stayed in hands of Earls of Warwick until 1978, when the Earl sold it to Madame Tussaud's waxworks. You can climb twelve-sided Guy's Tower and clover-shaped Caesar's Tower; alas, the Canaletto paintings have gone but still fine collection of paintings, tapestries. Arms from Middle Ages to 17th century in armoury and inhumanity in the torture chamber.

Royal Leamington Spa: Queen Victoria made it 'Royal' in 1838; grew from village to fashionable spa around 1815; salty springs feed Pump Room baths still

Leamington Spa
continued

Crown, Coventry St
(tel 42087): good value.
Meals FP £4.50; card £6. BB
£8.50.

At Leamington, Landsdowne,
Clarendon St (tel 21313):
charming Regency house,
well restored; excellent
value. Resident owners
British, Swiss-trained. Fine
home-made soups, pâtés.
Dinner FP £5.70; BB £8.25–
12.95. SB (2 days, good
value).

Regent Hotel, 77 The Parade
(tel 27231): a favourite of
mine, built 1819; Prince
Regent stopped here; also
Queen Victoria, General
Grant when US President,
Duke of Wellington,
Napoleon III, Dickens,
Longfellow, explorer H. M.
Stanley. Beautifully
decorated, superb staircase;
in same family since 1904,
excellently managed by
Vernon May for 24 years.
Fine Italian chef in main
kitchen; young English chef
in outstanding Vaults
gourmet restaurant. Lunch
FP £5.25; dinner £7.50;
Vaults dinner card from
£8.50. Vaults closed Sun.
House wine £4; 100 others.
BB £17–24. SB weekends.

used for rheumatic
treatment. Taste waters in
Pump Room annexe to work
up thirst. Lovely little town
with fine houses – Georgian,
Regency, early Victorian.
Good touring centre. Grand
Union Canal meets river
Leam here.

A452 towards
Kenilworth, right
on A444
Stoneleigh,
Coventry (8 m)

At Kenilworth, Clarendon
House (tel 54694): Tudor
hotel built 1538 round an oak
tree which still supports roof.
Family owned – Mrs Lea is
expert on antique maps –
walls covered with them;
Tavern restaurant in former
stables; Cromwellian
garrison during Parliament
siege of Kenilworth; good
game dishes; try pheasant in
Madeira wine with oranges,

Kenilworth: impressive ruins
of famous castle on green
slopes; Norman keep; John
O'Gaunt remodelled it as
palace in 14th century.
Setting of Walter Scott's
novel *Kenilworth*. Earlier held
by Simon de Montfort's son
against Henry III's army;
castle was then surrounded
by 120-acre lake. Henry's
army tried to cross in barges
but failed. On same lake Earl

grapes, walnuts; wild duck in red wine; venison casserole; barbecued beef. Meals: card £7; 5-course FP £5.50; wines reasonable; BB £11.50–16.50. SB.

Ann's Bistro/Restaurant Diment, 121 Warwick Rd (tel Kenilworth 53763): award-winning chef-owner; two operations under same roof; bistro speciality home-made lasagne, Basque chicken; restaurant more exotic French dishes; game in season; bistro £4; restaurant lunch FP £3.95; dinner card around £9–10.

of Leicester, Queen Elizabeth I's favourite, welcomed her here with floating artificial island and £60,000 party. Lovely old streets, as well as new town.

Stoneleigh: in churchyard of tiny village is buried Duchess Dudley, died 1669 aged 98, first woman to be created duchess in her own right. Timbered Elizabethan houses include some cruck-framed (curved oak beams as support). Grounds of abbey are National Agricultural Centre for research, training; site of Royal Show.

Coventry: industrial city, difficult driving for strangers, but *do* see cathedral. On night 4 November 1940, 40 acres of city centre destroyed by German bombers. Rebuilt after war; new cathedral in modern style by Basil Spence consecrated 1962. Blackened ruins of old cathedral form approach; cross made of two charred roof timbers on original altar inscribed 'Father Forgive'. Graham Sutherland's vast, superb tapestry in nave. Bright, light, friendly church; after Sunday morning service, clergy and congregation drink and chat at tea and juice bar. Fine musical concerts.

A427 Brinklow, small road alongside Oxford Canal on to B4112 at Newbold on Avon small road across A426 and A5 to Calthorpe, under M6 and M1 to Swinford, Stanford on Avon (10 m) small road to join B5414 to North Kilworth, right on A427 Market Harborough (14 m)

At Market Harborough, Frank Taylor's Fish Restaurant, 6 Adam and Eve St (tel 63043): second oldest fish and chip shop in world, with downstairs self-service restaurant, upstairs restaurant; awarded Accolade of Campaign for Mushy Peas. All the great fried fish dishes, plus chicken, ham, starters and desserts. 21 wines from £2.85; beers.

Angel (tel Mkt Harborough 3123): cosy old inn; snacks, Stable bar and Fodder Grill; restaurant. Lunch card average £3.75; FP, includes choice 6 roasts £4.95, children's portions £1.95, grandparents' portions £3.95. Dinner FP £6.50; £7.50. Several English wines on list. BB £11–12; SB midweek.

Three Swans, High St (tel 66644): once owned by Fothergill (*Innkeepers' Diary*), now by politer Dutch chef. Comfortable. Lunch £4.75; dinner £9.20. BB £12.50–17. SB weekends.

Stanford on Avon: village divided by river. Stanford Hall stables have motor collection, also replica of first aircraft to fly in England; Percy Pilcher crashed it here and was killed. Hall (handsome William and Mary mansion) includes collection of Stuart portraits and religious objects which belonged to Cardinal Henry Stuart (called King Henry IV of England by Jacobites). When electricity came to the house, ferrets were used to run wires under floorboards! Open Easter–end Sept, Thur, Sat, Sun pm. Stanford church has organ thrown out of Charles I's Whitehall Palace by Cromwell.

Market Harborough: small town, big square for market (general Tues, Sat; cattle Tues). On river Wellend.

A6 towards Leicester 3 m B6074 East Langton, Church Langton, B6074 1 m turn right to Hallaton, Horninghold, on to B664 Uppingham A6003 Oakham (20 m)

At Uppingham, Lake Isle, 16 High St (tel 2951): for wine addicts, like me. 500 wines, from Blanc de Blancs at £2.75 to lovely items like '57 Leoville Barton £12, '71 Hospice de Beaune £11.50, '49 Richebourg £27, '76 Pouilly Fuise £5. Dinner: 5 courses FP £9.50.

At Oakham, George, Market Place (tel 56971): chef Douglas Hamilton-Dick prides himself on caviar and lobster dishes, but takes equal trouble with humbler fare. Hotel lunch around £2.50;

At Wing, off A6013 near Oakham: turf maze 40 ft across; used in Middle Ages for wrongdoers who were put in middle and left to find way out!

Oakham: once proud capital of England's smallest county, Rutland; alas people with tidy minds and little sense of history merged it into Leicestershire in 1974 when so many old names and boundaries fell to bureaucrats. County museum fascinating show of agricultural vehicles and

Stable restaurant dinner around £7. Tempting wine list with 14 around £4.25, including Alligoté and fair Côtes du Rhône. BB £10–17.

Crown, High St (tel 3631): most bedrooms recently refurbished and very comfortable, with bath or shower; pleasant hotel, privately owned. Lunch FP £3.80; dinner FP £5.50; card £8.50. Italian house wines £3.85. BB £11–19. SB weekends.

machinery. Collection of horseshoes on wall of Norman banqueting hall of castle. Custom requires any peer passing through the manor to present one; donors range from Queen Elizabeth I to present Queen. Reason? Original lord was Earl of Ferrers, meaning farrier or blacksmith. Rutland Water, largest reservoir in England, alongside town; landscaped, picnic spots, excellent fishing, sailing.

**A606
Empingham,
Stamford (11 m)**

Ye Olde Barn, St Mary's St (tel Stamford 3194): in much-photographed Olde Barn Passage; beamed and suitably decorated; run 33 years by Duncan McKechnie, brother of radio actor the late James McKechnie. Big choice of grills. Meals around £5; wine from £3.25.

Bull and Swan, St Martins (tel 3558): Portuguese owner-chef makes super bar lunches: guinea fowl, trout

Pre-Roman Britons forded river Welland here; Queen Boudicca chased the shattered Roman 9th Legion across it in AD 61; and my generation queued for hours in cars until the notorious A1 road was moved to bypass it, leaving behind good inns. Fine looking town; stone houses from Middle Ages or built by prosperous wool merchants in 17th/18th centuries.

Stamford
continued

with almonds, paella, rack of lamb duck, beef stroganoff £3–5. BB £8–10.

George, (tel 2101): great historic inn; 900 years ago hostel gave food and lodging to pilgrims on way to Holy Land. Present building 14th/ 16th-century. Became coaching inn on London– York–Scotland route; 40 coaches a day stopped here. Gallows sign across road, as warning to highwaymen, didn't stop them using it. Duke of Cumberland stopped on way home from beating Scots at Culloden. Biggest customer was Daniel Lamber, who weighed 52 st 11 lb when he died in 1809. Comfort, good food. Interesting starters. Sensible wine list includes elusive Brouilly '79 £6.65. Dinner card around £10; lunch bar meals. BB £16–20.

Burghley House, 1 m E: truly magnificent house built by William Cecil, Lord Burghley, Elizabeth I's treasurer. Intended for show, with superb towers and chimneys, finished 1587. Heaven Room painted by Verrio 1694 is remarkable; almost limitless treasures, including 700 paintings. Home of Marquess of Exeter, better known to sportsmen as Lord Burghley, Olympic hurdler.

A6121 Caldcot A6003 Rockingham 1 m on to edge of Corby, left on small road to Deene Park, Deenthorpe, across A43 to Upper Benefield left on A427 Oundle (23 m)

Talbot, New St (tel Oundle 3621): historic (see opposite), comfortable, good atmosphere; French and English cooking. FP meals £6.50; also card. BB from £17.

Barnwell Mill (A605 3 m S Oundle): here's history with your meal; lovely peaceful spot on river Nene; first mill built here AD 875. Henry VIII gave it to Queen Catherine Howard. She was chopped, so her successor as queen, Catherine Parr, got the mill. It was still grinding corn until 1930s. Renovated 1976. Now serves lunch to passing travellers and dinner by candlelight. Midweek candlelit supper from £5;

String of historic houses on this route. Rockingham Castle: royal retreat through Middle Ages; much altered by Watson family, owners since 1553. Includes Post-Impressionist paintings. Nice grounds – views of five counties; open Thurs, Sun Easter–30 Sept. Kirby Hall, near Gretton village: eerie; from afar, it looks like lovely Elizabethan house, closer you find roofless halls, gaping windows; still lovely; gardens planted with thousands of roses.

Fotheringhay Castle, Oundle: all that remains is a mound of castle where Richard III was born and Mary Queen of Scots executed; castle stone

dinner card £9.50. Offer to cater for wedding receptions might not have appealed to Catherine Howard.

used to build Talbot Hotel in 1626; oak staircase was 'won' from castle, too.

Oundle Marina, on river Nene, is inland waterways leisure boating centre.

A605 S at Lilford Park, left on B1662 through Clapton to Alconbury Weston, under A1, A14 by B1043 into Huntingdon (15 m)

At Godmanchester, Huntingdon, Black Bull, Post St: 300-year-old inn still serving good simple English food; bar £1–4; restaurant £2.40–6.50. Wines £3.30–6.30. BB £9.50.

At St Ives, Slepe Hall, Ramsey Rd (tel St Ives 63122): very pleasant; owner Peter Scott writes poetry about Fens. Very palatable cooking; bar buffet; dinner FP £6.75; card around £10. BB £14–18. SB.

Lilford Park: famous aviaries restored, stocked with hundreds of birds, including Little Owl, Lilford Crane. 220-acre park; flamingo pool, children's farm, Jungleland play area, woods, lake, river.

Huntingdon: Oliver Cromwell, whose grandfather owned George Inn, born here, attended grammar school where Samuel Pepys was pupil thirty years later; now Cromwell Museum.

A1123 E St Ives, B1040 Etisley, A45 St Neots (20 m) A428 Bedford (12 m)

At Bedford, Swan, Embankment (tel 46565): lovely riverside 18th-century building by great architect Henry Holland; fine old staircase (possibly by Wren) with twisted balustrades brought from Houghton House ('House Beautiful' of *Pilgrim's Progress*). You can sleep Edwardian, Georgian,

St Ives: Cromwell's farm was nearby and his statue, booted, wearing his famous hat, is in marketplace. Lovely bridge over river Great Ouse has chapel in the middle; museum has souvenirs of days when river iced up in winter – primitive ice skate, Charles Whynter's fine painting of skating in 1891.

Bedford
continued

modern or Parisienne (100 bedrooms in different styles). Good value. Lunch FP £4.95; dinner FP £6.50; house wine £3.45. BB £14–20.

Greek Villager, 36 St Peter's St (tel 41798): Cypriot owner Costas Andreou 'dedicated to bringing Cypriot and Greek food to Bedfordshire'. A touch of dancing, too. Try his Masedonia – roast lamb in wine, cheese, spices, fennel sauce. Dinner only: £8. Wines from £4.10, including Cypriot and Retsina.

St Neots: named after 10th-century priory dedicated to Saxon holy man, spiritual adviser to King Alfred. Pleasant town on Great Ouse; large marketplace with old houses, inns.

Bedford: Saxon settlement in AD 915. Four fine old churches; by St Peter's (Saxon-Norman) is statue of John Bunyan, born in nearby Elstow village 1628, wrote *Pilgrim's Progress* when in Bedford gaol for Nonconformist beliefs. Bunyan Meeting House displays relics; library has his works. Five-arched Georgian bridge spans Great Ouse with gardens on each bank. Market Wed, Sat in St Paul's Sq.

A428 Gold
Brayfield
B565 Olney
(9 m)
local road to
Weston
Underwood
B526 very short
distance to
Gayhurst, then
right on small
roads, over M1
to Wolverton
(11 m)

Olney: museum where poet William Cowper lived 1767–86. He wrote hymns ('God moves in a mysterious way') with vicar who was former slave trader (sea captain). Place where Shrove Tuesday pancake race held since 1445. 2 m S Emberton Park almost surrounds village; bounded by Great Ouse: shallow lakes with wildfowl, canoes, small boats.

Weston Underwood: Flamingo Gardens hold one of the world's finest collection of birds and mammals. Rare flamingos (open Easter–Oct, Wed–Sun). Pretty village, stone with much thatch.

Gayhurst: Gunpowder Plot to blow up Parliament hatched at Gayhurst House 1604 by Sir Everard Digby and friends.

B4033 Winslow
(13 m)

Winslow: thatched cottages with overhanging gables; ancient books in church; Bell Inn was favourite of Dick Turpin, notorious highwayman.

---

small road to Claydons (East Claydon, Middle Claydon, Steeple Claydon, Botolph Claydon) small road to Bicester (15 m) A421, A43 Oxford (12 m)

At Weston-on-the-Green (5 m past Bicester), Weston Manor (tel Bicester 50621): pleasant spot for food or bed away from Oxford. High reputation for food, comfort, service. Nothing elaborate on menu but well-cooked dishes with some good sauces; dinner £8.50; 10 house wines under £5. BB £17.50–27.50.

Around Claydons, quiet and lovely; old churches, little bridges, thatched cottages. Claydons were all manors belonging to Verney family, who built fine mansion Claydon House at Middle Claydon in 1752; has Chinese Room, rococo state rooms and Florence Nightingale museum, including her diary; her sister married a Verney (open Mar–Oct, not Mon).

Bicester: old market square with 16th-century buildings.

Route 4

East Anglia: Colchester – Cambridge – Ely – Lincoln –
King's Lynn – Norwich – Ipswich – Colchester

Colchester

George, High St (tel 78494):
Pauline Beer is the first lady
head chef in the Grand
Metropolitan Hotel group;
her speciality – roast beef.
So carve as much as you
want in Carvers Restaurant.
Meal FP £5.95; house wine
£4.10. BB £10.35–14.35. SB
all year.

Wm Scraggs Seafood
Restaurant, 2 North Hill (tel
41111): the real thing. Best
fresh fish cooked to order.
Oysters £4.60 a dozen when I
was there; try clams in the
pot (cooked in cider, herbs,
cream); sole Wm Scraggs
(with prawns, mushrooms,
tomatoes in cream and wine
sauce); we had splendid
grilled Dover sole. Well-
chosen wine list; French,
German bottled house wines
£3.90. English Felstar, from
Felsted, Essex (fine for fish)
£5.25. Meals: card around
£8. Shut Sun.

Bistro Nine, 9 North Hill:
cordon bleu cook Penny
Campbell owned her first
restaurant at 21; now ripe
old age of 24. Says her
speciality is 'brown bread ice
cream', but try any of her
dishes; super pie of game in
port; ham and asparagus
crêpes; Chicken Pillow
(creamed chicken and
mushroom in pastry case);
constantly changing card.

Colchester: still holds
October oyster feast but
oysters and roses mostly
replaced by lathes and
diesels as main industry.
Founded by Belgic tribe;
capital of SE England under
King Cunobelinus
(Shakespeare's Cymbeline);
taken by Romans but sacked
by Queen Boudicca.
Normans took stones from
Roman buildings to make
castle. Castle keep, largest in
Europe, remains as museum
(interesting – treasures from
Stone Age to medieval
times; include Roman figure
of Mercury). Lovely castle
gardens. Minories
(Georgian): art gallery with
works by Constable,
Georgian furniture, china,
silver. Col Fairfax with
Parliamentary forces
besieged town during Civil
War; his HQ, 15th-century
Siege House, now open,
complete with Royalist bullet
holes in wood.

Chappel Station: Stour Valley
Railway Centre, steam locos,
rolling stock; signal box;
open weekends.

River Colne skirts northern
edge; lovely medieval
houses beyond North Bridge.
University of Essex in
Wivenhoe Park. Bourne Mill
(1 m S): 1591 fishing lodge;
became mill; restored to

Excellent value meal around £6. House wine £3.95; good '73 Rioja £5.95. Shut Sun, Mon.

working order (open Apr–Sept Wed, Sat, Sun pm).

B1026 Layer de la Haye Abberton Reservoir, over Causeway, small road right back over reservoir to Layer Breton, Layer Marney, Tiptree (10 m)

King's Ford Park Hotel, Layer Rd, Layer de la Haye (tel Colchester 34301): lovely Regency house in 15-acre woodland park. Italian owner and chef, so beautiful home-made pasta and veal dishes; international card, with Spanish paella, French sole Veronique. Lunch or dinner FP £4.50; card from £5. Italian house wines £3.80, BB £11.50–15.

Colchester Zoo (2 m Layer de la Haye on road right): centrepiece Stanway Hall, built Henry VIII's reign. Zoo, well stocked, also has model railway.

Amberton Reservoir: 12 m round, mostly man-made; flocks of waterfowl and migrating birds rest here. Stopping on causeway disturbs them, so 'hide' and car park for viewing built on Colchester side.

Layer Marney Tower: Italian-style gatehouse with giant towers built as entrance to estate of Henry Marney, powerful in Henry VII's reign. Open 1 April–1 Oct (Thur, Sun; also Tues July, Aug). Views from top over Essex.

B1023 Coggeshall (4 m)

White Hart, Market End (tel Coggeshall 61654): attractive, very old historic inn; sitting room dated 1420 (ghost haunts corner furthest from TV set); place of public entertainment since 1489; Great Dining Room was gambling casino; duels fought in what is now car park. Lady ghost haunts West Wing corridor ringing her hands. 3 FP dinner menus £7.50, £9.50, £11.50; card lunch and dinner; bar lunch; 350 wines £4.45–150. BB £11.50–20.

Paycock's House, one of best Tudor homes in Britain. Elaborate wood carvings. Woolpack and White Hart hotels even older.

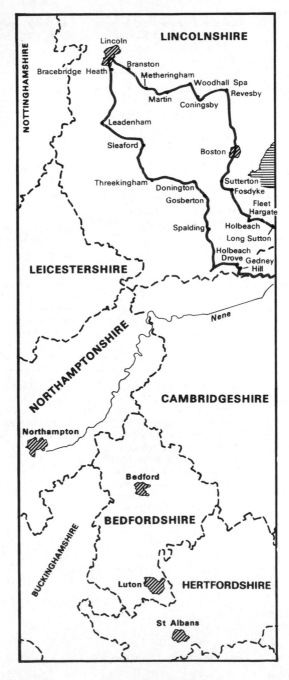

A120 Braintree (5 m)	At Braintree, Tudor Rose, Lt Square (tel 45349): 17th-century; Antonio and Christina came from Sicily; chef is British; so excellent pasta, plus pork fillets in cider sauce, apple and cream, flavoured with cranberry or in Marsala. Delicious veal in wine and cream. Meals card £5–10. house wine £3.75.	Braintree: attractive mixture of old and new. Many ancient houses; Swan Hotel (medieval) has fine courtyard. On river Blackwater; market dates back to 1199.
A120 Rayne, small road left Little Dunmow, Felsted B1417, then A130 to Howe Street small road right to Pleshey, High Easter, Leaden Roding (on B184) (18 m) A1060 White Roding, small road right (just past Whalebone pub), right again at T-junction to Hatfield Broad Oak, right again to join B183 through Hatfield Forest A120 at Takeley, turn right to Great Dunmow A130 Thaxted (18 m)	At Great Dunmow (Stebbing, 2 m NE), Priors Hall at Parsonage Farm (tel Stebbing 316): delightful, but you *must* book ahead. The Fishers accept only six guests, blending atmosphere of historic private home with standards of good hotel. Magnificent timbered old house, built over four centuries (14th–17th); rich in old beams, fine fireplaces; modern kitchen and heated indoor swimming pool. Belonged once to Knights Templars; stream and ponds in garden; members of family include cats, dogs, a goose, ducks, and 20 peacocks. Mrs Fisher's cooking highly praised. 4-course dinner £9.70; wines, include Bruisyard from Saxmundham, £3.50. BB (private bath) £15–24. SB 2 nights. Star, Great Dunmow (tel 4321): pricey but already very good reputation for meals, though opened only July 1980. Daily change of menu on blackboard. Fish specialities on Thursday and Friday, brought direct from Billingsgate by owner. Unusual in England – fresh	Pleshey – Norman knight built castle on turf mound 60 ft high, 900 ft round. Castle has gone; lovely 15th-century redbrick bridge remains. For 200 years it housed Lords High Constable of England. Richard II's uncle Duke of Gloucester had it in 1397 when Richard kidnapped and murdered him, fearing treachery. The Rodings: eight villages along valley of river Roding in lush country; moated halls, old churches, half-timbered cottages. Known locally as 'Roothings'. Hatfield Forest: 1000 acres left from royal hunting ground; good rides, picnic glades, lake with boating, fishing. Places to hide in complete peace. Great Dunmow's Flitch held every four years is a mock trial of couples claiming they have 'not had a brawl in their home nor wished to be unmarried for the last twelve months and a day'. Winners get flitch of bacon. Fine timbered guildhall, old inn Saracen's Head, and Doctor's Pond, scene of first lifeboat experiments by Lionel Lukin 1785.

pike used for quenelles as starter. Good wine list with fair house wines £4.50; local Felsted Müller Thurgau dry white £4, and tempting Loire dry whites for fish dishes. Dinner card £10–14. Shut Mon and most Aug.

Thaxted: gorgeous timber-framed 14th/15th-century overhanging houses; superb arcaded 15th-century guildhall; grand 14th/15th-century church with battlements, buttresses and grotesque gargoyles; inside fine early 18th-century organ; Gustav Holst organist here.

as A130 bends right (just past Thaxted church) turn left downhill to Cutlers Green, Debden, Saffron Walden (9 m)

At Saffron Walden, Cross Keys, High St (tel 22207): one of our finest timbered inns – built 1450; bar meals; restaurant meals around £5; wine from £3. BB £9.25–13.

Eight Bells, Bridge St (tel 22790): have not eaten here yet but reliable spies tell me it is excellent value. Robin Moore tries to offer sort of value-for-money meal he would like to find as a customer. Imaginative bar dishes; try hot crab-meat with spices, topped with melted cheese, served with garlic bread, salad £1.65; saffron chicken (whole chicken breast, stuffed with prawns, garlic gilded with saffron); speciality roast rib beef carved from trolley. Lunch FP £4.50; dinner card around £6–7; Italian house wine £4.50. Chilford Hundred English £4.60.

Saffron Walden: name came from yellow saffron blooms grown here for centuries for medicine, cooking and dye. Huge church with 193 ft tower-spire. Many timbered houses. Youth hostel in superb 15th-century Myddilton Place. Medieval houses in Church St decorated vividly with figures, foliage.

Audley End: magnificently elegant mansion begun 1603 by Thomas Howard, Earl of Suffolk, Lord High Treasurer; house originally as big as Hampton Court. James I, something of a wit ('he never said a foolish thing nor ever did a wise one'), remarked, 'It's too big for a king, but might do the Lord Treasurer.' Still huge. Present interior and fine grounds mostly by Robert Adam in late 18th century; he also designed temple in grounds, Palladian bridge with summer house on it, and several lodges; main house has lovely furniture. House cost £200,000 to build – about £10 million now. Charles II fancied it, bought it for £55,000 but never paid it all. William III returned it to the family. (Open Apr–early Oct, except Mon).

A130 Cambridge (12 m)

A thousand years before the university was established, the Romans built a camp here called Granta. It became a Saxon market town, Danish army base, then in 11th century a Norman military base where William the Conqueror himself directed operations against Saxon leader Hereward the Wake. 700 years later a student Charles Kinglsey was to climb out of Magdalene College in the night to go fishing in the Fens – which led him to write a brilliant novel, *Hereward the Wake*. Students came in 13th century – novice monks from Ely, Oxford students fleeing from riots. Peterhouse College (1284) came first. Now there are thirty colleges. You need a book to tell you of their history, treasures and people who passed through them.

Do not miss King's College Chapel, one of the finest buildings in Britain, started by Henry VI, 1446, magnificent glass in reds, blues, yellow and grey; Rubens' colourful, vital masterpiece *Adoration of the Magi* behind the altar; the choir, whose Christmas carol festival is broadcast; spring daffodils in surrounding meadows. See too Old Court of Corpus Christi; Wren Library of Trinity; modern architecture of Churchill and Robinson colleges if only to argue about it. See the gardens of Christ's College, its mulberry tree planted by student John Milton; medieval chapel of Jesus with Pre-Raphaelite ceiling and brilliantly vivid stained glass by William Morris and Burne-Jones; New Bridge over river Cam at St John's in Venetian style – Bridge of Sighs; wooden bridge over the Cam at Queen's, built 1749 on mathematical principles without using a nail, taken apart by inquisitive Victorians who needed nails to rebuild it! Samuel Pepys left his library to his old college Magdalene; his diary, written in shorthand, was found among books and transcribed only in 1922. See treasures of Fitzwilliam Museum, one of Europe's greatest, spanning time from ancient Egypt, Rome, Greece to the 1960s; works by Breughel, Samuel Palmer, Blake, Augustus John, Epstein, Stanley Spencer, Graham Sutherland. Constable's *Hampstead Heath*, Epstein's *Einstein*. Stroll the Backs, riverside meadows, take a punt on the Cam. A city for strolling and browsing.

Hotels and restaurants

At Great Shelford, on way in to Cambridge, King's Mill House (tel Cambridge 843125): Regency house, cross between staying with family and guest house; evening meals by arrangement (or short notice); remarkable value: £3 or £6 dinner party. BB £7.50–8.50. Shut Nov–Mar.

Arundel House, 53 Chesterton Rd (tel 67701): convenient, overlooking river Cam; Victorian terrace converted; baths in most bedrooms. Bar lunch; supper card; wine prices low; main dish £1.60–3; dinner FP, fair choice £6; also card. BB £13–20. SB.

Garden House, Granta Place, off Mill Lane (tel 63421): 4-star, gorgeous position in lovely grounds down to river Granta; pricey. Prestige hotel (rather like French Châteaux hotels but not so in architecture); bathrooms to each bedroom; meals FP £6.30–7.75; card £10–12. (AA rosette for cooking. BB £23.50–34.50.

University Arms, Regent St (tel 51241): 1831 hotel replaced by box-like but comfortable pile; overlooks Parkers' Piece, so dream of hearing again the sound of young Peter May using the cricket bat as an offensive weapon. Hotel in Bradford family for 80 years; excellent chef, here 35 years. Dinner £8; house wine £3.40 to '45 Chateau Latour £45. BB £18–24.50.

Shades, King's Parade (tel 59506): good reasonable priced snacks in wine cellar; restaurant excellent, lunch and dinner, Tues–Sat; card £8–10. Shortish well-

Cambridge
continued

chosen wine list, many by glass, bargains: Loire
Gamay £2.60, '79 Côtes du Rhône £3.10, DOC '79
Chianti £2.95, Beaujolais '79, Bordeaux Sauvignon
£3.50. House wine £2.50.

Varsity, 35 St Andrews St: Greek taverna in old
Cambridge listed building; Retsina and Old Lace;
excellent value; really good Greek dishes, charcoal
grilled English steaks; French escalopes; nice chicken
dishes; except steak, main dishes £1.95–2.30. Meal
around £3.50–4.50; house wine £2.60. Retsina
available.

Hobbs Pavillion, Park Terrace (tel 67480): named after
my boyhood hero, Jack Hobbs, greatest batsman
England ever had. Sir Jack was born in Cambridge,
son of a college servant. Counter service Tues–Sat
until 5pm. Table service evenings only when university
is 'up' (term time). Lunch £3.50; evening FP £5.50
(simple); card £6–7. Wines reasonable; ordinary
Burgundy '78 £3.35.

Arts Theatre, 6 St Edwards Passage (Pentagon
Restaurant): excellent cold buffet; four hot dishes a
day. Reasonable prices; meal £4–5. House wine £3.50
(French, Italian).

A45 towards
Newmarket,
B1102 to
Swaffham
Bulbeck,
Swaffham Prior;
left fork on to
small roads to
Reach and River
Bank on river
Cam (11 m)

Anglesey Abbey (B1101):
Augustinian priory 1135,
rebuilt as country house in
Elizabeth I's reign. Once
owned by mayor of
Cambridge and horse-renter
(livery stables) Thomas
Hobson, who would offer
customers 'Hobson's choice'
– the horse he chose or
none. Contains Lord
Fairhaven's superb collection
of clocks, furniture, porcelain,
silver, tapestries, paintings,
including Constable's
Waterloo Bridge. 100 acres
landscaped garden with huge
herbaceous border. National
Trust (open 1 Apr–Oct, pm;
house shut Mon, Fri).

River Bank: hideaway hamlet
on river Cam used by
knowledgeable students. At

Reach, Devil's Ditch: earthwork dyke runs straight for 7 m; defence for East Anglians against Mercia in 7th century. Rare flowers in chalk – bee orchid, purple pasque, also harebells.

small road to Upware, on to join A1123 near Wicken Fen A1123 Stretham A10 Ely (8 m)

Stagecoach, 39 Market St (tel Ely 2584): still has notice outside offering stage to London, King's Lynn. Bargain lunches – FP £3 includes choice of roasts. Same chef-owner 20 years. Dinner card average £5.50. Shut Tues, Sun eve.

Nyton Guest House, 7 Barton Rd (tel Ely 2459): useful overnight; quiet. BB £8–10; dinner in winter only on SB (2 nights).

Wicken Fen: before Fens were drained men travelled them on stilts. Almost natural condition; sedge and reed land, like Danube delta, with many wild water plants and flowers, birds and fish; the swallowtail butterfly is back.

At Stretham, beam-pumping engine of type which took over from windmills is kept in working order; diesels took over pumps in 1925.

Ely: delightful place; beautiful, peaceful, with fascinating, violent history beginning long before Normans built present cathedral in 1083; island until Fens drained in 17th/18th centuries. Hereward and Anglo Saxons beaten only because traitorous abbot let the Normans across in Hereward's absence. Far bank of river Ouse now a yacht harbour. Lovely old house where Oliver Cromwell lived near St Mary's Church. Cathedral – seen from miles away – not only beautiful but amazing piece of engineering, with huge tower held up by eight 64 ft oak trunks. Ely got its name when St Dunstan found monks living with women – he didn't like that sort of thing and turned them into eels.

A10 Littleport
A1101 Upwell
Wisbech B1168,
B1166 Gedney
Hill, Holbeach
Drove; on to
A1073 Spalding
(45 m)

At Downham Market (W of Outwell 5 m), Crown (tel 2322): old coaching inn famous for English cooking, especially steak and kidney pie, Welsh lamb pie, also old sauces made with honey, red currants, port, ginger; fresh roasts. Try fillet of beef with Stilton, horseradish sauce. Stables Grill meals £5; Fox Restaurant card £8–9. House wine £2.95. BB £11–15; SB weekends.

At Spalding, Isabel's Pantry, 4 Church Gate (tel 2193): imaginative dishes; try Silton and celery pâté; Dover sole stuffed with prawns, mussels, mushrooms, wine and lobster sauce; salmon in casserole with white wine, cream, mushrooms, prawns and asparagus. Good fish. Bar meals; lunch FP £3.50; dinner card around £8. House wine £4.35/litre.

Farmworkers of Littleport started revolt in 1816; starving while corn they grew went to London at high profit. They marched on Ely with a tank – six guns on farmcart. Six hanged by Bishop of Ely.

Wisbech: very attractive town on river Nene with fruit orchards and bulb fields round it; still small port, but gets further from Wash as land reclaimed. Lovely Georgian houses beside Nene on North Brink, including Peckover House, built by Quaker banker, rococo décor in wood, plaster; fine Victorian garden (open Apr–mid Oct pm except Mon, Fri). Centre of town attractive. Route from Wisbech across fens rather tortuous but signposted.

Spalding: bulbs – all round it, packed in it; daffs, tulips, tens of others over 10,000 acres. Fine old market town with seven bridges over river Welland. 13th-century church, 14th-century inn.

A16 Gosberton,
A152 Donington,
A52 through
Threekingham,
shortly after,
right on to A15
Sleaford (23 m)

Sleaford: nice little town; marketplace with one of the oldest church spires in England, 144 ft. Mounds all that remains of castle where King John died of fever in 1216.

A15, then left on A17 to Leadenham A607 Bracebridge Heath A15 Lincoln (13m)

At Lincoln, D'Isney Place Hotel, Eastgate (tel 38881): 18th-century house converted to BB hotel for comfort and peace. All rooms have bathroom, TV, phone. BB £11.50–18.

Lincoln: same story all over flat East Anglia; given a ridge and a river, Romans built a fort; then Normans built a castle and big church, and a town went on growing. Castle, ordered by William

Harveys Cathedral Restaurant, 1 Exchequer Gate (tel 21886): right in front of cathedral; much improved by Harvey family. Formula: simple lunches, superb dinner. Bob Harvey cooks the savoury dishes, Adrianne the sweets. Lunch not too simple; try Crewman's Catch. All good value. Lunch card £4–5; 5-course dinner FP £8.50. Wine list includes 12 PAYD bottles – pay as you drink, not for what you leave.

Roman Ruin, High St (tel 41750): lunch/dinner 4–course, fair choice FP £5.50; wines from £2.70.

the Conqueror, is in ruins but the cathedral is one of our finest buildings; 365 ft high, honey-coloured stone, a medieval masterpiece built after an earthquake knocked down the old church in 1185. Fine views over Lincoln from Observatory Tower. I find Museum of Lincolnshire Life fascinating, with agricultural implements like a fine old haywain, and story of the Lincolnshire poacher.

B1188 SE from
Lincoln to
Branston,
Metheringham
B1191 Martin,
Woodhall Spa,
B1192 Tattersall,
Coningsby
(23 m)

Dower House, Manor Estate, Woodhall Spa (tel 52588): pleasant house in 2½ acres gardens, woodlands; good English cooking with fresh vegetables all year. Dinner FP £6.50; card £8. Small dining room, candlelit; dishes cooked to order; wines from £4; BB £12–16 with bathroom.

At Coningsby, Ratty's, 43 High St (tel 42285): friendly service, home cooking, using local ingredients in season. Owner Hans Hanson trained at Savoy, London. Dinner FP £6.75. Wines £3.95–13.50, fair list.

Woodhall Spa: out of Fens into heath, pines and silver birch. Still has pump room; also championship golf course.

Tattersall: castle built by Ralph Cromwell in 14th century – another Lord Treasurer; he is buried in Holy Trinity Church which he also built. Castle, with 22 ft thick walls at base, restored by Lord Curzon in 1911; National Trust since 1925; long views from battlements; open all year.

Dog Dyke pumping station, Bridge Farm, has 1855 beam engine once used for land drainage.

Coningsby: church has early 17th-century one-handed clock, largest of type in world. Lincolnshire Aviation Society has museum, open most weekends, with complete old aircraft; in old warehouse.

A153 towards
Horncastle; right
at Tunby on
A115 Revesby
right on B1183
Boston (15 m)

At Boston, New England Hotel, Wide Bargates (tel 65255): Anchor Chain hotel; in pretty old house; all bedrooms with bath, TV, phone, teamaker. Carvery dining room so mostly roasts; fresh veg, salads; lunch/dinner FP £4.35. House wine £3.65. BB £12.50–24. SB all year, weekends, also fishing breaks for coarse fishermen.

Three Tuns: wine bar, restaurant with cheap meals under £3.

Church's, Church St (tel 67400): Italian chef-owner, English-style card apart from fine osso bucco; pizzaiola

Boston: important seaport in 13th century, but silting, land reclamation and build-up of America moved ports to west coast; still handles cargo ships, pleasure boats; famous Boston Stump – octagonal tower of 14th-century St Botolph's Church, still used as navigation mark by boats in The Wash; 272 ft high, fine views from top. Old buildings include 13th-century Shodfriars (Dominican) hall, now a theatre. Cells in which Pilgrim Fathers were imprisoned 1607 after first attempt to escape to America, in 15th-century guildhall, now museum. Any

(steak in white wine, onions, herbs, garlic). Lunch £2.25–4; dinner card around £7 good value. Wines reasonable: Frascati, Gaillac white, Roussillon red £3.65, Barolo '74 £4.25! Chianti Classico '77 £4.25.

good Bostonian will tell you how, ten years after the *Mayflower* sailed, emigrants led by John Winthrop went to found Boston, Mass; in Fydell House, built 1726, is an American Room for use of visitors from there.

Revesby: attractive village round green. Sir Joseph Banks, naturalist who sailed with Captain Cook, lived in Revesby Abbey – different house now but still deer in the park. Reservoir lures fishermen and waterfowl.

A16 Sutterton
A17 Fosdyke,
Saracens Head;
small road right
to Holbeach East
on A151
rejoin A17 at
Long Sutton,
Sutton Bridge,
King's Lynn
(33 m)

At King's Lynn, Dukes Head, Tuesday Market Place (tel 4996): Trust House Forte with their usual strength and weakness (BB prices). Meals splendid value: lunch FP £5.75; dinner FP £6.95; English cooking; card around £8; lovely old building of various periods; all bedrooms with bath, TV, phone, teamaker; beds per person £16–23 but £3.50 more for breakfast. Good SB, 2 days minimum.

Antonio's Wine Bar, Baxters Plain (tel 2324): good fresh Italian dishes; house wines £4/litre; Trebbiano £3.10. Shut Sun, Mon. BBC viewers say Antonio retains Italian charm after eight years in King's Lynn. Lucky for local lasses!

Holbeach: walk along the old seabank but don't try to walk out to the sea; treacherous marsh mud; market town surrounded by lovely spring bulbs.

King's Lynn: just Lynn to locals. Delightful old place still alive and working as a port. Once third most important port in England. Local lad navigated and explored north-west coast of America; had one of world's biggest ports named after him – George Vancouver. Superb modern glass made at Wedgwood Glass, Hardwick Estate (open Mon–Fri, last tour 1.45pm); glass-blowing, hand cutting, shop. Lively Tuesday market in place of same name. King's Lynn Festival in July started by Lady Fermoy, grandmother of Princess of Wales.

A148, left on A149 Castle Rising; small road right to gates of Sandringham House B1440 for short distance, then A149 Ingoldisthorpe, Snettisham, Heacham (14 m)

At Dersingham (by Sandringham House), Westdene House (tel 40395): simple comfortable private hotel; central heating; no single rooms. Dinner card around £5.50; wines cheap; BB £8–8.75. SB, 2 nights Oct–Apr, 3 nights summer.

Castle Rising: port from which sea has long since withdrawn; castle built by man who married Henry I's widow; Edward III shut his scheming mother up here after killing her lover Mortimer. Mostly ruined.

Sandringham, the Queen's country house, is Victorian and ugly; Edward VII bought it as a retreat because he disliked Osborne House, Isle of Wight. Possible to visit four rooms and gardens mid Apr–mid Sept provided no member of Royal Family in residence; usually closed last two weeks July.

Heacham: Caley Mill, just outside is centre for collecting lavender to be sent to Fring distillery. Fine walk along shore Snettisham to Heacham but watch sands – tide can cut you off. Heacham village sign and memorial in church honour Red Indian princess who married John Rolfe at Heacham Hall in 1614 – Pocahontas.

B1454, then right fork on small road to Fring lavender distillery back to B1454 at Docking B1155 Burnham Market, Overy Staithe A149 Holkham Wells next the Sea (16 m)

At Burnham Market, Fishes: Gillian Cape, oyster grower and chef; oysters from own beds £4.50/dozen; own smoked fish; seasonal fish dishes include splendid mussels in cider (Sept–Mar); lunch £4.25; dinner card around £8.50. House wine £4.

At Wells next Sea, Crown, The Buttlands (tel 710209): English cooking with French touches; comfortable; family run; good local oysters, fish. Bar lunch; dinner FP £6.50 and card. 50 wines from £3.90. BB £12.50.

Fring: distillery makes lavender water, extracting 2 oz fluid from an acre of lavender, then oil from that as base for perfume. Harvest late summer.

Burnham Thorpe: Thomas Coke, Earl of Leicester, had Holkham Hall built 1740 by William Kent in style of Palladio. Marble hall in rich purple, pink, green. Fine art collection includes works by Rubens, Poussin, Gainsborough, Van Dyck. Still owned by Coke family. Garden laid out 1762 by Capability Brown. Open June–Sept (check days).

B1105 Great
Walsingham,
Little
Walsingham,
small road south
through Great
Snoring, Little
Snoring
A148 Thursford
B1346 Blickling,
Aylsham (20 m)

At Great Snoring, Old
Rectory (tel Walsingham
597): turreted manor house
of around 1500, well
decorated and furnished to
resemble country home. Fine
English cooking, usually with
a roast. Beds for only 11
guests. Dinner FP £6.50; BB
£14–16.

Little Walsingham: the shrine
of Our Lady of Walsingham,
based on a pretty story of a
lady's dream and 'miracle' in
medieval days, became
England's top shrine for
pilgrimages, greater than
Canterbury. Every king from
Richard Lionheart to Henry
VIII paid homage; then Henry
VIII had the image burned.
From 1931 Anglo-Catholics
built a new shrine with 14
altars, including one for the
Eastern Orthodox Church.

Blickling Hall: superb
Jacobean house with red-
brick front, built 1619.
Pictures, tapestries, fine
furniture. National Trust;
open Apr–mid Oct (check
times).

B1354 Coltishall,
B135 Hoveton,
A1151 Wroxham
A1151 Norwich
(16 m)

Hotel Wroxham (tel 2062): large, modern; looks better fitted for Roussillon coast of France than Broads, but very comfortable; good value. Inventive chef. Lunch carvery £3.95; dinner FP £4.50; card £8. BB £12.50–17.50. SB weekends – value.

At Norwich, Maid's Head, Tombland (tel 28821): part of Norwich history for 700 years; one of Britain's oldest inns; some modern additions. Mostly old and attractive, especially bedrooms; all with bathroom or shower, TV, even heated trouser presses. Good service. Lunch FP £5; dinner card £7–10. BB £17.50–27.50 (higher prices are for singles). SB weekends – good value.

Heathcote, 17 Unthank Rd (tel 25639): just extended; good value; meals FP £4.50; English and Italian dishes; house wine £4.25; BB £11.50–12.50. SB weekends.

Oaklands, Thorpe St Andrew (tel 34471): on Yarmouth Rd, country club hotel overlooking Yare river valley; nice atmosphere; good English cooking; local fish; lunch FP £3.50; dinner FP £4.50; card £6–8; BB £11.50–12.50. SB (many).

Stower Grange, Drayton (tel Norwich 860210): Georgian house in own grounds; rural, 4 m Norwich centre; family run; good cooking, choice; lunch except Mon and Fri; dinner except Sun; meals FP £7.75. BB £11–14.

Broads are stretches of open water with navigable approach channels, thirty in Norfolk which, with linking rivers, streams, canals, make up 200 miles for motorboat cruising and sailing; usually crowded in summer when thousands of holidaymakers, are waterborne. Broads were created by medieval men digging for peat.

Wroxham: 'capital' of Broads – Mecca for those who like the look, sound, smell of boats. Huge store selling everything: tinned food, woolly hats, ropes; crowded in season. Wroxham Broad fine for sailing when not crowded.

Norwich: one of prettiest cities, despite huge insurance office blocks, moving of cattle market, and controversial 1930s city hall (one critic said, 'It looks like a public convenience which is what, I suppose, it is'). Norwich looks good from any angle. One of best Norman English cathedrals, beautifully topped by 15th-century spire. Lovely cloister arches, begun 1300. Close with old buildings which include grammar school where Nelson was pupil. Two fine gates lead from Tombland (meaning market): Erpingham Gate, built 1420 by knight who commanded victorious archers at Agincourt. St Ethelbert's Gate built after a riot between monks and townsfolk over monks levying taxes at annual Tombland Fair. The Pope excommunicated Norwich,

Mischief Tavern, Fye Bridge St (tel 23810): tavern since 1312; originally called Wine Vaults; newer name from sign, probably by Hogarth, which came from London – man with his wife, drinking gin and making lewd signs, on his back. Well run by friendly young couple. Good simple meals in bar or carvery; meals around £3.50.

Tatlers, 21 Tombland (tel 21822): local seasonal dishes, especially fish. Meal from £5. Wines from £3.70.

Marco's, 17 Pottergate: we have too few good Italian restaurants; Marco Vessalio is a fine Italian cook, as at home with a 'simple' grilled sole from Yarmouth as with his Italian specialities; mouthwatering list of good Italian wines from all regions. Meal card £6–10. Wines £5.50–10.

made monks and townfolk build arch as penance. Nurse Cavell, shot by Germans in 1915 for helping British prisoners escape from Belgian hospital, buried beside cathedral. Hugh Bigad, one of William the Conqueror's henchmen, built the castle, now a good museum (including collection Norwich School of painters). Maddermarket Rep Theatre is in old half-timbered building; Elm Hill, cobbled, has shops and houses from 14th/18th centuries. 16th-century timber-framed Strangers' Hall has 20 rooms furnished in different period styles. Guildhall (1407) still used as court. Pull's Ferry – 15th-century watergate, ferryman's house – is lovely. Interesting mustard shop in Bridewell Alley (Colmans have made mustard here since 1814; mustard grown locally).

B146 Beccles,
B1127
Southwold
A1095, B1125,
B1387
Walberswick;
back along
B1387,
left on B1125
Leiston,
Aldeburgh
(52 m)

At Beccles, Manor Farm, Shipmeadow (tel 715280): farm overlooking Waveney valley; good coarse fishing; birdwatching; modernized house; working farm of 140 acres. 2 nights minimum BB £8.70; dinner £5.

Waveney House, Puddingmoor (tel 712270): in gorgeous position right on river Waveney; country house 1592 with 1750 additions. Nicely furnished; some four-poster beds; chef 25 years with Cunard ships. Dinner FP £5.95; card £8; BB with bathroom £16–18.50.

At Southwold, Swan, Market Place (tel 722186): pretty, ivy-clad; comfortable bedrooms. English dishes, good choice. Wines from £3.60 good value. Lunch FP £4.85; also card; dinner FP £5.75; card. BB £13–18. SB.

Avondale, 18 North Rd (tel Southwold 722538): most bedrooms overlook sea; 5 min walk centre; dinner £4; BB £6.50. DBB £10. Wines from £3.

Beccles: in 14th century they built church tower separately in case its 3000 tons fell down; mostly 18th-century town by river Waveney. Lovely river walks; good sailing.

Southwold: pleasant family seaside resort of quiet sort. Built round greens. Almost Edwardian. In 1672 local people watched offshore naval battle of Sole Bay between English and Dutch, ending in a draw. Canons on front are reminders. Adnams' Southwold beers rated some of our best. Local fishermen still sell catch by harbour.

Walberswick: little fishing port gradually turned into chic retreat for fashionable people and amateur artists, but somehow holds its charm; some odd houses have joined the fine old ones; not many pro fishermen left; many boats owned by part-timers.

Aldeburgh: always a flourishing town, but two men made its name world

Sutherland House, 56 High St (tel Southwold 722260): the Joneses run restaurant because they enjoy it. In price, few can keep down with the Joneses. Lunch FP £2.60; grills with sweet £2. Shut Mon, Weds. Lovely 15th-century house.

At Walberswick, Mary's Manor House (tel Southwold 723243): English cooking. Lunch salads; dinner £4.95; wine reasonable (Muscadet £3.70). BB £6.

At Aldeburgh, Wentworth Hotel (tel 2312): in same family since 1920; good fish dishes. Dinner FP £6.50; card £7.50. BB £13–19.50; SB (including golf).

famous: 19th-century poet George Crabbe, who ran away to sea from here and wrote the scathing poem on the town *The Borough* on which the other famous local, Benjamin Britten, based his opera *Peter Grimes*. Britten founded the Aldeburgh Festival of Music and Arts in 1948; held each June, and smaller September season. One of the world's great music festivals. Concert hall is at Snape (5 m away) in maltings beautifully converted, burned down in 1969, now rebuilt. Concerts also in Snape Church. Nice walk along bank of river Alde from Aldeburgh to Snape.

A1094 Snape
A12 Wickham
Market, Ufford,
small road left
Woodbridge
A12 Martlesham,
Ipswich (25 m)

At Snape, Crown (tel 234): old smugglers' inn; secret room found since. Country casseroles, real stockpot soups, no deep frying; local foods. Meals around £6; wines from list chosen by a master, Simon Lofthouse. Meals around £6. BB £8–9. Real country inn used by locals.

At Woodbridge, Seckford Hall (tel 5678): Elizabethan house and lovely gardens with lily lake are sheer joy; superb beamed rooms, well furnished; one four-poster bed from 1587. Immaculately run by Michael Bunn, whose family have owned it more than 30 years. Chef John Heeley, 17 years at hotel, favours local products – Norfolk duckling, lobsters, sole from nearby coast, Orford smoked salmon. Pricey but not for such

Woodbridge: broad stretch of river Deben makes it look coastal; attractive position; yachts, cruisers, sailing dinghies give prosperous air of rich man's hideout. Old boat-yard which built a fighting ship for Drake; now builds pleasure boats. Elizabethan merchant Thomas Seckford left behind Shire Hall, now a court, and Seckford Hall, lovely hotel where Seckford's ghost roams in Elizabethan dress with tall hat; he is said to be complaining that the money he left to the poor only benefits the rich. Tide mill on quayside beautifully restored. Our word 'tawdry' came from goods sold at St Audrey's Fair at Woodbridge market each 23 Oct.

Ipswich: still some old buildings but most have been knocked down. Lively

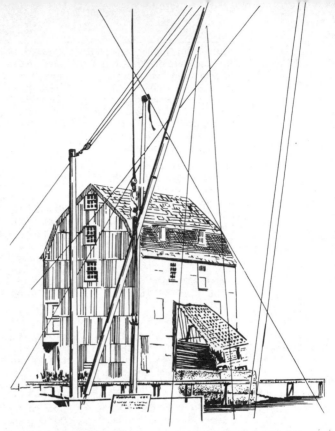

luxury. Lunch FP £5.50; dinner card £8–10. House wine £3.90. BB £15–22.50. SB.

At Ipswich, Marlborough, Henley Rd (tel 57677): furnished with taste; pleasant bedrooms; quiet area. Expensive but value. Lunch around £7; dinner FP £6.90; card £9–10. BB £22–32. SB.

Le Beaujolais, St Stephen's Lane (tel 212526); bistro wine bar and full restaurant, Parisienne owner-chef; classical and regional French dishes; meals card £5 wine bar; £9 restaurant. Wines from £3.80. Shut Sun, Mon.

museum in Christchurch Mansion in park; furniture, toys, dolls houses, model ships including some made from bone by French prisoners in Napoleonic Wars; paintings by Constable, Gainsborough.

A1071
Hintlesham
Hadleigh
B1070 East
Bergholt A12,
B1029 Stratford
St Mary,
Dedham A137
Colchester (21
m)

Hintlesham Hall (tel Hintlesham 268): in this beautiful house you will pay about £15 for your meal; but everyone should taste a Robert Carrier meal before they die! It was said that he 'changed single-handed the eating habits of the nation'. Well, *not* the nation but those with money to eat in his restaurants or time to digest his cookery books and follow them in the kitchen. BB £30–52.50.

At Hadleigh, Edgehill Hotel, 2 High St (tel 822458): 16th-century farmhouse converted into simple hotel; home cooking; dinner £4–5; wines from £2.24; BB £8.60–12.

At Higham (East Bergholt), Old Vicarage (tel Higham 248): 16th-century timbered house, own grounds, views to river Stour; own pool, tennis courts, boats on river. BB £8.

Dedham Hall (tel Colchester 323027): one of the Wolsey Lodge 'Englishman's Home' houses at which families accept paying guests. All extremely pleasant. 15th-century house in five acres; vegetables, eggs, honey from garden. Remarkable value. Dinner FP £5; wine from £3.20; BB £9–15. Shut Jan–March.

Marlborough Head, Mill Lane (tel Colchester 323124): fine 15th-century beamed inn, once a weavers' house. Bar meals; restaurant lunch FP £5; dinner FP £7. BB £10–12.50.

East Bergholt: delightful, but crammed with summer crowds and cars. Artist John Constable born here 1776; four of his greatest paintings were of nearby hamlet of Flatford on river Stour and its mill, and the scene has changed little – apart from crowds of pilgrims. Go in early spring or autumn. Thatched cottage now a café; other buildings leased by Field Studies Council as lecture centre.

Dedham; Constable painted its church spire several times. Sir Alfred Munnings, who painted dozens of horses, lived in Castle House; now a museum containing much of his work, including landscapes, gypsies, pleasant pictures he painted in Paris, and advertising posters for chocolates.

Hadleigh: fine 15th-century guildhall from days of wealth from wool; High Street is a pageant of different Suffolk building styles.

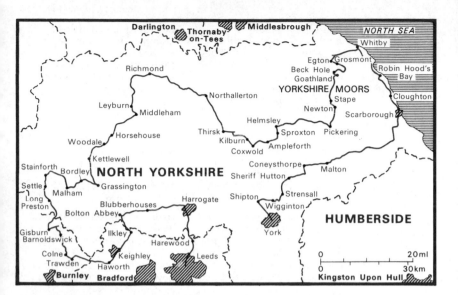

Route 5

**Yorkshire: Leeds – Ilkley – Brontë Country –
James Herriot Country – Scarborough – York
(join Route 7 Borders at Richmond)**

Leeds A61
Harewood,
Harrogate (14 m)

At Harrogate, West Park
Hotel, West Park (tel 63371):
comfortable, cosy old pub.
Steak bar restaurant with
stalls; bar snacks; meal card
£5.50; BB £9.25–11.

Russell Hotel and Hodgsons
Restaurant, Valley Drive (tel
503134): a find. Old hotel
taken over by family with
two sons with experience at
some of Europe's best hotels
and restaurants, one
management, other chef (ex
Imperial, Torquay; Frantel,
Rheims; Box Tree, Ilkley). Try
tomato and orange soup,
chicken leg stuffed with
apple in cider sauce;
residents FP menu (very
good) £6.90; card (4-course)
£9–11. BB £12.50–14.50.

Harewood House: superb.
Robert Adam's best interior
decorations, Adam's and
Chippendale's most exquisite
furniture, in a Palladian
house by John Carr in a park
and gardens by Capability
Brown. All done around 1759
thanks to Edwin Lascelles
(1st Earl of Harewood)
mostly from profits of West
Indian plantations. Current
Earl cousin to the Queen.
Great paintings, Sèvres
china, fine silver. Open April–
Oct daily; Nov, Feb, Mar:
Sun, Tues, Wed, Thur.

Harrogate: spa, 18th-century.
Town of flowers, turkish
baths, sauna, solarium in
Royal Baths; Royal Pump
Room now a museum with

| Harrogate *continued* | Youngs Hotel, 15 York Rd (tel 67336): Cambridge PhD and maths-graduate wife in hotel business ten years. Pleasant cooking, value meals: £5.50. Wine from £3.75/litre; BB £8.25–10.50. Quiet area.

Arden House, 69 Franklin Rd (tel 509224): real Yorkshire cooking; 4-course meal £3.50; BB £7–8. | concerts in hall, once served 1000 glasses of sulphur water in a morning; old Valley Gardens have lovely sun colonnade, 600 ft glass-covered walkway; trial gardens of Northern Horticultural Society (Harlow Car Gardens) attractive and interesting.

Ripley, 3 m N, remodelled 1827 like a French village with cobbled square, stocks, cross. Ingilby family have lived for centuries in castle – where Cromwell stayed after winning at Marston Moor. |
| --- | --- | --- |
| A59 Blubberhouses, Bolton Abbey (16 m) | At Bolton Abbey, Bolton Park Farm (tel Bolton Abbey 244): 900-acre working stock farm, charming building; Mrs Crabtree, farmer's wife, bakes and cooks: beef and lamb bred on the farm. What more could you ask? BB £6.25. BB with 4-course evening meal £8.50. Closed Oct–1 May. Children, babies welcome. | Bolton Abbey: a lovely ruin, among woods, waterfalls and meadows beside the river Wharfe; it has a throat-catching nostalgic look caught by Landseer's painting. Roads and footpaths follow the river, and stepping stones cross it just north. |
| small road alongside B6160 Ilkley (3 m) small road across Ilkley and Bombalds Moors to Keighley (4 m) | At Ilkley, Cow and Calf, Moor Top (tel 607335): lovely views over Wharfedale. Very comfortable; cordon bleu chefs. Meals card £7.50. BB £12–20. SB weekends.

Lister Arms, Skipton Rd (tel 608698): nice garden; teamakers in bedrooms; internationally trained chef Stephen Pollock fanatical about real bread. Lunch FP £3.85; dinner FP £5.95 plus card. Wines reasonably priced. BB £11–13.50.

Sangsters, 19 Church St (tel 600566): wine bar; wine prices cheap, no plonk; | Ilkley may be just a name in a funny song 'Ilkley Moor Baht 'at' to many non-Yorkshiremen, but it is an attractive town, with the river Wharfe flowing beside main street. Victorian spa. Moors, lovely in summer, bring *Wuthering Heights* back to life in autumn mists.

Cow and Calf rocks are practice ground for climbers.

Revived Worth Valley Railway, steam, runs Keighley–Oxenhope via Haworth. Used for *Railway Children* film. |

French house wine £3.15,
Bereich Nierstein £3.45. '71
St Emilion £5.95. Blackboard
menu daily (seafood
pancakes, beef carbonnade,
gammon in Madeira) from
£2.75 main dish. Shut Sun,
Mon.

A629 Haworth
small road NW
Haworth
Parsonage (5 m)

Haworth: Emily, Charlotte
and Anne Brontë walked the
moors. High Withins, eerie
ruin on the moors, was
setting for *Wuthering
Heights*. The Brontës lived in
Haworth Parsonage, where
each daughter wrote a
classic. Charlotte's *Jane Eyre*,
Emily's *Wuthering Heights*,
Anne's *Tenant of Wildfell
Hall*. Parsonage is Brontë
museum.

small road on to
Trawden, Colne
(5 m)
small road to
Barnoldswick via
White Moor
Reservoir B6251,
left on A59
Gisburn (9 m)
A682
Long Preston
Settle (11 m)

At Giggleswick, Settle,
Woodlands (tel Settle 2576):
ex-manager at London
Grosvenor Hotel, lecturer in
catering, and wife ex-flight
hostess TWA run very good
guest house (just extended);
fine country views. 4-course
dinner FP £5. BB £9. Good
value. SB off season.

Royal Oak, Market Place,
Settle (tel 2561): 17th-century
inn; meals card £3.75
(includes roast beef) to £6.
BB £11–16.

Colne: British-in-India
museum.

Gisburn: steam and fair
organ museum

B6479 Stainforth, small road right to Malham, Bordley Grassington (17 m)

Buck Inn, Malham (tel Airton 317): cosy, solid stone retreat; children's room next to bar, children's menu 5–6pm; pets welcome. Meals FP £5.50. BB £5.50; snacks. BB £8–12. Walker's Bar for climbers too thirsty to take off their boots.

At Grassington, **Wilson Arms, Threshfield** (tel Grassington 752666): attractive rooms, nice gardens, own fishing rights (trout, grayling). Lunch 4 courses FP £4.50; cold table dish £2.90; dinner FP £8; also card. BB £14–19; big reductions over 2 nights. Low season £6.50–12.

Ashfield House, Grassington (tel 452584): useful; 17th-century; warm, comfortable; fresh home cooking, Yorkshire portions. Meals £4.70 residents; BB £7.95.

Dales National Park: packhorse bridge at Stainforth where river Ribble cascades over Stainforth Force. Park scenery of fierce beauty; million years of flowing water has carved limestone into odd, dramatic shapes. Road to Malham and beyond passes waterfalls.

Malham, centre for climbers, set in amphitheatre of hills. Malham Cove (1 m) is sheer limestone cliff, 240 ft, streaked with black, which inspired novelist Charles Kingsley to write *Water Babies* with boy chimney sweep falling into river. Nearby Gordale Scar, spectacular rocky ravine with a stream falling and leaping down it.

Grassington: cobbled square, narrow streets, medieval bridge.

B6160 Kettlewell, small road right Woodale, Horsehouse, Middleham (20 m) A6108 Leyburn, Richmond (10 m)

(Route 7 Borders joins here at Richmond)

Bolton Castle Restaurant, Bolton Castle, Leyburn (tel Wensleydale 23408): in Great Chamber of castle; run by David Walker, former butler to Lord Bolton of nearby Bolton Hall. Lunch £1.50–4 (£5 Sunday); 4-course dinner £5–9, wine from £3.65. Open daily except Mon, Easter–Oct; weekends Oct–Easter.

Black Lion, Finkle St, Richmond (tel 3121): handsome old inn; saddle of lamb, sirloin of beef, loin of pork in cider. Lunch FP £3 (bargain); dinner FP £5.50 (value); fine value bar meals £2.30; BB £9–11.50.

Kettlewell: pretty village at foot of 2300 ft Great Whernside. From Middleham to the Vale of York already called 'James Herriot Country' in appreciation of the best-selling writer vet.

Middleham: racehorses trained here.

Jervaux Abbey, 6 m SE, ruined 12th-century abbey dissolved by Henry VIII.

Bolton Castle (12th-century), Leyburn: Mary Queen of Scots held here.

Richmond: romantic castle ruins among grass and trees (11th-century). Georgian theatre (1788) one of Britain's oldest. 'Sweet Lass of Richmond Hill' of song came from here.

B6271
Northallerton
(13 m)
A168 Thirsk
(8 m)

Golden Fleece, Market Place,
Thirsk (tel 23108): old market
inn where war-time aircrews
pretended to be at peace
between raids. Now well-run
Trust House Forte inn. Meals
FP £6; card £8; children
under 14 half price. BB £14–
20.

Beginning of Vale of York,
watered by many rivers and
beautifully fertile; bounded
by the Dales westward, North
Yorks Moors to east; green
vale of rolling farmlands,
tramped by prehistoric man,
Roman Legions, armies of
English fighting Scots,
Royalists and Roundheads
fighting each other. Now a
delight to travellers.

Thirsk: old market town with
racecourse, remembered by
thousands of bomber crews
who flew from round here in
the war; now known as the
place where James Herriot
and Helen lived at Skeldale
House.

A170, small road
right to Kilburn,
Coxwold,
Ampleforth,
Sproxton, rejoin
A170 Helmsley
(14 m)

Coxwold, Fauconberg Arms
(tel 214): good-looking 17th-
century inn. Menu includes
30 main courses; various
steak dishes. Lunch FP £4;
dinner (with wine) card £10.
House wine £3.15. BB £8.50–
13. Restaurant shut Mon.

Black Swan, Helmsley: 400
years old; Yorkshire chef
researches local and
traditional dishes; Steak Old
Peculier – strips of fillet in
strong ale and mustard sauce
served in Yorkshire pudding;
Wensley fowl, stuffed with
Wensleydale cheese, sauce
of port and walnuts; many
more. Enormous English
breakfast £3.75; lunch FP
£5.50; dinner FP £7.50; card
£10. Rooms double £32–35;
single £24; SB.

Feathers, Market Place, (tel
Helmsley 70275): very
attractive, some beamed
rooms, central heating. Local
food, big choice of dishes.
Lunch FP £4.50; dinner FP
£6.50. BB £11–13.

Kilburn: tiny village famous
for wood-carving started by
Robert Thompson, whose
trademark cut into furniture
and other carvings was a
mouse (a symbol of quiet
industry), retained by his
successors since his death
(1955). 700 ft escarpment 2
m N beloved by glider pilots.
White Horse 314 x 288 ft cut
into hill by schoolmaster and
pupils 1857.

Coxwold: Lawrence Sterne
(1713–68), author of *Tristram
Shandy* and *Sentimental
Journey* – a charming travel
book – lived at Shandy Hall.
He was reburied in 1969 in
the churchyard of the church,
where he was vicar.

Shandy Hall (1450) open
Weds 2–6pm, or any time by
appointment (tel Coxwold
465).

Newburgh Priory, ½ m SE:
mansion originally priory;
tradition says Cromwell's
body brought here by his

Helmsley
continued

Feversham Arms, High St (tel Helmsley 70766): charming family-owned hotel, log fires, all bedrooms private bath, colour TV, phone, hairdrier. Spanish owner, extensive menu; genuine paella (advance order); 4-course dinner £8 plus special dishes; BB £11.50–14; SB winter.

Crown, Market Square (tel 70297): good roasts, local meat; home baking; fish from Scarborough: Lunch FP £3.55; dinner FP £5.50; BB £11.

daughter after Stuart kings returned, buried in bricked-up vault never since opened.

Helmsley: most pleasant market town; stalls on Friday in market square with restored old buildings. Ruined castle enclosed by Norman earthworks.

Rievaulx Abbey (2 m NW, pronounced 'Rivers') is huge ghostly and majestic 12th-century Cistercian abbey built by twelve monks from France. Beautiful even in ruins. English Gothic style. 18th-century landscape terrace with fine views.

A170 Pickering (12 m)

Forest and Vale Hotel, Pickering (tel 72722): warm, cosy hotel; walled garden facing south. Built 1787 as mansion, recently modernized internally; most rooms own bathroom. Lunch FP £4.80; 4-course dinner FP £7; card around £8. BB £11.50–14.50.

At Cropton, 3 m N in Moors Park, New Inn (tel Lastingham 330): useful village inn; bar snacks; meals about £5; BB £5–7.50.

Pickering: entrance to wild, lovely North Yorks Moors, with few roads. One of Britian's oldest markets; founded by Celtic king, 270 BC; 12th-century church with wall paintings, including Salome dancing for Herod, George and Dragon, murder of Thomas à Becket. North Yorks Moors Railway runs from Pickering to Grosmont through heart of National Park. Glorious 18 mile ride. Opened 1863 with horse-drawn carriages; steam engines came 11 years later. Closed by BR 1965. Reopened by enthusiasts.

Flamingo Land, Kirby Misperton (3½ m S): claimed to be biggest private zoo in world; also children's farm, lakes, fun fair, big model railway. March–Oct. Road chosen could be difficult in winter. In that case, take A169 across moors to Whitby (check in Pickering with police).

small road signposted Newton on Rawcliffe; on to Stape, Mauley Cross (¾ m), for 2 m road *not* tar-sealed nor marked on some maps but reasonable; tar starts again after bridge where Wade's Causeway (Roman road) crosses; after 4½ m bear right at junction, sharp right again after ½ m continue 3 m to Goathland (20 m) left at Mallyan Hotel, left again (signposted) to Beck Hole; road climbs on to moor; left at junction, left again on to A169 almost immediately take left signposted Grosmont

At Goathland, Mallyan Spout Hotel (tel Whitby 86206): ivy-clad stone hotel on green where sheep graze; comfortably, pleasantly furnished; garden; views of moors and Esk valley. Fish fresh daily from Whitby; trout, lamb from the moors, local salmon, Yorkshire beef. Best English cooking. Vegetables 'cooked crisp – ask if you want them cooked longer'. A good hotel. Dinner FP £6.50; card £7–9. BB £11–16. Lunchtime hot bar meals £1.50–3.50. SB including summer.

Mauley Cross: cross marked end of family estates in Middle Ages; forest drive (toll) E to Cropton starts here. Wade's Causeway (restored) built AD 80 by Romans; large 'golf balls' seen across moor part of NATO's missile defence early warning system at Fylingdales.

Goathland: moors and grazing sheep encroach among houses of village. Several nearby waterfalls; nearest Mallyan Spout.

Beck Hole: pretty hamlet in wooded hollow.

Grosmont: end of North Moors steam railway from Pickering. Sheds where old steam engines are restored.

---

small road Egton, right to A171 Whitby (24 m)

Whitby: Bagdale Olde Hall (tel 603552): owner-chef catches seafood in own boat off Whitby coast. Dishes praised by *Gourmet* magazine (US). Meals FP 4-course £5.50; £8; £10 with wine. Dinner daily; lunch only if 6 or more reserve. Interesting old house.

At Ruswarp, 2 m, Old Hall Hotel (tel Whitby 602801): historic house converted to

Captain James Cook, explorer, started sailing among Whitby colliers in 1746; captain in nine years; joined Navy as simple AB, knew more about navigation than any man then living; became King's Surveyor, circled world twice; first man to sail round Australia, New Zealand; first to chart Newfoundland and North American Pacific coast;

Whitby
continued

hotel by industrial chemist and wife five years ago. Built 1603 by shipowner; son married daughter of Cromwell's General Fairfax (victor Battle of Marston Moor against King Charles' army). Kept changing sides between King and Parliament; finally executed. House has original Jacobean staircase with minstrel gallery; priesthole for 2 or 3 men to hide built into 4½ ft outer wall; occasional ghost; few minutes' walk from river Esk (fishing). Meals from £4; BB £8.50–9.50.

Antarctic discoveries. Sailed from Whitby on expeditions in Whitby-built ship *Endeavour*. Killed by natives in Hawaii 1779. He discovered that scurvy, killer of whole crews, could be avoided by eating fresh fruit, vegetables, drinking lime (reason English sailors were called Limeys). His house in Grape Lane is small museum. Whitby is photogenic old port; in 18th century had big whaling fleet; now only a cut-down fishing fleet but still a tang of salt air and fish; houses ascend from harbour in steep tiers.

Whitby Abbey founded AD 657, where Synod of Whitby was held (English churches decided to tie up with Rome); home of our first known Christian poet, Caedmon. Ruins of 13th-century abbey; Count Dracula landed here in Bram Stoker's novel (1897); damage partly caused by German navy shelling 1914. Whitby craftsmen still make jewellery from jet (fossilized wood, black or smoky colour).

A171, B1447
Robin Hood's Bay, small road past Ravenscar to Cloughton
A171, very soon A165
Scarborough (20 m)

Raven Hall, Ravenscar (tel 870353): lovely position; splendidly run by family for 20 years; same chef (Donald Holmes) 20 years, second chef a mere 10 years; swimming pool, tennis courts, golf, putting course; 60 single malt whiskies. A fine hotel with typically English eccentric history. I like it. Built on Roman early warning signal station against Saxon raids. Dr Willis, who made a fortune

Robin Hood's Bay: hurry – the honeycombed cliffs are losing 20 ft to erosion every 100 years! Rocky reefs below; fossils in cliffs 150 million years old; narrow main street of town dives down to sea, houses seem to lean on each other. Once fishing and smuggling town; now turned to tourism. 3 mile sweeping bay to headland at Ravenscar. Small ships have been deposited ashore in storms. Robin Hood hid here.

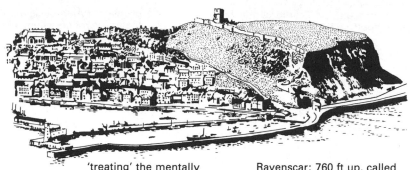

'treating' the mentally disturbed King George III built it; Count Dracula supposed to have stayed here. Owners Gridley family have plant-nurseries in the grounds. Meals £4–7.50, good wine list from £3.50. BB and DBB rates vary according to type of room, length of stay, season. BB standby price (on day) from £8.50; DBB £17.59–35. SB. Closed Jan, Feb, Mar.

Majestic, Norstead Manor Drive (tel Scarborough 63806): remarkable value. Family run; modern. 4-course dinner FP (including roast) £3 high season, £2.50 early/late; wines £4–65. BB £7–13, DBB £9–15. Shut Nov–Mar.

The Outlook, 18 Ryndleside (tel 64900): another good family hotel; sauna, solarium, in handsome building. BB £7.50–8.60; DBB £9.20–10.60.

Green Gables, West Bank (tel 61005): comfortable, spacious, bright décor; heated indoor swimming pool; baby listening. BB £6.30; DBB £8.60. Good value.

Royal Hotel, St Nicholas St (tel 64333): a delight. Part of

Ravenscar: 760 ft up, called 'resort that never was'. Developers put in sewers, mains water, roads, laid out plots last century, but few people bought land; so a nice village remains. Pony-trekking country; amateur geologists work on cliffs.

Scarborough: fishing village grown into resort long ago, but still also a fishing village. A favourite of mine. Few better places for really fresh shellfish – stalls by the harbour; oysters, lobsters, whelks, prawns as pre-dinner appetizer. A spa since 1622, became one of most famous in Europe in 19th century. So fashionable hotels such as Grand and Royal appeared on south cliff; below them and over headland are all entertainments of modern seaside resort. In countryside and on sea are action holiday centres – fishing, sailing, parachute jumping, sub aqua, flying and a Yorkshire county cricket pitch. Norman castle on headland (1158), played vital roles in history, ruined by Cromwell after a siege. Plenty for children. Model passenger-carrying railway a favourite; good art gallery. Big choice of theatre shows from musicals to

| Scarborough continued | Scarborough's history. *All profits go to medical research.* Tasteful period décor; another £1 million spent last year on furnishings; Churchill suite, where Winston stayed often, has Union Jack. Extra 'gourmet' restaurant with own chef. Hotel restaurant lunch FP £3.50 plus special dishes; dinner FP £6 plus. Gourmet restaurant dinner £10–12. BB £17.50–22. DBB £24–28. SB. Good wines from £4.50. 'Gourmet' closed Sun night; all Jan.

Scarborough. Contact Tourist Board, St Nicholas Cliff (tel 72261). | playwright Alan Ayckbourn's theatre-in-round where all his new plays are first shown. |

| A64 Malton small road to Coneysthorpe; left to crossroads at edge of Welburn right to Sheriff Hutton, Strensal (33 m) small road Wiggington, Shipton, left on A19 York (12 m) | At Hackness, 4 m NW Scarborough, Hackness Grange (tel 82281): true relaxation; Earl of Listowel's former residence on banks of the Derwent, with its gracious rooms, trout pool, river trout fishing. Now a delightful hotel with indoor heated pool which seems out of doors, all-weather tennis court, house-party atmosphere. Family run. Real Yorkshire cooking; traditionally, Yorkshire pudding often served with sauce before roast. Lunch card £4.50–6; 4-course dinner FP £9. BB £21; DBB £28. Pricey, but still value.

At Malton, Green Man and Fleece, (tel 5662): comfortable inn run by Tate-Smith family for 116 years; lunch from £4.50; BB £8.50–13; also family rooms (3–4 people).

At Hovingham (4 m N Coneysthorpe), Worsley | Malton: passing motorists often miss its old market square round Norman church, markets still held Friday, Saturday, include livestock. Racehorse training centre.

Castle Howard (5 m SE), designed by Vanbrugh for Howard family, 1699, still one of Britain's grandest houses. Vanbrugh, an artist, had never designed a building before. Baroque style, except west wing (Palladian – built later). Painted Hall is brilliant. Paintings include Holbein's *Henry VIII*. Park dotted with lodges and odd 'follies' (purposeless ornamental buildings. Open daily Easter–Oct. Richard III's son Edward, Prince of Wales, buried in church at Sherif Hutton. Effigy on his tomb.

2 m Shipton, Beningbrough Hall: 1716 – redecorated to house 18th-century portraits |

Arms (tel Hovingham 234): deservedly well-known hotel in Georgian house, garden, pleasant atmosphere; all rooms with bath. Lunch £4.50; dinner £8. BB £15–16. DBB £22.

Malt Shovel, Hovingham (tel Hovingham 264): pub run by a farmer; famous for steaks from local farm. Meals £6.50. Shut Tues.

from National Gallery. Lovely carvings; pleasant garden; open Apr–end Oct, pm.

York

Delightful place, if a bit crowded in midsummer. One of Europe's most attractive and interesting cities.

The Minster is fourth cathedral to stand on site of Roman fort of AD 71. Started 1222, it was finished 250 years later. Dwarfs most European cathedrals, including Westminster Abbey, and has a solid grandeur few possess. In 1969 foundations were dug out to repair 20,000 ton tower. Beneath they found Roman fort foundations, Viking strongpost, Norman church pillars and 13th-century foundations of present Minster. The undercroft was not filled in but made into a spectacular museum of history. Minster has more than 100 stained-glass windows, covering 800 years. York's medieval city walls, most complete in England, with four magnificent gateways, have walkway on top. 18 medieval parish churches exist, some turned to other uses – 13th-century St Martin Micklegate (youth centre); St Mary's, Castlegate (heritage museum); St John's, Micklegate (live arts centre).

National Railway Museum, with famous steam locomotives, world's fastest Mallard (128mph), and wealth of railway items; superb Castle Museum with reconstructed Victorian cobbled street with houses, shops, lamps, tavern, hansom cab in recognition of inventor Joseph Hansom, born in Micklegate, a lovely collection of ornate sentimental Valentine cards, and the condemned cell where highwayman Dick Turpin spent three months before being hanged in 1739. Whip-Ma-Whop-Ma-Gate, road where lawbreakers used to be flogged, passes home of Margaret Clitherow, tortured to death in 1586 for hiding Jesuit priest; recently made a saint. The Shambles, Butchers' Street, has overhanging timbered gables.

River Ouse running through city passes walls of stone houses then flows through woods and meadows;

boats for hire, cruises. The new university, with
attractive modern buildings grouped round a lake.
Treasurers' House (17th-century), lovely building in
peaceful walled garden with fine period furniture.

King George V said, 'The history of York is the history
of England.' Not a museum, but a lively city.

Information: Tourist Board, De Grey Rooms, Exhibition
Square (tel York 21756).

Hotels and restaurants
At Acaster Malbis, beside river Ouse, 3½ m S, Ship Inn
and Wheelhouse Restaurant (tel York 703888):
charming inn, lovely position; own moorings and
fishing; garden bar; hot and cold lunch bar meals;
'Wheelhouse' dinner Tues–Sat £6–7. BB £9–10.50.
Book ahead.

Dean Court Hotel, Duncombe Place (tel 25082): in
house beneath Minster West Towers, once used to
house visiting clergy by archbishop, Ian Washington
runs pleasant hotel immaculately; all bedrooms have
bathroom, colour TV, phone. Good English cooking,
fine service. Lunch £6; dinner £8. BB £21. SB Oct–mid
May.

Grasmead House, 1 Scarcrott Hill (tel 29996): family
owned; bedrooms good value; all rooms have bath,
colour TV, teamaker, mostly four-poster beds; limited
meals, dinner if ordered ahead £3.50; some snacks. BB
£12–15.

Abbots Mews, Marygate Lane, Bootham (centre of
York) (tel 34866): run by couple who converted coach
house and stables. Comfortable, pretty bedrooms;
meals FP £6; card £8–9. BB winter £12.50; summer
£18. SB winter.

Young's Hotel, 25 High Petergate (opposite cathedral)
(tel 24229): birthplace of Guy Fawkes, Catholic
enthusiast who tried to blow up Houses of Parliament;
he was old boy of York's public school, St Peters.
Locals use Young's restaurant; generous portions;
meals: card around £8. Simple bedrooms. BB £12.50.

Jeeves, 39 Tanner Row (tel 59622): family run; young
son trained chef, makes excellent sauces; not cheap,
but good value. Popular with young set local people.
Little bistro-style building. Dinner FP £5.95; card £7.50.
List of 140 wines, vintage clarets £6.95–48.50; French
house wine £3.75. Shut Sun; Mon in winter.

Route 6

**Manchester – Forest of Bowland – Lake District –
Yorkshire Dales – Manchester**

Manchester
A56 Rawtenstall,
A646 on edge of
Burnley, left to
Padiham (21 m)
(6 m from Colne,
Route 5)

Rawtenstall- beginning of
Forest of Rossendale,
museum with Egyptian
antiquities; craft of clog-
making; 18th-century musical
scores, instruments.

A6068 Higham,
left on small
road to
Newchurch in
Pendle,
Roughlee, left,
left again to
Downham, left
to Chatburn
(12 m)

Pendle Forest is a wild area;
on church tower at
Newchurch is carved the 'all-
seeing eye of God' (1544) to
protect faithful from wiles of
local witches who used to
meet in 16th/17th centuries
on Pendle Hill (1831 ft
footpath). Ten of them were
hanged at Lancaster Castle in
1612. On Pendle Hill in 1652
George Fox claimed a vision
telling him to found the
Society of Friends, became
known as Quakers.

small road
through Forest
of Bowland to
Slaidburn (6 m)

At Slaidburn, Hark to Bounty
(tel 246): a 19th-century
hunting parson had a hound
called Bounty who would call
him to return from the pub to
the parsonage. Good lunch
snacks, home-made
sausages. Attractive
bedrooms; real ale; meals
around £8; BB £14.85; DBB
£22.50.

Parrock Head Farm,
Woodhouse Lane (tel
Slaidburn 614): 200-acre
stock-rearing farm; 17th-
century farmhouse. Won

Forest of Bowland has few
trees; rugged, lonely hill
country, with narrow roads,
rocky peaks and wild scenery
– at its best when heather
turns purple in late summer,
autumn. Check road
conditions in winter before
crossing it.

Slaidburn: moorland town on
river Hodder; cobbled
pavements; grey-stone
houses flank narrow streets.

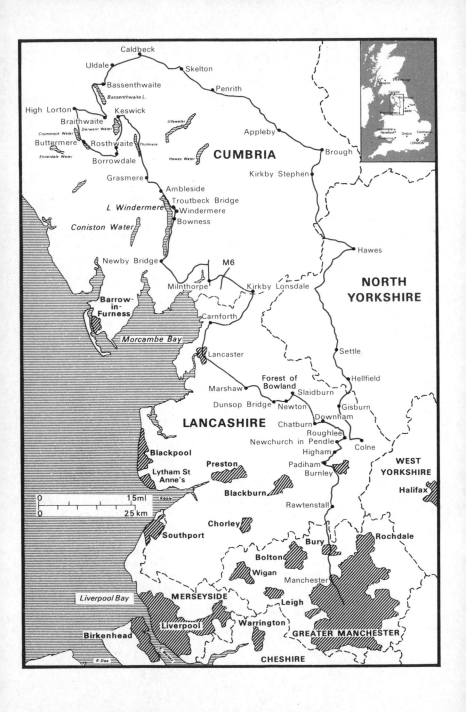

Forest of Bowland *continued*

AA's Farm Guesthouse of the Year 1980 (North). Dinner around £5.50; house wine £3.20. BB £10.

At Bolton by Bowland (between Chatburn and Slaidburn), Harrop Fold Farm Guesthouse (tel Bolton by Bowland 600): 280 acres, with streams rising to 900 ft. Bedrooms with bathrooms. Real Lancashire hotpot, local trout, lamb, nettle soup. Dinner open to non-residents; card £8.50; BB £10–14; DBB £18.50. SB, including winter game.

---

small road left to Newton, right to Dunsop Bridge, through Trough of Bowland Pass to Marshaw, Lancaster (18 m)

At Lancaster, Farmers' Arms, Penny St (tel 36368): useful overnight hotel; bar meals; help-yourself cold table £1.80. Dinner £6 (roasts and grills). BB £9–16.

At Caton (on A683), Ship (tel Caton 770265): nice 17th-century coaching inn; old beams; good cheap bar meals (around £3); dinner by arrangement. BB £7.50.

Bowland Pass climbs to 1000 ft above sea level. Highwaymen used to waylay travellers, and Yorkshire smugglers carried goods through it when trading with Isle of Man. Rugged in winter.

Lancaster: attractive city; fine Norman castle, built on site of Roman camp, is a prison and court. Museum in 15th-century Hadrian's Tower. Many elegant Georgian buildings of grey stone and one ornate Victorian monster – Jubilee Tower, built for Queen Victoria's golden jubilee. Views from top sometimes to Snowdonia (75 m), Lake District mountains and Isle of Man. Friends' Meeting House (1695) museum (closed Sun) has superb furniture by Gillow. University fine modern architecture. Lancaster Canal good for lazy holiday cruisers – few locks.

A6 Carnforth,
B6254 Kirkby
Lonsdale (16 m)

At Carnforth, New Capernwray Farm, Capernwray (tel Carnforth 4284): built 1697, its oak beams have not rotted; no longer a working farm, so extra quiet and peaceful; reputation for hospitality; good cooking of fresh food. Guests help themselves to as much as they like – or as little. Dinner 4 courses £4.75; bring your own wine; BB £8.75–9.50.

At Kirkby Lonsdale, Craggs House Hotel, High Casterton (tel 71551): 18th-century farmhouse. 4-course dinner with surprising choice 'real bargain' at £6; especially when hare with calvados, mustard and cream sauce is offered; lunch at £3.75 looks a bargain too; heaven for true whisky drinkers – 93 of 117 known single-malt whiskies on offer. BB £7.50: you should sleep well if you try even half the malts. Restaurant closed Tues.

Whoop Hall Inn (tel 71284): 17th-century inn; extensive bar menu; full children's menu £3.50; dinner card £7–10. BB £8–9.

Carnforth: Atlantic shore has crept away; until end 18th century was shipbuilding port. Processed iron ore followed; furnaces closed in 1931 Depression. Steam town, live steam museum, has over twenty locomotives, many working; some unusual industrial machines.

Kirkby Lonsdale: John Ruskin, 19th-century artist and fighter for social justice, called the view across the river Lune to the fells 'one of the loveliest in England, therefore in the world'. Turner, a greater artist, painted it. Likeable little market town, with fine old buildings. The Devil built the 13th-century bridge in a night, made a beautiful job of it; truly unspoiled England.

A65; just after
going under
motorway, left
on B6385 at
Crooklands to
Milnthorpe

Crooklands: very comfortable, well run; Swiss chef; game specialities; buttery-coffee shop open all day for light meals. FP lunch £4.30; FP dinner £7.50; card £10. Wines £4.30–20. BB £17–23. SB 2 days.

At Milnthorpe, Bluebell at Heversham (tel 3159): FP lunch £4.75; dinner FP £8.25; BB £11–16.50. SB winter.

north on old A6 for 3 m, left on A590 close to Grange over Sands, to Newby Bridge on Lake Windermere (21 m)

At Grange, Kent's Bank Hotel (tel 2054): built 1872 by a parson; Betjemanesque architecture, high, lovely views; friendly; locals use bar. Meals £4.40–7.25; BB (seasonal) £7.25–13.75. SB winter.

Grange Hotel (tel 3666): independent first-class hotel known for good straightforward English cooking. Dinner 4 course FP £7.50. BB £13.50–17.50.

Aynsome Manor, Cartmel (tel Cartmel 276): fine old manor house, furnished like country home. 5-course dinner £8.45. DBB only £20–24. SB winter. Cold buffet only Sunday night.

At Newby Bridge, Swan (tel 681): long white old inn beside Leven river and edge of Windermere. All bedrooms with bathroom, teamakers, colour TV; buffet bar for light lunches; dinner FP £8.50; card £8–12. BB £16.50–18.50. SB Oct–Apr.

Lakeside Hotel (tel Newby Bridge 207): famous Victorian hotel beside lake; boats for hire; dinner FP 4 courses £7; BB £16.50, own bath.

New A590 near Grange, less car queues. Sheltered mild climate; views across to Morecambe coast. Two golf courses, pony trekking, fishing. Bathing dangerous – tide rushes in; outdoor seawater pool. Sea disappears as fast at low tide to reveal miles of sands with 'river' channels. Called 'over Sands' because stage coaches and carriages once crossed sands most dangerously from Morecambe.

Levens Hall (nr junction A6–A590): Elizabethan, contains some of the finest furniture in any stately home. Magnificent topiary gardens laid out 1690. Collection of steam engines, open Easter–30 Sept, gardens daily; house Tues, Wed, Thurs, Sun.

Holker Hall (Cark, 2 m W of Grange): 17th-century, altered 19th century when it was favourite of Duke of Devonshire; much Victorian furnishing; screen embroidered by Mary Queen of Scots. Park with deer; children's park. Motor museum. Open Easter–end Sept (not Sat).

Newby Bridge: beautiful Windermere scenery begins here, with wooded slopes and hills folding to the water; Newby is delightful village with slate bridge over river Leven leading into lake; beautiful old boats run by Sealink to Bowness, Ambleside; join at lakeside, Newby Bridge to Lakeside and Haverthwaite steam railway running 3½ m.

A592 by east side of Lake Windermere to Bowness, Windermere village (9 m)

At Bowness, Bardriggs Country House, Longtake Hill (tel Windermere 3567): peaceful family-run hotel ½ m from lakeside; 1½-acre gardens. All home-made dishes, including bread. Dinner £6.50; BB £11.65. SB.

B5284 4 m at Crook, Wild Boar Hotel (tel Windermere 5225): delightful old inn, finely furnished, very well run, but pricey. All bedrooms have bath or shower; golf course next door. Mouthwatering menus, superbly cooked. Wild boar in season. 4-course lunch £5.40; dinner FP 5-course £9.25; card £10–12; 150 wines from £3.30 (Yugoslav) to '71 Richebourg £22, '66 Latour £44. BB £16.70–19.55.

Hideaway, Phoenix Way, Windermere (tel 3070): many accolades for Tim Harper's friendly hotel which I have not yet stayed in. Maybe unusually well-stocked bar with cocktail called Hideaway Hair-raiser helps, but meals get highest praise; all bedrooms have bathrooms; lunch bar meals; dinner £6; wine £3 (Burgundy) to £30. DBB £17. SB Nov–April.

Langdale Chase (tel Ambleside 2201): another high-quality, pricey hotel; magnificent lakeside position, superb views, fine grounds, beautiful furnishings; lunch FP £5.25; 4-course dinner £9.25; BB £15.50–24. SB Nov–April.

Pleasant road with glimpses of lake; too narrow and hilly to hurry. Windermere is 10½ m long, only 1¼ m across at widest; deeper waters have char, salmon-like fish.

Bowness, original Windermere village, now tourist centre with water skiing and yacht club. 14 isles – biggest is Belle Isle with cylindrical house (1774).

Troutbeck Bridge, left on A591 Ambleside, Grasmere alongside lake Thirlmere on minor roads on West side, rejoin A591 at tip of lake for Keswick (18 m)

At Troutbeck, Askew Rigg Farm (tel Threlkeld 638): farm cooking; BB £5, plus £3.50 4-course dinner; no meals Sun, Wed.

Rydal Lodge, Rydal (tel Ambleside 3208): lovely old house 5 mins from Rydal Water; river Rothay flows through garden; country cottage furnishing. Very pleasant. FP dinner £6 (little choice); BB £9.80–10.80.

Nanny Brow Hotel, Clappersgate, Ambleside (tel 2036): magnificent views from charming house of 1906. 5-acre woods, garden, peaceful; local produce; English country cooking. Dinner FP £5.75; BB £12.50; DBB £17.25; SB winter.

Wateredge Hotel, Ambleside (tel 2332): a winner. In garden leading to water's edge, 17th-century cottage intelligently modernized; tasteful décor, lake views.

Roads round here get packed in summer – not surprising, when you see scenery; no alternatives, so grin and bear it. Kirkstone Pass dominates Troutbeck. In village is Town End, yeoman farmer's house of 1623, almost unaltered; same family, the Brownes, lived here for 300 years. Original oak furniture, some home-made, kitchen utensils, books, 18th-century local fabrics.

Ambleside: stone-built town with mountains on three sides; lovely position; 1 m from lake. Bridge House, tiny two-roomed 17th-century summer house built on bridge over stream; now National Trust information centre. Climbing centre; guides can be hired.

Rydal: Wordsworth lived in Rydal Mount 1813 until his death in 1850; 16th-century house, open to public (except Feb); he laid out 4½ acre garden.

Sally Collier, 'Outstanding Young Chef of 1977' at London's Cordon Bleu College, produces imaginative meals beautifully cooked. Lunch £4.50; 5-course dinner £9. BB £16.50.

Travellers Rest, Grasmere (tel 378): useful inn; bar meals; dinner (book) FP £5. BB £8.

Skiddaw Grove, Vicarage Hill (tel 73324): family hotel, 6 of 12 bedrooms with own bathroom; swimming pool, views to mountains; meals good value. 3-course bar-meal lunch £2.30–2.75; 4-course dinner £5; wines from £3. BB £8.50–12.50. Shut mid Nov–mid Mar.

Yan-Tyan-Tethera, 70 Main St (tel 72033): *not* Chinese – means 'one, two, three' in lakeland shepherd dialect! Farmer's daughter cooks mouthwatering daytime snacks such as savoury pancakes; in evening venison casserole, giant shrimps, veal dishes. Supper around £7 inc wine. Shut Mon eve, Sun– Wed eve in winter.

Chaucer House, Derwentwater Place, Keswick (tel 72318): comfortably furnished hotel run by same family since 1941; six members involved; grandma, Irene Stone, still runs it, grandson David Stephenson is chef. Dinner FP £5.50; card £6. DBB £13–15.

Grasmere: 'The loveliest spot that man hath ever found,' said Wordsworth, who lived at Dove Cottage 1799–1808. Museum nearby. Little lakeside village set in ring of mountains; a touch of Austria but softer.

Thirlmere Lake: 3 m long, flanked by forests; once two lakes, joined to make reservoir to supply Manchester with water through 96 m aquaduct. Outcry at the time against flooding of land led to formation of National Trust. Small roads on west side give much better views than from A591.

Old market town of Keswick has a dozen magnificent views. Best are from Castle Head (529 ft) over Derwent Water, and Bassenthwaite Lake, and Latrigg (1203 ft, 1 m NE) wide panorama. Interesting Moot Hall (town hall, 1813); poet Robert Southey lived in Greta Hall.

B5289 S by Derwent Water to Rosthwaite, Borrowdale Pass, through Honister Pass to Buttermere (14 m)

3½ m S Keswick, Lodore Swiss Hotel (tel Borrowdale 285): not cheap but fine value. In 40 acres which include Lodore Falls. Modern furnishings; lovely views; all bedrooms with bath or shower, TV. Indoor and outdoor heated swimming pools, sauna, solarium, sun bed, massage; steam bath, paddling pool; squash, tennis courts, trampoline; free weekday golf; nursery; film shows, dancing. Chef Kurt Hartman just returned from refresher course in Bordeaux. Try guinea fowl and crayfish dishes. Lunch FP £5.50; dinner FP £7.50; card £9–10. BB £23. Full board £33.

Borrowdale Hotel, (tel Borrowdale 225): comfortable old hotel with good imaginative dishes; famous bar lunches, with dishes from many countries. 4-course lunch FP £5.80; 6-course dinner FP £8.50. DBB

More superb mountain lake scenery; Bowder Stone, near Rosthwaite, weighs 2000 tons and seems to be about to fall down hill; perfectly safe – a ladder up it gives lovely views from top. Castle Crag (900 ft, 20 min walk): views over Derwent Water.

At Grange, stone bridge crosses river Derwent at narrow point called Jaws of Borrowdale. Magnificent scenery through Honister Pass (1200 ft). Seatoller village (E end of pass) beginning of Johnny Wood Walk through forest of old oaks, some pines, to High Doat to see Borrowdale and fells. Path marked by Naturalists' Trust.

Seathwaite, 1 m upriver, lovely but wettest place in England (rainfall four times London's – driest months May, June, Sept).

Barnard Castle *continued*	only £22.90. SB winter. Shut Jan. Yew Tree, Seatoller (tel Borrowdale 634): useful restaurant; local trout; good value. Meals about £4–5. Shut Mon.	Buttermere is a gorgeous valley; small village and 1¼ m wooded lake huddled between mountains; lake joined to larger Crummock Water by river which tumbles down Scale Force, lovely waterfall. Mountains here 500 million years old, among world's oldest.
B5289 High Lorton, right B5292 Whinlatter Pass to Braithwaite (12 m) A66 beside Bassenthwaite Lake, right on B5291 to Bassenthwaite village (7 m)	Ivy House Hotel, Braithwaite (tel 338): 1630 house, balconied dining room, antique furnishings. Elegant, comfortable. Try Neptune's Feast (mixed seafoods in creamy sauce); and dish made for actor John Cleese – pork stuffed with apples, apricots, in brandy sauce (Pork Fawlty Towers – what else?) Dinner £7–10. BB £17.50–20. Pheasant Inn, Bassenthwaite Lake (tel Bassenthwaite 234): real 16th-century pub, chintzy; lunch £4.50; dinner from £7.50; wines £3 to Châteaux Leoville '64 £24.50. BB £15–16. DBB £20–21.50. SB.	Whinlatter Pass rises to 1043 ft. Bassenthwaite Lake fringed by Wythop Woods with eastern backcloth of Skiddaw mountain; sailing (steady breeze), canoeing. Rare white fish, vendace, found in this lake and Derwent Water – sort of freshwater herring; also pike, perch, trout.
small road Uldale, Caldbeck (8 m) B5299, right on B5305, small road right to Skelton, Penrith (16 m)		My illusions shattered; John Peel, the huntsman about whom the song 'D'ye ken John Peel?' was written, is buried in Caldbeck churchyard. But he was not killed riding like a knight of the hunting field. Lakeland fashion, he followed the hounds on foot – a sort of mountain beagler. He lived to 77, to sing the song of his own 'death' himself! But at 20 he *did* elope to Gretna Green to marry and he did give the girl thirteen children.

A66 Appleby, Brough (20 m)	At Appleby, White Hart (tel 51598): 17th-century inn run by ex-mechanical engineer and wife. Useful overnight stop. Dinner around £5; BB £8.50; bedrooms closed Jan–March. Gale House (tel Appleby 51380): working dairy farm; Mrs Wood takes guests Easter–end Sept. BB £5.50; DBB £8.	Appleby: the saying 'before you can say Jack Robinson' was born in Appleby's attractive main street, Boroughgate; Jack, secretary to the Treasury and intolerant of delay, built his White House here before you ... well, very quickly! Gipsy Horse Fair draws gipsies from whole North each June. Brown trout fishing in river Eden. 11th-century Brough Castle was home of Baron Clifford, called the Butcher for his cruelty in Wars of the Roses; now ruined.
A685 Kirkby Stephen, B6259 over Mallerstand Common just before Garsdale Head, left on A684 Hawes (17 m)	At Kirkby Stephen, King's Arms (tel 71378): 17th-century inn; good English food – salmon, Wensley chicken, baked ham, roasts, steak. Upstairs, Adam doors and ceiling. Meal £7.25; BB £12–16. Lunchtime snacks. At Hawes, White Hart, Main St (tel 259): special meat pie, local trout, lamb steak. 3-course meals £2.50–5.75; BB £8.60.	Kirkby Stephen: centre for walks, views southward across Pennines. Mallerstang Common, lonely, lovely stretch; valley below Wild Boar Fell (2324 ft). Hawes: little town hidden among slopes; views N on road to Hardraw Force (1 m), waterfall cascading direct over 100 ft ledge; sheep market sells 100,000 sheep a year. Town makes Wensleydale cheese – 3 tons a day from 7000 gallons of milk.
B6255 by Widdale Fell B6479 Settle (22 m) A65 Hellfield A682 Gisburn Colne (22 m) A6068 Burnley A56 Rawtenstall, Manchester (26 m)		Joins Route 5. Colne – see Route 5.

Route 7

North Yorkshire – Teesdale – Hadrian's Wall – Scottish Border – into Scotland and return

Richmond
small road NW
Kirby Hill,
Ravensworth; on
to A66, left to
Greta Bridge,
small road to
Egglestone
Abbey,
Startforth,
Barnard Castle
(19 m)

Richmond – see Route 5.

At Greta Bridge, Morritt Arms (tel Teesdale 27232): Charles Dickens stayed here. In lovely setting. Dorchester-trained chef specializes in game; lunch £4.50; dinner FP £7.50; FP £9.50. BB £12.75–18.50. SB.

At Barnard Castle, King's Head, Market Square (tel Teesdale 38356): parts built 1300, rest 1700; newly renovated; baths to all bedrooms. Family-owned and run. English cooking. Meals FP £6.50; BB £12.50–17; SB winter.

Blagraves House Restaurant, The Bank (tel Teesdale 37668): delightful; medieval hall once owned by Richard III; restored by local farmer and wife who run it as restaurant/antique shop. Not cheap but good imaginative cooking, includes Elizabethan dishes. Dinner FP £9.90; 62 wines. Shut Sun, Mon.

Montalbo Hotel (tel Teesdale 37342): good fish dishes. Lunch FP £4.25; dinner card £6–7; BB £7.50–9.

Red Well Inn, Hariture Rd (tel Teesdale 38023): long list; bar meals £4–5; longer choice in restaurant; 7 steak dishes; meal card £9; house wine £3.65/litre.

Teesdale, an area of rugged beauty, deserves to be better known, though parts are strictly for very fit walkers and climbers.

Barnard Castle named after castle on rock above river Tees; rebuilt in 1112 by Bernard Balliol, ancestor of founder of Oxford's Balliol College; owned by 15th-century Richard Neville, Earl of Warwick, called 'the Kingmaker'. Cobbled marketplace, wide streets falling steeply to river. Bowes Museum one of Britain's best – something for most people. Built like French château in 1869, nice grounds; fine art collection, including Goya, Tiepolo, El Greco (*Tears of St Peter*). Pottery, porcelain, jewellery, watches, snuff boxes and period settings showing furniture, (lovely French 18th-century) dolls, dolls houses, toys including musical silver swan which picks up fish (18th-century).

B6277 Cotherstone, Middleton in Teesdale (10 m)	At Middleton, West Park, Lunedale on B6276 (tel Middleton 380): old farmhouse in peaceful spot overlooking Grassholme Reservoir; building once a packhorse inn; now beef-breeding farm. Mar–Oct for riding. Good fishing; super bar made from old butter cellar. Riding, for adults. 4-course meal £5.50; BB £6.50; DBB £12 (phone ahead); Nicolas and other wines. Teesdale Hotel (tel Middleton 264): old coaching inn; lunch bar meals £2–4; dinner FP £6.90; card £9; wines reasonable; SB 1 Nov–30 Apr.	Middleton in Teesdale: beautiful situation with lovely walking country around, but it can be unkind; hence Fell Rescue Association HQ here. 4 m on B6277 is High Force Waterfall, highest in England; double fall of water boiling down sheer drop 70 ft; ferns and flowers grow in cracks of gorge. Cast-iron drinking fountain in Middleton Square commemorates lead mines; formerly run by Quakers. Romaldkirk, just left before Middleton: an attractive village, round green with stocks and pump.
B6277 past High Force to Alston (21 m)	Lowbyer Manor Hotel, Hexham Rd (tel Alston 81230): pretty 17th-century manor house; white stone; quiet, comfortable with nice bedrooms (8 out of 12 with bath); enthusiastic new owners. Meal FP £8.50; BB £12.25–16.50. Open 1 May–31 Oct.	Rugged Moors: road all right but check conditions in winter. Alston has special attraction for me; cosy in winter, pleasant in summer; surrounded by highest fells of Pennine chain; three major rivers rise in them – Tees, Wear, South Tyne; rockpools waterfalls, wooded cliffs, meadows; alpine flowers. Alston is highest market town in England.

B686
Bearsbridge,
Haydon Bridge,
Fourstone,
Chesters
(Hadrian's Wall)
(23 m)

At Allendale, pleasant old town 4 m E Bearsbridge, Ashleigh Hotel (tel 351): pleasant hotel, good value restaurant; in five acres secluded gardens; peacocks; meals around £5; try Northumbrian leek pudding; BB £9.50–10.50.

Dale Hotel (tel 212): run by same family for 60 years; Elizabethan (1st), once called Tinkler House, faces market place, garden views; not licensed these days. Lunch £2.30; dinner £4. BB £7; DBB £9.20.

At Haydon Bridge, Anchor (tel Haydon Bridge 227): meals £5–5.65; wines from £3 (Calvet); BB £8.50–9.50.

Haydon Bridge: old church on hillside where medieval village stood; stones from nearby Roman camp used to build nave; Roman altar used as baptismal font.

1800 years ago the Romans built Hadrian's Wall – a 73-mile chain of lookout towers, forts and barracks, to defend the frontier of their empire. Most came from Andalucia, Spain, Costa del Sol!

Remains of Chesters fort give clear idea of a base for 500 cavalry – barrack blocks, stables, troops bath-house, commander's quarters with hypocaust central heating (charcoal-heated air blown through stone ducts). Museum with many interesting items such as soldier's 'discharge papers' on bronze tablet, coins with Emperor Hadrian's head and Britannia on the back, leather sandals amazingly preserved of a design like those we still wear on beaches; the Romans abandoned the Wall in AD 383.

B6320 Wark, Bellingham, small road across Kielder Forest signposted to Kielder (36 m)

National Park – Wark Forest, Kielder Forest, Redesdale and Wauchope Forests across Scottish Border.

Simonburn, 2 m S, village where St Mungo, Glasgow's patron saint, baptised people in the well in 6th century.

Bellingham: small market town called Bellingjam locally. 12th century church of St Cuthbert has stone roof to frustrate firebrand marauders (called 'reivers') from across Scottish border. Hareshaw Burn has 30-ft waterfall.

Kielder Forest – a magnificent great forest of Canadian Sika spruce, Norway spruce (Christmas trees), Scottish pine and others, with flowing rivers, pools, lakes; produces 110,000 tons of timber a year, growing at the rate of 1000 tons a day. Magnificent recreation ground. All planted by Forestry Commission since 1926 on grouse moor and poor upland sheep pastures. Half original trees grown from seed collected from Prince Charlotte Isles of British Columbia. Deer, wild goats, otters, birds. Walking, riding, fishing, canoeing.

cross Scottish Border at Deadwater, small roads to Sautree, turn right along B6357 through Waychope Forest to Bonchester Bridge, left to Hawick (26 m)

At Hawick, Kirklands Hotel, West Stewart Place (tel 2263): ornate Victoriana with garden and good outlook. Helpful owners; bedrooms vary in size. Nice dining room. owner-chef; 4-course dinner FP £7.50; card £7–8. BB £12.50–15.50.

Hawick (pronounced 'Hoyk'): with sheep market; famous for woollens. 250,000 sheep a year sold here. History of border fighting, Battle of Flodden, most Hawick men killed. English raiders held off by local youths on horseback – Horse Monument in High St, and ceremonial ride round boundaries in June.

A698 Denholm,
B6358 Jedburgh

At Jedburgh, Carters' Rest, Abbey Place (tel 3414): local 'penny' grammar school where pupils paid penny a week; then inn used by carters at horse market. Hay loft and stables now dining room and bar. Three chef's special dishes daily; châteaubriant steak. Lunch FP 2-course £3.50; 3-course £4; Scottish high tea (hot main course) £3.25–4.25; dinner, card around £8; bar supper (hot dish and salad) £2.20–4.

Jedburgh Country House Hotel (tel Camptown 274): Norman Dalgetty puts hotel stables to good use – trains National Hunt horses; winners at Kelso, Hexham, Market Rasen. Roasts, steak and curries in dining room. Lunch FP £4.35; dinner from £5; bar meals from £1.65. Wines from £3.50. BB £9.50–16; DBB £14.50.

Denholm: village on river Teviot, round green, has thatched cottage where John Leyden, poet friend of Walter Scott, was born. Jedburgh lies in lovely valley of Jed Water; good touring centre. Attractive, many old houses. Centre for centuries of some of the toughest fighting between Scots and English overlords who raided each other's lands for loot, cattle, women, and destroyed what they could not take away. When Scots clans were not fighting English, they fought each other. English took the castle so often that Scots destroyed it as being more use to the enemy. Now a prison on the site, with a prison museum. Jedburgh Abbey, founded by King David I (12th century), still beautiful in ruin. Stone house where Mary Queen of Scots stayed is now a museum; she lay ill after a tough ride to see Bothwell, lying wounded in Hermitage Castle. The things even queens will do for love. . . .

A68 S over Border to Otterburn (35 m)	Otterburn Tower (tel Otterburn 20620): castle-like mansion, huge bedrooms, being renovated; friendly. Disco nightly. Chef ex-Reids, Madeira's historic hotel. Dinner card £7; BB £11–15. DBB £16.50–20.50.	Otterburn is part of Scots history. Here the Earl of Douglas (one of the Black Douglases) won a battle but got himself killed (1388). Ballad of the fight was 'The Battle of Chevy Chase'.
	Percy Arms (tel 20261): two bars named after Chevy Chase battle rivals Hotspur and Douglas. Log fires; lunch FP £3.50, £4, £5. 4-course dinner £7.50. BB £12–16.	
B6320 through Old Town, right on A68 Ridsdale, Great Swinburne right on A6079 Hexham (22 m)	At Hexham, Country Kitchen, Market Place: useful quick lunch spot; home cooking, vegetables grown by owner; wine; lunch £2–3.	Hexham: attractive old town on river Tyne; Tuesday market for sheep and cattle 1300 years old; held beside Hexham Abbey; Anglo Saxon crypt remains from first church built by St Wilfrid in year 674; present abbey 12th century. 15th-century hall used as council chamber till 1838.

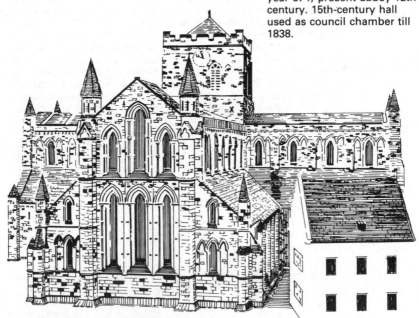

A69 Corbridge (3 m)	Ramblers of Corbridge, 18 Front St (tel 2424): owner-chef Heinrich Hermann is German. Outstanding starters; try smoked chicken, kidney-mushroom vol-au-vent; cold apple soup with cream and wine. House wines £3.50 – 2 German, 2 French. Meal card around £8.50. The Hayes, Newcastle Rd (tel 2010): nice rooms but limited, so phone ahead. 7½ acres with lovely views. Wonderful value; English dishes like roast beef, mixed grill – changes daily. BB £5.50; with 4-course dinner £8. Children's reductions. Not licensed.	Corstopitum was Roman supply base for Hadrian's Wall. Remains of fort still on outskirts of Corbridge; interesting relics in museum; attractive resort; quiet now; for long a historical storm centre. King Ethelred murdered here in AD 796. Battles raged until 1349 when a more ruthless conqueror, the Black Death, almost wiped out the population. Now a town of pleasant houses and gardens.
B6037, B6306 Blanchland (8 m)	Lord Crewe Arms, Blanchland (tel 251): next to church, part of old abbey; truly historic; priesthole where Catholic Jacobites were hidden during rebellion; bar, once abbey crypt, to bury your troubles; resident lady ghost; Italian owner well-known nationally in hotels; English chef cooks classic English dishes with local ingredients (salmon, lamb, game); excellent value. 4-course dinner £6.95; good wine list; BB £16–18. SB weekends.	Route crosses on to Tourist Map of North Pennines and Lakes. Area I have only just discovered; little known. Across Blanchland Moor to stone village on river Derwent by Derwent Reservoir (known to sailing and trout fishing enthusiasts). Steel town of Consett, sadly depressed at present, at other end of reservoir. Name Blanchland comes from White (Blanc) monks who built abbey in 12th century; village was town-planned (1800), one of our least spoiled villages; you must park and walk a few yards to old church, gatehouse and monastic prior's house now converted into fine inn (Crewe Arms, see opposite); Pow Hill Country Park by reservoir for picnics.

small road S to
join B6278
Stanhope (11 m)
A689
Wolsingham,
small road right
Bedburn, forest
drive (toll)
through
Hamsterley
Forest to
Woodland to
Cockfield
right on A688
Staindrop (17 m)

Stanhope: moorland market town; 250-million-year-old fossilized tree stump in churchyard. In 1843 Iron Age implements were found, including parts of wheel and harness, showing horse-drawn transport was used in England more than 3500 years ago (now in British Museum).

Stanhope Castle (1798 fake medieval) now a school; fortified manor house Stanhope Hall, superb mixture medieval, Elizabethan, Jacobean styles (not open). Stanhope is holiday walking centre.

Hamsterley Forest: 7000 acres laid out by Forestry Commission; motor routes, car parks, picnic and camp sites. Roe, fallow and red deer; slopes, valleys, streams.

Staindrop: 18th-century stone houses round village green; Raby Castle nearby mainly 14th-century fortress; nine towers surrounding courtyard; Baron's Hall, 136 ft long with minstrels' gallery, could hold 700 knights. Neville family lost it after plotting to put Mary Queen of Scots on English throne in place of Elizabeth I. Dutch, Spanish, English paintings, including Reynolds and Lely. Open Easter-end Sept; Wed, Sun till July, then daily except Sat.

B6274 Winston,
Forcett,
Richmond (16 m)

Joins Route 5 here.

Route 8

**Scotland – South West – Burns Country –
Loch Lomond – Carlisle – Dumfries – Galloway – Ayr –
Loch Lomond – Stirling**

Carlisle A7, A74
Gretna Green
A75 Annan
(19 m)

Gretna Green: perhaps the young need to be told that in Olden Times (until 1940) runaway lovers could be married in 18th-century Gretna Hall and smithy, though Daddy disapproved. A loophole in Scottish law allowed it. Now the law has changed and Daddy isn't consulted anyway. But tourists still make nostalgic, romantic visits to the smithy. Scots and English tried to make a truce here in 1398 – obviously without success.

B724, B725
Dumfries (16 m)

County Hotel (tel Dumfries 5401): historic – and good. Started 150 years ago by Jane Williamson with £700 given her by American government; she was niece of local man, John Paul Jones, father of American Navy, scourge of Royal Navy. Prince Charlie's Room (Charles Edward Stuart commandeered hotel as HQ in 1745 and heard of approach of Duke of Cumberland's forces here – see opposite column). MacLachlan family have run hotel since 1914. Inventive chef. Choice of meals: quick lunch £1.35–2.50; grill room meal £5–7; 3-course supper £3.15–3.95; 4-course dinner £6.50. BB £11.50–21; DBB from £16.50. SB good.

The story of Robert Burns, Scotland's very human and wayward national poet, starts here for us. In 1791 Burns came to live here, as exciseman, wrote 'Auld Lang Syne' and 'Ye Banks and Braes o' Bonnie Doone'; he died in Mill Vennel (now Burns St) in 1793; his wife Jean Armour lived in the house until her death (1834); now a museum; they are buried with several children in St Michael's churchyard and his pew in the church is marked with a plaque. He was more often in his 'favourite howff' – Globe Inn, opposite County Hotel, the place to drink his health. Good memorial statue to Burns.

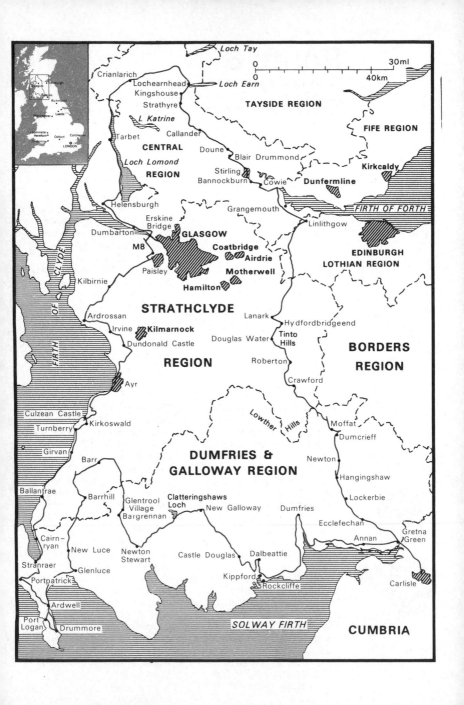

Robert Bruce gets only a plaque in Castle St for murdering in 1306 'Red Comyn', English King's envoy, thus launching his fight for Scottish independence, ending in his Bannockburn victory. Old Bridge (now pedestrian) reminds us of its builder Devorguilla Balliol, who founded Balliol College, Oxford. When he left County Hotel (see hotel column), Pretender Charles Edward Stuart demanded £2000 and 1000 pairs of shoes for his army. People of Dumfries could not raise them so he took a local dignitary hostage until Dumfries paid the difference. Dumfries, like other parts of Scotland, did not find Prince Charlie so Bonnie.

A710 close to Rockcliffe and Kippford to Dalbeattie (26 m)

At Kippford, Anchor (tel 205): old fishermen's inn, quayside position with backcloth of wooded hills; loved by yachtsmen, so book for beds. Nice meals; good choice of bar meals; dinner (fair choice, good value) £5; BB £9. Bar meals and BB only Oct–Easter.

The Granary, Barend, Sandyhills, Dalbeattie (tel 663): restaurant in old farm buildings, attached to new development of self-catering log houses. Imaginative cooking; dinner FP £6.50. ½ m inland, riding stables, pony trekking, tuition. Shut Nov–Xmas except Sat; early Jan–Easter.

Inlets here used by smugglers for centuries. Rockcliffe has narrow sand beach; Kippford, in tidal estuary, is tiny fishing village used mostly by yachtsmen. Very attractive when tide is in; islet joined to village by mysterious stone causeway hidden at high tide; believed to be a prehistoric path. Used by smugglers. Burns was one of the excisemen trying unsuccessfully to combat smuggling. Spanish Armada was due to make a landing here in 1588 – with help of the Maxwells from Lochmaben Castle, N of Dumfries. Scots Catholics were to join in marching on England. Dalbeattie's grey stone is used all over the world, including Thames Embankment.

A711 Palnackie small road right, then left on to B727 right on B736 Castle Douglas

At Auchencairn, 4 m Palnackie, Balcary Bay Hotel (tel 055664 217): super setting on edge of Balcary Bay; one of nicest hotels I know in Scotland. Built 1625, used as smuggling base; goods stored in underground passages reached through back of fireplace. Looks across to Heston Isle, once smugglers' lair, now providing lobsters for hotel table. Italian manager, Scottish chef. Lunch from £4 and card; dinner FP £8 and card. Superb choice, excellent cooking. Try Mary Queen of Scots' favourite soup Feather Fowlie (chicken with bacon, herbs, cream); salmon poached in wine with strips of smoked salmon in cream (salmon Balcary) or Italian saltimbocca ('jumped in the mouth'), slices of veal, ham, mozzarella cheese cooked in marsala wine. Wines from £4.95 litre. BB £17–20. DBB £24–27.

At Castle Douglas, Douglas Arms (tel 2231): 200-year-old coaching inn; bars lively with locals. Satisfying meals, bar lunches. Meals FP £6.85; BB £14–16.50.

All over Scotland are little guest houses with friendly welcome, also families who take a few guests in spare rooms. Find out about these from local information centres. This is typical:

Rose Cottage Guest House, Gelston, Castle Douglas (3 m) (tel 2513): good plain home cooking and baking; rooms with hot and cold running water. BB £6, DBB £8.50

Castle Douglas: market town, convenient touring centre; on Loch Carlingwark you can sail, row or canoe but not use power.

2 m west is Threave Castle on a river Dee islet, now a ruin but once all-powerful; built in 14th century by Archibald the Grim, Earl of Douglas, it was home of Black Douglases who terrorized area, raided constantly into England and had long feud with English Northumbrian Percy family (Hotspur); over doorway of Threave a gallows knob for hanging anyone who upset them, and they boasted it 'never wanted for its tassel'. James II took the castle in 1455 with a cannon Mons Meg, now in Edinburgh Castle. Threave House, baronial style mansion, has gardens open to the public (Scottish National Trust) showing the truly mild climate of this sheltered coast washed by Gulf Stream; gardens especially lovely in April, May (gardens open daily). House is School of Practical Gardening; graduates hold top gardening posts all over world.

Wildfowl refuge nearby on river Dee, roosting and feeding place for wild geese and ducks (open Nov-March).

To me, with its mild climate, coves, inlets and little fishing villages, this coast to Mull of Galloway is like Cornwall with fewer people. Many retire here.

| A713 New Galloway (13 m) | Milton Park Hotel, Dalry (2 m N New Galloway) (tel Dalry 286): inviting hotel overlooking Ken Valley; meals served on fine china. Odd looking (1920–30s styles, including towers and mock Tudor), but nice gardens. Fine fishing in well-stocked lochs; bar lunch; 4-course dinner £8. BB £11. Breakfast choice includes fried haggis and black pudding. | Road alongside long, narrow Loch Ken, superb for watersports – fishing, sailing, canoeing; water skiing at Loch Ken Watersports (tel Parton 220) restricted to one stretch for sake of fishermen. |

| A712 past Clatteringshaws Loch right on to A75 Newton Stewart (20 m) | At Newton Stewart, Bruce Hotel, 88 Queen St (tel 2294): modern, almost luxurious, small; social centre of town. Good chef. Try smoked haddock in cream, cheese, and breadcrumbs as starter; steak with brandy cream sauce and asparagus. Dinner £8. BB (good bedrooms) £13–16.50. | Clatteringshaws Dam has turned Black Waters of Dee into reservoir loch; on left is Raiders' Road, open for driving in summer, 25mph limit necessary for sake of you and your car; in winter international rally drivers do 70mph, and many run out of road. Road used by old-time cattle rustlers; few miles on, right side, you may see wild goats; if you want a picture, bring sweet buns as bait. Part of Galloway Forest Park (240 sq m). |

Kiroughtree Hotel (tel 2141): I like it. 1719 country house converted; I have known it some time. Newish owners have 'upgraded', so higher prices for more elaborate meals. Good cooking. Delightful bedrooms. Exclusive club atmosphere. Meals 3 FP £9, £11, £13; also card. Superb wine list from £4.20 to Latour '65 £17.60, Clos des Mouches Beaune '73 £14.60. SB.

Creebridge House (tel 2121): charming old building, creeper clad; family owners trained at Scottish Hotel School; exceptional value; lunch £3.50; dinner £6; try smoked roast pork; BB £10.30–12.60.

Crown (tel 2727): old inn where you meet real Scottish characters. Dinner £5.50; also card; BB £11.50–13.50.

A714
Bargrennan,
small road right
to Glentrool
village (lane to
Loch Trool,
signposted)

House o'Hill, Bargrennan (tel
243): real old Scots country
inn, loved by fishermen
(including me). 3½ m of own
salmon and trout fishing on
river Cree (£4 a day, max 3
rods). Stay here and you get
to know foresters, farmers,
possibly poachers if there are
any (as an outsider, I
wouldn't know, would I?).
Anyway you'll probably get
poached salmon for dinner –
or grilled salmon, trout fresh
from river or loch, or local
Galloway beef. True Scottish
fashion, high tea is served as
well as dinner – a cooked
main course. High tea £2.40–
4; dinner card £5–6.50; wines
£2.80–4.20; BB £7 (book
ahead, few bedrooms;
shooting lodge available
also, beds for nine).

Land of huge fir forests,
steep hills, lochs, and rivers
rich in trout and salmon.
Bare mountain until Forestry
Commission replanted;
seven forests covering
130,000 acres. Chief forester
encourages public to use
forest, if they avoid damage
and fires. Car park beside
Bruce's Stone – memorial to
Robert Bruce, whose men
ambushed English soldiers
on opposite hillside and
rolled stones on to them
(1307). Marked hill-walks
start here; foresters ask you
to leave name, time, path
you mean to take and
expected return time for
rescuing parties in case of
mishap. Rich in wildlife – fox,
otter, deer, red squirrel, wild
goat, rarer birds. Lovely view
down to loch, rising to green
and mauve hills opposite.

---

from Glentrool
village, N
through forest to
North Ballach
left on small
road to Barr; left
on B734 to
T-junction of
A714, left again
to Barrhill (27 m)

This is a wanderer's route
through wild and lovely
country of forest and rivers;
steep twisty roads but well
surfaced; check road
conditions in winter (A714
leads Bargrennan–Barrhill,
but misses wonderful
scenery).

Barr: charming village on
Upper Stinchar river; angling
resort.

---

small road
New Luce,
Glenluce (18 m)

Barrhill, village in Duisk
valley between high moors –
narrow roads to New Luce
across hilly moorland beside
waters of Luce; fine views.

A715 Drunmore (19 m)		Glenluce: Lochinch Castle gardens between two lochs, inspired by Versailles. Open April–end Oct (except Sat).

B7065 Port Logan, minor road (a drive) past Logan Gardens to A716 Ardwell, left to Portpatrick (19 m)

Portpatrick, Fernhill (tel 220): small family-run hotel (two former teachers); attractive décor; spacious grounds; views over harbour. Home cooking, local ingredients; 4-course dinner £6.50; wines; BB £11.50–14.50. SB. Shut Nov–Mar. Golf nearby at special rates.

Knockinaam Lodge (tel 471): old dower house in lovely wooded glen with lawns to sandy cove. 30-acre grounds, sheltered; Churchill and Gen Eisenhower met here in war. Superb meals, so not cheap; FP £9.50; card around £10. Wines hand-picked by owner Simon Pilkington, a great expert, bottled in country of origin, shipped direct. BB £16–22. Shut Nov–Mar.

Logan Botanic Gardens: subtropical plants prove again mild climate of what has been called the 'Land's End of Scotland'. Open daily 1 Apr–end Sept. Logan Fish Pond: tidal pool in rocks, 30 ft deep, 53 ft round, made 1800 to supply fish to Logan House. Holds about thirty fish so tame they can be fed by hand. Good sands at low tide.

Ardwell House: fine gardens (daffodils and azaleas especially) autumn tints. Open March–end Oct, Mon–Fri.

Portpatrick: 19th-century ferry port; lost out to Stranraer. Now a fishing port and holiday spot.

A77 Stranraer (9 m)

Bay House Restaurant, Cairnryan Rd (tel Stranraer 3786): the Murdochs have been fishermen for generations; Stewart Murdoch serves fish caught by his own boat. Try local oysters cooked in cream and cheese, lobsters, crabs, scallops in sharp Armoricaine sauce, Luce Bay salmon, Galloway beef, whisky pâté. Meal card £5.50–7. Wines from £3.65/litre.

George Hotel (tel 2487): well modernized; bar lunch £2; dinner FP £6; 4 courses £7.25; card £8.50. BB £12.50–14.50.

At head of Loch Ryan, which forms natural harbour, Stranraer is commercial port for Irish cargoes and car ferry to Larne, Northern Ireland. Fishing, sailing. North West Castle, now hotel, built in shape of a ship, by Arctic explorer Sir John Ross (1777–1856).

| A77 Cairnryan, Ballantrae, Girvan (30 m) | Girvan – many hotels of all sizes, including pleasant family-run hotels such as: | Cairnryan: village with harbour built in Second World War; road passes through lovely wooded Glen App. |

Hotel Westcliffe, Louisa Drive (tel 2128): most rooms have bath or shower; centrally heated, laundry room, suntan bed, bar; BB £6.50–8.50; dinner £3.

King's Arms and Coachlamp Restaurant, Dalrymple St (tel 3322): privately owned, comfortable; dinner FP £6.25; card £6.50–8. Wine from £3.80; BB £12–16.

Cairnryan: village with harbour built in Second World War; road passes through lovely wooded Glen App.

Ballantrae: rock shingle, some sand by muddy river estuary; isle of Ailsa Craig out to sea; its granite used to make stones for Scottish ice sport of curling. Dramatic coastal drive to Girvan along Kennedy's Pass.

Girvan: small resort with sands, harbour, entertainment. Grant's distillery, one of the most modern, makes blended and single-malt whisky, open Mon–Fri for visits.

A77 Turnberry, Kirkoswald, small road across to A719 to Culzean Castle (11 m)

Turnberry Hotel (tel 202): perfect hotel for rich golf fanatics; 360 acres on Ayr coast; tennis, horse riding, fishing, private beach, indoor pool, gymnasium, sauna, solarium, real luxury; immaculate service, very good cooking, and two championship golf courses, Arran and the tough Ailsa, where British Open was held

Footsteps of Robert Burns. Kirkoswald churchyard is where originals of Burns's poem 'Tam o'Shanter' lived. Tam was a farmer (Douglas Graham), Shanter his farm, Johnnie Davidson (Soutar or Cobbler Johnnie) lived in thatched cottage, now with life-size stone figures from the poem in the garden (open to public).

in '77. Famous 9th hole across rocky creek with waves below; don't use championship tee unless you have plenty of balls with you. FP lunch £4.50 or £7; FP dinner £11; card around £15. BB £29–35. Landing pad for helicopters on front lawn – if you have one!

Culzean Castle: a magnificent sham; clifftop mansion built for one of the Kennedy family, Earl of Cassilis, in 1780 by Robert Adam; truly beautiful interior, with lovely staircase; top floor flat given to General Eisenhower. Contains mementoes. Country park with swan lake round the house; 18th-century walled garden, aviary, camelia house. Guided nature trail walks Mar–Oct (¾–1½ hrs).

A719 Ayr (12 m)

County Hotel, Wellington Square (tel Ayr 63368): good value meals; lunch FP reasonable choice £3.50; high tea £2.25–4.30 (steak); dinner £4.70; wine from £3.45. BB £10.75–14. SB.

Kylestrome Hotel, 11 Miller Rd (tel 262474): extended Victorian house; comfortable; known for good fish dishes. Lunch around £4; dinner £8. BB £14.50–17.50.

Usual resort hotels and accommodation in Ayr. Information: 30 Miller Road.

Savoy Park Hotel, Racecourse Road (tel Ayr 66112): run by one of Scotland's most respected hotelkeepers. Good soups and sauces. Dinner £8; house wine £3.50. BB £13–16.50.

Ayr: West Scotland's major seaside resort. Tam o'Shanter Inn in High St, with sign showing Tam mounting his grey mare Meg, no longer serves a dram; it's a Burns museum. I wonder if Burns would have approved.

River Ayr still spanned by Burns' 'Auld Brig' (Old Bridge): Burns was born at Alloway, on edge of Ayr, in 1759 in a simple thatched cottage, now a museum. A Burns monument, built 1832, overlooks the bridge over river Doon (Brig o' Doon) which Tam crossed on his mare when fleeing from Auld Nick the Devil. Tam had seen him in the churchyard of the Auld Kirk of Alloway (now a ruin). Emboldened by whisky, Tam had dared to make a pass at the sexy witch Cutty Sark, and Auld Nick objected.

Burns wrote of Ayr: 'Wham ne'er a toon surpasses. For honest men and bonnie lasses.' Ayr has two championship golf courses, owned by town. Four more at Prestwick (3 m N) and five at Troon (6 m N) – British Open Championship 1982.

A719, A77
towards
Kilmarnock left
on B730
Dundonald
Castle on to A71,
left to Irvine
(17 m)

Dundonald Castle: high on
isolated hill. built by first
Stuart King, Robert II, who
died there 1390.

Irvine: main port of Glasgow
until Clyde was deepened in
18th century. Explosives first
made on dunes northward in
1873 by Alfred Nobel,
Swedish chemist who
invented dynamite and
founded Nobel Prizes,
including the *Peace* Prize!

A70 Ardrossan
B780 Kilbernie,
A760, 737 to
edge of Paisley
left on A761,
very soon right
on A740
join M8
motorway
(Junction 10)
towards
Greenock right
on M898
(Junction 11) to
cross Clyde at
Irvine Bridge
(29 m) on
leaving bridge,
left on A814
through
Dumbarton to
Helensburgh
(8 m)

Ardrossan: port for Isle of
Arran, Isle of Man, Belfast
ferries; South Bay is resort
with long sandy beach (safe
bathing), running into
Saltcoats, where Customs
House Museum has relics of
Betsy Miller, first woman in
Britain to be a ship's captain.
She died in 1864. Horse
Island is bird sanctuary.

In 11th century, Dumbarton
was capital of independent
kingdom of Strathclyde.
Helensburgh, popular resort
on Gare Loch; sailing,
fishing, golf, centre for
exploring mountains and
valleys of Dunbartonshire.
Lovely scenery; alas few
roads. John Logie Baird,
television inventor, born
here.

B832, A82
alongside Loch
Lomond to
Tarbet (16 m)

Tarbet: views across Loch
Lomond to peak of 3192 ft
Ben Lomond. West beyond
Loch Long is 2891 ft peak of
Ben Arthur (known as The
Cobbler). When laying waste
the country in 1263, King
Haakon of Norway
'persuaded' the crews of his
ships to haul them from Loch
Lomond across land to Loch
Long.

Loch Lomond is lovely when mist clears, not only for its backcloth of mountains but its thirty isles. Isle of Inchmurren, largest, 1½ m long, believed to have been monastic retreat of St Mirren from marauders. Largest Scottish loch, 23 m long, ½ to 5 m wide, and deepest point 630 ft. Fishing for trout, pike and powan (white fish found in Scotland and Wales).

A82 Crianlarich (16 m)

In superb mountain scenery, centre for climbing and walking.

A85 Lochearnhead

Wooded Loch Earn is lovely and this is a great spot to enjoy it; walking, sailing, water-skiing. In the distance the lofty peaks of Ben Vorlich (3224 ft) and Stuc o'Chroin. Flame nasturtium (red tropacolum) grows wild on hillsides.

A84 Kingshouse Strathyre, Callander (14 m)

At Balquhidder, Ledcreich Hotel (tel Strathyre 230): excellent cooking with some unusual dishes by Duncan Hilditch, true master chef, well-known judge of cooking contests. David Hilditch an expert wine buyer. Their combined expertise shows at table. That's another thing about Scotland – you never know when you will run into the master touch. Try Stilton and green pepper soup; pork cutlets in mushrooms, cream, lemon and herbs; especially Scottish duck, with raspberries, Drambuie and haggis – how Scottish can you get? Wines from French 'gamin' £3.80 to Meursault '76 £9.20. Dinner FP £9;75. BB £13.50. DBB £21.50.

2 m to right at Kingshouse, prettily situated at end of Loch Voil, Balquhidder: charming place with terrorist past. Here the freebooting MacGregors, led by Rob Roy – brigand, cattle thief and protection racketeer – having cut off the head of the King's Forester John Drummond, swore over it that they would never grass on the clan members who had murdered him. Sir Walter Scott wrote a novel about Rob Roy. Other locals were Clan Laurin (McLarens to you), outlawed for killing one of their own members who was vicar of Balquhidder, and got into various other murderous situations. Rob Roy MacGregor's son was

At Strathyre, The Inn (tel Strathyre 224): value; all bedrooms with bath; bar meals £2.50, meals card £3–7. BB £8.50 Rob Roy fought here.

At Callander, Dalgair House, 113 Main St (tel 30283): Brown family reconstructed this house with their own hands; comfortable, friendly; 'good honest food' but rather unenterprising; card, mostly grills; many of my readers satisfied and appreciative. 'Regular' menu about £3.50; card £5–9. BB £7.50–9.

Arden Guest House, Bracklinn Rd: 'Arden House' in TV series *Dr Finlay's Casebook*. BB around £6. DBB £9.

hanged for killing a McLaren in a land dispute. Nice people, those old clan chiefs. Now Balquhidder is a superb hideaway for travellers and even the English are not murdered.

Strathyre, in hills beside a new forest: attractive village in summer for walkers, fishermen.

Callander: now known as 'Tannochbrae' of TV's *Dr Finlay's Casebook*; most attractive town in lovely setting. Touring centre for The Trossachs – land between Highlands and Lowlands with tree-covered hills, sharp crags, steep streams, moors and glens.

A81, B8032
Doune A84,
small road left to
Blair Drummond,
back on to A84
to Stirling
(Bridge of Allan)
(16 m)

At Doune, Woodside Hotel (tel Doune 237): long stone house with bright interior; Angus beef, including entrecote Glencoe (*not* massacred, says chef Bill Morrison); sea trout, venison, lobster in season. Bar lunches, including steak £2.50–5; dinner around £8. BB £11–16. SB (2 nights or more).

At Stirling, Heritage, 16 Allan Park (tel 3660): very pleasant period furnished; French chef-owner Georges Marquetty, winner Escoffier medal in USA; cooks brilliantly without offending the peculiar palates of the British. Lunch £5; dinner £10. French house wine £2.90; 100 wines. BB £12–17.73.

Doune: in Doune Park, gardens laid out by 18th-century Earl of Moray, is a motor museum with some gems, like 1923 Citroën 5 and an alluring 1938 Alfa Romeo built for Le Mans 24-hour Race. Old Bentleys too. Open 1 Apr–31 Oct.

Doune Castle, highly publicized by Walter Scott in Waverley novels. Its 14th-century builder, Duke of Albany, Regent of Scotland, almost inevitably got himself beheaded. Earls of Moray took it over. 'Bonnie Earl of Moray' of the song lived here. Illegitimate son of James V of Scotland, half brother to Mary Queen of Scots, he became her friend and adviser, turned against her, led an army against her. He, too, was murdered. Open 1 Apr–31 Oct.

At Bridge of Allan, Royal Henderson St (tel 2284): solid Victorian hotel where Dickens stayed. Comfortable and professional. Buffets; also dinner FP 4 courses £7.50; card £11. BB £17–20. SB (3 days).

Blair Drummond: lions, elephants, baboons, giraffes and others in safari park of Blair Drummond House; performing dolphins; boat trip to Chimpanzee Island. Previously famous for land reclamation scheme; after 100 years had removed 12 ft thickness of peat, by washing it away into river Forth.

Stirling: pleasant historic city made pleasanter now missed by main traffic on M9. Imposing castle on 250 ft rock overlooking battlefield of Bannockburn (1314) where Robert Bruce defeated much bigger force of England under Edward II, making Scotland an independent nation; Edward had to flee to coast, escape by ship. Edward I had taken castle ten years earlier. Castle became Scottish royal residence. Present castle built 15th century; James II and V of Scotland born here; Mary Queen of Scots, crowned as infant in fine Church of Holy Rude nearby, lived in castle. General Monk took it in 1651, Charles Edward Stuart failed to take it back in 1746. Now houses regimental museum of Argyll and Sutherland Highlanders.

Abbey Craig, beyond Stirling Bridge, topped by monument to Sir William Wallace, who defeated Earl of Surrey here in 1297 to become ruler of Scotland. He lost at Falkirk next year and was executed in London.

Bridge of Allan (2 m), spa for 150 years, still has pump room and baths.

A9 Bannockburn,
B9124 Cowie to
A905 right
through edge of
Grangemouth on
to A9 Linlithgow
(15 m)

Statue of Robert Bruce,
mounted and armoured,
looks over the field of the
Scots victory so long ago.
Most of the battlefield built
over. 58 acres belong to
National Trust. Borestone, in
which Bruce's colours stood,
surrounded by rotunda
showing course of battle.

Linlithgow Palace – ruined
but still splendid, overlooking
loch; Mary Queen of Scots
born here while her father
James V lay dying in
Falkland Palace.

A706 Lanark,
New Lanark
(25 m)

Beside market town of
Lanark in 1784 was built
what was then a New
Jerusalem – social-industrial
experiment with houses and
cotton mills remarkable in
days when mills really were,
in Blake's words, dark and
satanic. David Dale built it.
his son-in-law Robert Owen
started workers' welfare
schemes and reduced the
working day sensationally to
10½ hours; gave them cost-
price shop and schools for
their children.

New Lanark overlooks Coral
Linn, spectacular 90 ft
waterfalls of river Clyde.

A373 Hydford-
bridgeend, A70,
for 1½ m, then
small road right
to Douglas
Water; cross A70
to join B7055 to
Tinto Hills small
road right to
Roberton
(14 m)

Little-known country,
charming; Roberton is
attractive hamlet with
Borthwick water near. Hill
walking, fishing, solitude.

A73, A74
Crawford fork
left on to B719
A701 Moffat
A708 for 1½ m
right on small
road Duncrieff,
Newbigging,
Newton,
rejoining A74 at
Hangingshaw to
Lockerbie (38 m)

At Moffat, Beechwood
Country House (tel 20210):
run by Manchester couple
recently retired from printing
business, deservedly
successful. Handsome stone
house. Delicious cooking –
smoked venison, local trout
with prawn stuffing, guinea
fowl, home-made sweets.
Dinner £6.90; Italian house
wines £3.25, good list. BB
£10.25–14.

Hartwell House (tel 20153):
country house; good value
meals, well cooked. Trout
Montrose (local salmon trout
with mustard and whisky
sauce) delicious. Dinner
£4.60. BB £6.90. SB (4 days);
golf holidays.

Arden House, High St (tel
20220): useful guest house;
BB £5–6; DBB £8–9.
Unlicensed.

Lockerbie House Hotel (tel
2610): built 150 years ago.
Now a health-without-tears
holiday spot and good hotel.
In 78-acres park and woods,
with deer, it has qualified
beauty therapists, saunas
and solarium, planned
programme of treatments;
also a fine hotel for people
like me, beyond hope! Meals
good value, some bedrooms
most attractive; dinner FP
£4.95; card £6–7; BB £11.50–
17.50.

Moffat: attractive town on
river Annan, sulphur spring
made it once a minor spa.
Good fishing. Centre of
sheep country, hence ram on
fountain in High Street.
Lovely hills around here with
wild and green slopes.

Lockerbie: another pleasant
town with a violent history.
One of the last clan feuds in
which the Johnstones routed
the Maxwells and cut off
their ears with a cleaver –
known since as the
'Lockerbie nick'. Delightful
area.

A74 Ecclefechan,
Gretna A74, A7
Carlisle (27 m)

At Kirtlebridge, Wyseby
House (tel 429): delightful
house in park with trout
stream haunted by
kingfishers. Large bedrooms,
good food. Lots of fresh fruit,
vegetables from garden,
home-baked bread, own free-
range eggs; bring your own
drinks. Dinner £4; BB £6.50.
Fine value.

Thomas Carlisle, historian,
critic, essayist, born in 1795
in cottage in Ecclefechan.
Now a museum. Once his
word was a power in the
land. I wonder who reads
him now? Yet we all quote
him without realizing it.

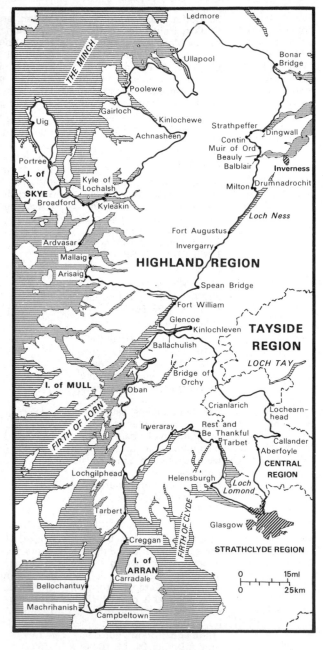

Route 9

Glasgow – Mull of Kintyre (diversion) – Loch Lomond – Oban – Isle of Skye – Dingwall – Loch Ness – Glencoe Pass – Trossachs

Glasgow A184
Helensburgh,
B832, A82 Tarbet
see Route 8.

A83 Rest and Be
Thankful,
Inveraray,
Lochgilphead
(48 m)

At Inveraray, Fernpoint Hotel (tel 2170): historic house, became hotel 1977; on headland overlooking Loch Fyne. Comfortable. Loch Fyne fish; trout from streams and farm. Bar meals; dinner FP £6; also card. BB £9.75–14.75.

Once there was a steep rough road through Glen Coe rising to 900 ft with a rough stone seat at the top marked 'Rest and Be Thankful'. Wordsworth wrote a poem about it. A new gentler road has come, the seat has gone, the old road is not used much now even for motor trials, but the name remains. Ben Ime (3318 ft) rises to NE. Ben Arthur, known as the Cobbler (not, I must say, for my sake), rises 2891 ft E.

Inveraray: seat of Clan Campbell, Dukes of Argyll, for 600 years beside waters of Loch Fyne; present castle built mid 18th century; Dr Johnson stayed here during his 1773 Highland tour. Has collection Highland weapons, paintings, French tapestries, Church has wall down centre so that services could be held simultaneously in Gaelic and English. Stevenson's *Kidnapped* written about unfair trial of James Stewart, accused of killing a Campbell.

Lochgilphead
continued

Auchindrarin: last tenant farmers left in 1963, but recreated as museum of crofters' life. Includes school, and old farm implements in barn.

Crarae Gardens: created 65 years ago by Sir George Campbell; rare plants, lovely shrubs at best May, June.

---

recommended diversion here south through Knapdale to Mull of Kintyre A83 Tarbert (12 m)

At Tarbert, Bruce Hotel (tel 577): meals excellent value; Swedish chef in Scotland some time. Uses Loch Fyne fish splendidly – herring, sea trout; try salt-cured salmon, Scotch topside in red wine; 4-course dinner with fine choice £6.95. Wines from £3.50. BB £12. Shut Dec–Feb.

West Loch Hotel (tel 283): cosy, reliable cooking, good vegetables; good hot and cold bar lunches around £3; dinner FP £8.50 (lobster in season £2 extra): house wine £3.55; fair list. BB £12–17. Shut Nov.

Road alongside Loch Fyne, to Tarbert: attractive, sheltered by hills; village port with fishing boats on isthmus between Knapdale and Kintyre. Centre of Loch Fyne herring industry; herrings caught to smoke for Fynnan Haddock. Good sands and bathing; nice centre for people who like boats. From 4 m SW, on other coast, car ferries sail to Isle of Gigha. Gigha can be seen on coast road Tarbert–Bellochantuy.

A83 Bellochantuy, Craigs, small road past airfield to Machrihanish B843 Campbeltown (44 m)

At Bellochantuy, Putechan Lodge (tel Glenbarr 266): old hunting lodge of Dukes of Argyll; antique furnishings; central heating. Comfortable and well-plumbed. Good restaurant, especially for locally caught seafood; dinner; card £6.50–9.50; BB £12.50–16. Shut Jan.

At Campbeltown, Ardshiel, Kilkerran Rd (tel 2133): useful little hotel; meals from local produce, home cooked; dinner FP £6; wines £4.50–5. BB £12.50–13.50.

Bellochantuy: lovely sandy bay on Atlantic, a little unprotected from wind. Just north, attractive village of Glenbarr. Machrihanish, wartime Naval airport, now NATO, not a pretty village, but fine golf course and superb sand beach.

Campbeltown: pleasant if not pretty town, with protected harbour in tiny loch; fishing boats land their catch mostly elsewhere but some lobster and white fish landed; once had 34 distilleries, boats could find their way there through fog by following their nose. Now it has two.

B842, B879
Carradale, B879,
B842 Creggan,
B8001 A83
Tarbert,
Lochgilphead
(52 m) (diversion
108 m)

Carradale is a hideaway for holidays; several little beaches, one big one; fishing harbour, a few houses built for holidays by the knowledgeable. Views of Isle of Arran; hills behind planted by Forestry Commission. Novelist Naomi Mitchison opens gardens of her home Carradale House to public 1 April–30 Sept pm.

A816 Oban
(37 m)

At Kilmartin (on A816 7 m from Lochgilphead), Kilmartin Hotel (tel 244): former advertising researcher and Crufts dog judge now devotes her energies to feeding humans with Scottish beef in red wine, steaks, haddocks, cream of trout soup, and raspberry Pavlova (Sassenachs forget that Scotland is the home of the raspberry). Everything home-made, from breakfast marmalade to dinner mints; splendid value, 4-course candlelit dinner FP £6; lunch or dinner bar meals £2.50–3.50. BB £7.

Kilmartin: charming little village among pretty hills. Nearby Neolithic cairns 3000–2000 BC; one 134 ft in diameter. Kilmartin Church has remarkable old gravestones and early Celtic crosses. 4 m NE begins Loch Awe, beautiful and fisherman's heaven – salmon, sea trout, brown trout.

Small left road on far side Loch Craignish leads to village of Ardfern and Craignish Castle (gardens open), riding; sailing dinghies for hire (instruction). Fishing – trout, salmon, sea trout. Wildlife

Oban
continued

At Kilmelford (pretty end of loch with isles alongside), Cuilfail (tel Kilmelford 274): friendly; fine cooking – game, fish; try salmon in lemon cream sauce. Bar lunches; dinner card around £7. BB £10. Good value.

At Isle of Seil, Willowburn Hotel (tel Balvicar 276): small hotel, already has AA rosette for dinners. Fresh local oysters, prawns, salmon, Loch Fyne smokies (haddock), lobster in season, venison. Bar lunch; dinner; card £6–8; house wine £2.50; some fine wines. BB £9.50–13.50. SB off season. Shut Nov.

At Oban, Alexandra, Corran Esplanade (tel 2381): member of high-class Scottish Highland group; excellent service, good position, sea views; good fish dishes. Dinner £6.90; BB (own bathroom) £16.65. SB (4 nights, much cheaper).

McTavish's (tel 63064): real tourist spot, with Scottish evenings (flings, pipes, patriotic ditties); but remarkable value meals; good 'budget special' with several choices £3.75; 'Scottish' FP menu £6.50 4-course (smoked or fresh salmon; haggis; Drambuie syllabub); also card.

Le Bistro, Breadalbane St (tel 64849): chef from Café Royal, (Edinburgh), Gleneagles. Good local seafood; good sauces; value. 2-course lunch £1.75; dinner FP £4.40; card £6–9.

(deer, wildcat, badger, otter, eagle). Loch littered with isles. Next left to Clachan and Isle of Seil – joined to mainland by high-humped bridge designed 1792 by Thomas Telford, known as Bridge Over the Atlantic.

Oban has an atmosphere I like; ferries to islands (Mull, Colonsay, Lismore, Staffa, (Fingal's Cave), working fishing fleet, pleasure yachts; sand beach; odd folly above town, lit up at night. McCaig, local banker, decided in 1890 to build local granite copy of Rome's Colosseum – to help unemployed stonemasons and glorify McCaig; blessedly never finished, and interior makes nice garden. Shinty – highly dangerous hockey – is local sport. New town hall (award winner for modern architecture) sensibly separated from older Oban. Sea and island views round here charming in summer, spectacular in winter, though Oban is sheltered.

A85, A828 South
Ballachulish, A82
North
Ballachulish Fort
William A830
Mallaig (93 m)

At Port Appin, Airds Hotel (tel Appin 236): pleasantly furnished; lovely position looking across Loch Linnhe to Isle of Lismore and Morvern mountains. Old ferry inn, built around 1700. AA rosette. Eric and Elizabeth Allen aim to promote Scottish cooking. Fishing, boat trips, walking in forest, pony riding. Dill salmon, scallop soup, local prawns, salmon; venison; try sole stuffed with salmon mousse, served with cream. Dinner £9; 100 wines from £3.25. BB from £13. DBB £19–22. Shut Nov–Apr.

At Onich, past North Ballachulish, Creag Dhu (tel Onich 238): beside loch, sheltered garden, fine scenery, good fishing, weekend off-season courses in arts and crafts; local produce well cooked. Dinner FP £7; bar lunch £1.30–3. BB £11.50–13.50. Hotel name rallying cry of Clan MacPherson – means 'Black Rock'.

At Fort William, Angus Restaurant, 66 High St (tel 2654): single courses or full meals; local salmon, trout; 3-course meals under £5. House wine £3.75/litre.

At Banavie (N of Fort William), Moorings (tel Corpach 550): Mary Sinclair's own recipes lure travellers to small hotel. Try Lochy pâté (salmon, cream); lovely sweets; dinner FP 4-course £7.25; BB £7.50–13.

At Mallaig, Marine Hotel (tel 2217): try Mallaig grilled sole and whatever fish are landed

Winding road round loch shores; small road left from Strath of Appin takes you to Port Appin, nice quiet village with ferry across to north end of Lismore Isle. Appin was for centuries scene of clan feuds, murders and massacres, with men murdered on their wedding days and their families plotting revenge for years. Mostly between the Stewarts, related to royal Stuarts and Jacobins, and the Campbells, supporters of the English kings and still hated as 'fifth columnists' by some Highlanders. That's true, believe me. I was a POW with the Campbell heir and even a Macdonald from New Zealand hated him for his ancestry! Yet Bruce gave Campbells much of their power after war against MacDougalls; the MacFarlanes were mixed up in the blood-letting, too.

Bridge now joins North and South Ballachulish. Wonderful hill scenery around here with changing colours in different lights.

Fort William: touring centre for Lochaber and West Highlands; below 4406 ft Ben Nevis, Britain's highest mountain, but you have to go up Cow Hill to see it. Fort built originally in 1655 by General Monk. Rebuilt in stone by order of William III in 1690. West Highland Museum interesting; reconstructed croft kitchen shows what a dog's life a girl used to lead; 'secret' picture of Prince Charles Edward reflected on curved cylinder.

Mallaig
continued

each day. Near harbour, looking to sea; nice overnight spot for Skye boats; views of Eigg, Rhum and Cuillins of Skye. Meals FP £4.50; card £5–7. BB £8–9.50.

West Highland Hotel (tel Mallaig 2210): venison, salmon, local seafood. Dinner FP 4-course £6.40; BB £10.50–13. DBB £18.

Mallaig: still important fishing port despite EEC arguments, but, like Oban, could do with some good news from Europe. Herrings still smoked in kilns to make kippers; lobsters farmed in ponds. Photogenic harbour. Boats carry people to Eigg, Rhum, Carna, and cars to Arnadale on Skye. Climb Carna Ghobair (1749 ft, no definite paths) to see magnificent views – 25 years ago I last made it! Charles Edward hid in these hills in 1746.

car ferry
Mallaig–
Arnadale,
Isle of Skye

There's talk of bridging half-mile strait of Kyle Akin to join Skye to mainland at Kyle of Lochalsh, but Skye is still a world apart. Alas, it has never been a very happy isle; crofters renting farms have had a hard fight for existence, there are few trees except those planted in recent years by Forestry Commission on Macleod and Macdonald estates, and its beauty is mostly from stark rocks; those in Quirang, NE corner of isle, are almost fantastic. But it is a sailor's and fisherman's paradise, with lochs and bays running deep into land, giving it more arms than a Buddhist god. Norway owned it until 1266, when it was given to Macleods, who fought over it with Macdonalds with the usual clan murders, double-crossing and brutality until both backed Prince Charles Edward against the English and lost. Both still own lumps of Skye. Macleods have had oldest inhabited castle in Scotland, Dunvegan, since 13th century. Macdonalds have Arnadale Castle in south, built 1815.

As wool trade fell off with development of man-made fibres, Skye became depressed and the young unemployed left for jobs on mainland. Schools closed, so children stayed with mainland relatives. Tourism, new capital and new enterprises had raised hopes until recent depression. Landowners from outside have introduced some capital, including Dutch investment (with mixed blessings for crofters).

suggested tour:
Arnadale A851
Broadford A850
Portree (42 m)
A850, A856 Uig
(15 m) A855
round north of
Skye back to
Portree (33 m)

At Isle Ornsay (on A851, not an isle), Duisdale Hotel (tel Isle Ornsay 202): in 60 acres woodland, garden, facing sea; popular, informal; boats for hire, sailing, cruising. Good seafood, fresh veg, home-baked shortbread. Bar lunch £2–4 (includes haggis and neeps); high tea £3.75; dinner FP £7.85. BB £10.50–13.50. SB spring, autumn.

Broadford Hotel (tel Broadford 204): a place of pilgrimage to true Scots; here, in hotel started by Sir Lauchlin Mackinnon in 1611, a descendant first prepared for Charles Edward, to Prince's own secret recipe, a drink called Drambuie. One of only two good things Charlie did for Scotland. Salmon and sea trout fishing on river (free to residents). 4-course dinner FP £7.47; wines from £2.30 (Nicolas): BB £13.80–17.20. Shut Nov–Mar (even for Drambuie).

Sligachan Hotel on A850 at end of loch (tel Sligachan 204): fishing in river running past hotel (sea trout; salmon rare). views of Cuillin Hills beloved by climbers and poets; turreted hotel looks as if it came from Normandy; lunch card £3–3.50; 4-course dinner FP £7.80. BB £16–18.

Portree, Coolin Hills Hotel (tel 2003): fine position overlooking bay; own grounds; boat for sea angling, excursions. Venison, Skye salmon, Skye lamb. Dinner £6.60; BB £10–14.

Rosedale Hotel (tel Portree 2531): on original waterfront;

Broadford: biggest crofting township; shops; hotels; lovely Red Hills westward. Airport nearby with services to Glasgow, Inverness.

Portree: nice little town with sheltered anchorage for fishing and pleasure boats; running 2 m into land. Hills alongside drop from 1300 ft steeply to sea. Fine views of Applecross mountains on mainland, Isle of Raasay in between. Ferries no longer call from Kyle of Lochalsh. West coast of Trotternish to Uig is richest soil of Skye with many crofts; centre has spine of brown hills.

Uig: harbour village with car ferries to Harris, North Uist. Charming place, quiet. 1½ m N is Monkstadt House. Here Lady Margaret Macdonald was wining with commander English royal forces when sailors landed on beach below with Flora Macdonald and her 'maid' – Prince Charles Edward in drag after 30 m row from Isle of Benbecula – Over the Sea to Skye – thus giving Scotland one of its greatest songs (the other good thing Charlie did for Scotland). Prince got away, Flora eventually arrested. She lived to marry, and to entertain Dr Johnson and Boswell on their Highland trip.

At Kilmuir is Flora Macdonald's tomb, marked by an ugly cross; she deserved better – and did have better but tourists of other generations chipped it away in pieces as souvenirs.

Portree *continued*	Andrew family-run 30 years; local lamb, beef, salmon; dinner FP £5.75; BB £11.25–13.75. Shut Oct–Apr. At Kensaleyre (6 m N Portree), Macdonald Hotel (tel Skeabost Bridge 339): modern, single-storey building overlooks loch; views of Cuillin Hills; all rooms with shower, teamaker; boats for fishing, pleasure; Mrs Macdonald former lecturer in food studies; Mr Macdonald former lecturer in horticulture, now runs own nursery supplying hotel; not licensed – bring your drinks; dinner £6.90; BB £10–12. Shut Oct–Apr.	Skye Cottage Museum (N Kilmuir): thatched croft restored; most interesting; includes a Paisley shawl covering a cot 300 years old, still nearly perfect. Do they make them like that now in Paisley? Probably, judging by the superb woollens you can still buy in Scotland. Road down east coast passes the Storr, mass of bare rocks up to 2358 ft – space fiction scenery. Old Man of Storr a mere 160 ft – solitary pillar, incredibly climbed in 1955 by Don Whillans and James Barber. Some pinnacles around here still not climbed. Any takers?
A850 Kyleakin (27 m) car ferry to Kyle of Lochalsh	Lochalsh Hotel (tel Kyle 4202): an old favourite of mine. Right beside water, pretty; friendly; local game, meat and splendid fish. French chef cooking Scottish, French dishes. Dinner FP £7.25; 4 courses £7.75; also card. BB £17.50 (high season); winter DBB £15. SB all year.	Kyle of Lochalsh: I can sit in the pleasant hotel here watching the rushing waters of Kyle Akin strait between here and Skye (½ mile away) doing their worst in any weather. A cosy feeling.

A87, A890
Achnasheen
(40 m) A832
Kinlochewe,
Gairloch (29 m)

Balmacara Hotel (3 m from Kyle) (tel Balmacara 283): happy inn; own brown trout fishing; good traditional Scottish cooking; meals FP £6.50; also card. Wines from £3.50; BB £12.50–15.50.

At Achnasheen, Ledgowan Lodge (tel 252): peaceful, dinner £6.75; BB £11.50–15. SB. Shut Nov–Mar.

Gairloch, The Steaiding (tel 2449): byre and stable converted, with tables in original cattle stalls. Run by very experienced hotel catering lady; local seafoods (prawns, whole crab, fresh salmon, smoked mackerel), local venison; self-service; open 10am–9pm. Attached to Gairloch Heritage Museum, national heritage award winner. Meals £3.50–6.20; wines reasonable prices. Open mid Apr–early Oct except Sun.

Old Inn (tel 2006): original coaching halt of 1730, most bedrooms with bath or shower; fishing, including lobster and crab; own catch cooked for you in kitchen; trips on hotel's sailing yacht. Dinner £6.25–8; BB £9–12.50; DBB £15–16.50.

Creagmore (tel Gairloch 2068): by old harbour, but new. Dinner £5.75; BB £9–10.50.

Lovely views and rugged country on this road. Until mid 19th century. Loch Carron was so packed with salmon that almost anyone could take twenty a day with a rod. They almost disappeared around 1845 – over-fishing.

Kinlochewe: hill-walking, climbing, fishing centre; Beinn Eighe Nature Reserve first in Britain (1951): wildlife includes martens, wildcats; also Forestry Commission have replanted bare hillsides which were forests centuries ago. Country very rugged, wild, especially westward.

Road alongside Loch Maree cuts across to coast at Gairloch, in superb setting with views to Outer Hebrides; sandy beaches, fine fishing, golf course. Fishing port, including lobster, crab. History of clan violence – this time Macleods v. Mackenzies.

A832 Poolewe.
through
Dundonnell
Forest, left on
A853 Ullapool
(56 m)

At Aultbea, Loch Ewe, Aultbea Hotel (tel 201): small hotel on loch shore, run by same family since turn of century. Trout fishing; sea, mountain views; a true taste of Scotland; good bar meals (grilled salmon, steak, local

Remarkable little-known Highland road beside lochs, sea, sand beaches; wild interior.

Poolewe: river here joins Loch Maree to Loch Ewe and sea – still rich in salmon. Poolewe more northerly than

Ullapool
continued

haddock) £2.50–4, 3 courses; dinner FP £5.50–6; BB £10–11. Shut end Oct–Easter.

At Ullapool, Ferryboat Inn (tel 2366): friendly, good fish – scallops in white wine, local prawns. good home-made soups; bar lunch. dinner FP £6.50; BB £8.25–10.50.

Harbour Lights, Garve Rd (tel 2222): dinner around £6.50; BB £8–10. Shut Dec–Feb.

Ceilidh Place, West Argyle St (tel Ullapool 2103): actor Robert Urquhart started with coffee shop in boat shed 'to play music and hang pictures'; now clubhouse, hotel, restaurant, coffee shop; weaving, art courses, sailing, field studies, climbing, sea angling, pony trekking; club rooms for 4 or 2 let without meals if wished, £4.25–6.25; hotel BB £12.50–16. Dinner coffee shop £3.60; 'Good Table' room 4-course £7.50.

Altnaharrie Inn (tel Dundonnell 230): reached by regular ferry from Ullapool – opposite side of loch; old drovers' inn; ferry free to guests (owned by inn). Very peaceful; fine deep sea fishing, cruising, walking, canoes, dinghies for hire. Fish from local boats, beef from local farms, home-baked bread. Lovely scenery. Chef Scandinavian, so dishes Scots-Scandinavian. Bar lunch; dinner £7–8. BB £10.50.

Moscow, on 58th parallel which runs through Hudson Bay and Siberia, yet thanks to Gulf Stream warmth, sub tropical plants and trees thrive in Interewe Gardens, one of the greatest places of Scotland. When Oswood Mackenzie started these gardens over 100 years ago, all that grew was one 3 ft high willow bush. He drained sour ground, excavated rock, planted treeshelter belts; brought in soil, cleared woodland garden. Magnolia 28 ft high and 75 ft circumference possibly world's largest. Gardens open dawn-dusk.

Road climbing over Dundonnell Forest is fairly bleak. Called Destitution Road, made in 1851 to give work to starving men in a potato famine. From Braemore through Strathmore is parkland scenery with wild rhododendrons.

Ullapool: interesting fishing port founded by British Fisheries Society in 1788 to help herring industry; sea-angling centre – European championships held here; skate of nearly 200 lb caught. Biggest fish off Summer Isles; once inshore fishing centre until big herring shoals were fished out. Bays, creeks, sounds, of Loch Broom give small boats sheltered waters. Ferries Ullapool–Stornaway on Isle of Lewis. Ullapool good base for pony trekking, sailing (including tuition), water skiing, canoeing. Wild, rugged country, not for midwinter pleasure.

A835 Ledmore,
A837, A836
Bonar Bridge,
A9, A836, A9
Dingwall (74 m)

Interpolly Forest, just before Ledmore, a nature reserve with three mountain peaks; covers 27,000 acres of wild loch, mountain, river, moor, crag and cliff; few people; splendid fishing in Loch Sionascaig. Land of deer, wildcat, pinemarten, eagles. Near meeting of A837 and A836, Falls of Shin, natural staircase up which salmon leap to breeding grounds. Viewing platform.

Carbisdale Castle (5 m NW) now youth hostel.

Dingwall: royal burgh since 1226, on Cromarty Firth.

A834
Strathpeffer
(6 m)

Kilvannie Manor (tel 389): parish church in 1801; manor house; now hotel. Handsome. Good traditional cooking. Dinner FP £6.25; house wine £3.25; BB £7.50.

Holly Lodge (tel 254): meal may include pheasant, venison, trout; meal FP £7.50; BB £11–14.

Strathpeffer Hotel (tel 200): good value; salmon in season, venison. Dinner FP £5.50. BB £9–11. Sauna. Shut Nov–Apr.

Ravenscroft Guest House (tel 403): traditional, varied meals. Good value. 4-course dinner £6; BB £7. DBB £11–14. Shut Dec–Jan.

Strathpeffer: Robert Louis Stephenson wrote in 1880: 'No place was ever so delightful to my soul'. Surprising, with all those Victorian buildings, but it is pleasant, in fine scenery, and good touring centre. In 1772 locals urged Royal Society in London to build a village near local healing well, but little was done until in 1819 Dr Thomas Morrison found the waters cured his own ailments, so built a pump room; European royalty and rich then addicted to spas, soon came; railway in 1885 brought lesser mortals; golf course and social life followed. Alas, spas dwindled, Grand Pump Room became army weapon store, then dismantled; its tiled floor shows in a car park. But sulphur waters still drunk in small pump room.

| A834 Contin, left on A832 Muir of Ord, A9 Beauly, Balblair (11 m) | Ord House Hotel, Muir of Ord (tel 492): fairly recently changed hands. Dinner £7.50. House wines £3.70. BB £15–18. | Beauly: on a salmon river. |

Ord Arms Hotel (tel 286). very popular inn; try fillet of beef Rob Roy (in oatmeal); pretty bedrooms. Dinner FP £7; bar lunches; BB £12–15.

| A9, A833 Milton left briefly on A831 Drumnadrochit (12 m) | Polmaily House, Milton (tel Drumnadrochit 343): lovely position; nice bedrooms; dinner: FP not great choice but good cooking, 5-course plus cheese £8.50. 100 wines from £2.80; BB £10–14. Own river fishing, tennis court, swimming pool in grounds, pony riding nearby. | Drumnadrochit: angling, riding centre. 2 m from Loch Ness at place frequented by Loch Ness monster (several sightings) Urquhart Castle blown up by owners (Grants) to stop Jacobites using it. |

| A82 along Loch Ness to Fort Augustus (19 m) Invergarry, Spean Bridge, (22 m) | At Fort Augustus, Inchnacardoch Lodge (tel 6258): gorgeous position, raised above Loch Ness, views across loch to Great Glen mountains and Inchnacardoch forest around it. Highland cattle in pastures near the windows; I have dined but not stayed here – but I shall stay. Own boats for salmon and trout fishing on loch, or try local rivers. Hire sailing dinghy on loch, pony for the forests. Locals meet here. Dinner FP £7 (good value), fair wine list. BB £10–14. SB. | Loch Ness in spring or summer looks friendly. But see it in mist or whipped up by a wind in unkinder months and it can look sinister. I like it in the spring; beautiful but not crowded. The 'monster' is probably friendly but frightened. They were talking in the 14th century of 'waves without wind, fish without fins, islands that float'. |

On A82, 7 m from Spean Bridge, Letterfinlay Lodge (tel Invergloy 222): overlooking Loch Lochy; spectacular views of mountains, forests; good traditional meals – Angus beef, Scottish hill lamb, fresh salmon, sea trout from local lochs, rivers. Dinner £6.95; good cellar; BB £9–15.

Fort Augustus: named after dreaded Duke of Cumberland, victor at Culloden; now Catholic school and Benedictine abbey on site of fort.

Spean Bridge: hamlet in glen with bridge built by Telford in 1819 over turbulent river. High on nearby hill is memorial to wartime commandos, many of whom trained here. Put up 1952, a spectacular group of three soldiers, by Scott Sutherland. Views of Ben Nevis.

A82 Fort William, Kinlochleven, Glen Coe, Glencoe Pass Bridge of Orchy (61 m)	At Glencoe, Kings Head (tel 259): one of Scotland's oldest inns, now modern hotel, well run. Meals, card £6.50. BB £12–13.75. Shut Nov–Feb.	Glencoe village is climbing and skiing centre, though ski slopes 11 m away. Glencoe Pass notorious for the massacre by the Campbells of the Macdonalds in 1692 after accepting their hospitality for 12 days; order for massacre written on nine of diamonds playing card, now called 'Curse of Scotland'. Pass of Glencoe is not pretty; bare, with few trees or heather; fearsome.
A82 Crianlarich (14 m) A85 Lochearnhead (joins Route 8) A84 Callander (30 m) A892, A821 Aberfoyle (14 m)	At Aberfoyle, Covenanters Inn (tel 347): these covenanters came in 1949 to pledge fight for Scotland's own parliament, free of Westminster. Two years later two million Scots had signed. Inn changed its name. Dinner FP £5.50; BB £13–14.50. SB.	See Route 8. Trossachs, called Highlands in Miniature, popularized by Sir Walter Scott in *Rob Roy* and *Lady of the Lake*. Rob Roy was Robert MacGregor (1671–1734); some called him a Robin Hood, robbing the rich to feed the poor, others a bandit and cattle rustler; depended which receiving end you were on. Aberfoyle: views of lochs; part of Forestry Commission's Queen Elizabeth Forest Park; pony-trekking country. Fine area for activity holidays.

Route 10

Edinburgh – Perth – Aviemore – Inverness – Balmoral

Edinburgh,
A9 past
Edinburgh
Airport
Linlithgow
Palace (12 m)
(See route 8)
A9 Falkirk,
Larbert,
Bannockburn,
Stirling, Bridge
of Allan (19 m)

A9 Dunblane,
Gleneagles
Auchterarder
(15 m)

Dunblane Hydro (tel 822551):
one of Stakis group; very
good value considering its
luxury. Fort-like Victorian
pile, well modernized;
bathroom or shower, TV,
teamaker every bedroom.
Sauna solarium, heated
indoor pool, tennis courts.
Dinner 4-course £7.25; also
card; house wine £4.20/litre;
nouveau Bordeaux £4. BB
£18–24; DBB from £19.

Altair Neuk Hotel, Doung Rd
(tel 822562): family run,
home cooking; dinner card
around £8; bar lunches; high
tea £3.50. BB £9.20–16.

Gleneagles, Auchterarder (tel
2231): right outside our
scope for price but one of the
world's greatest hotels – and
at least we own it; British

Dunblane: 13th-century
cathedral on Allan Water;
narrow streets of old town.

Gleneagles Auchterarder *continued*	Transport Hotel. Tennis courts, croquet, bowling green, squash court, swimming pool and *four* golf courses, used for championships. 640-acre estate. Lunch FP £11; dinner FP £14; and card. Eagle's Nest lunch £6.75; one of Europe's great wine cellars. Wines from £5.75. BB from £37. Shut Nov-Mar.	
A823, B822 Crieff (11 m)	Star, East High St (tel Crieff 2632): very nice place to eat; card has lobster, salmon, Dover sole, local trout at reasonable prices; bar lunch; dinner FP £6.75; card. BB £8–9. Crieff Hydro (tel 2401): another castle-like Victorian hotel, modernized; good value. Heated indoor pool, sauna, riding stables, badminton, croquet, 9-hole golf course, squash courts; children's dining room, playroom, paddling pool, baby listening. Lunch FP £4.60; dinner FP £6.20; BB £10–12; DBB £12–18. Gwydyr Hotel, Comrie Rd (tel 3277): small hotel, good value. Dinner FP £4.60; card £7; BB £7–8.	Crieff: charming little hillside town overlooks lovely Strath Earn; river runs in waterfalls from north. Innerpeffray Library, founded 1691; many fascinating books, including 17th-century 'treacle' Bible (words 'is there no balm in Gilead?' printed as 'is there no treacle in Gilead?').
A85 Methven, Perth (17 m)	On A85 from Crieff just before Huntingtower Castle, 3 m Perth, Huntingtower Hotel (tel Almondbank 241): two invading Sassenachs stole two local girls, married them, and set up very good hotel. Pleasant gardens; good English cooking – Scottish beef, but Yorkshire pudding. Lunch FP £4.95; dinner FP 4-course £8; also card; shut Sun eve. BB (limited) £14–19.50.	Methven: another historic battlefield; English beat Robert the Bruce in 1306; James Graham, Marquis of Montrose, pin-up boy of Charles I's army and great general, defeated Campbell, Duke of Argyll and army of Protestant covenanters in 1645. Montrose later fled to Holland, led invasion of Scotland in 1650 for Charles II and was killed.

At Perth, County, 26 County Place (tel 23355): Welcome Inn group hotel; comfortable; good service. Buttery lunch from £1.95; dinner around £6.50. BB £9.50–11.

Salutation, 34 South St (tel 22166): the old Sally, born 1699, still social meeting spot of the young, as when I flew from Scone airfield in 1939. Sallie's Disco added since. Very good value meals. 3-course bar lunch (choice usually includes a roast) £1.65; restaurant lunch FP £3.75; dinner FP £6; also card lunch or dinner with reasonable prices. Wines from £3 (Soave). Very comfortable hotel; all rooms with bath or shower. BB £16–18. SB. Disco 3 nights, dancing live music 3 nights, cabaret. Two Highlanders in dress flanking doorway are 19th-century ships' figureheads.

Penny Post, 80 George St (tel 20867): was a snuff mill, then post office 1803–62, saw Penny Post launched 1840, then bank. Now restaurant with pizza bar below. Lunch £3.45; dinner card around £7; wines from £3.55.

Timothy's, 24 St John St (tel 26641): useful eating house; all dishes cold except soup, jacket potatoes. Scandinavian smörrebröd (single-deck sandwiches); wine in jugs £4.50 a quart.

Perth: still the Fair City despite some ill-placed new buildings. Capital of Scotland until 1437 when Earl of Athol arranged murder of poet-king James I; his widow and son moved capital to Edinburgh. In St John's Kirk, consecrated 1243, John Knox, returned from exile 1559, preached first rousing sermon against idolatery in Catholic church. Protestant Earl of Gowrie kidnapped James VI (later James I of England) in 1582 and held him in Huntingtower Castle for a year to try to make him sack his Catholic advisers. Huntingtower (3 m W) open weekdays.

Salutation Hotel, 1699, in South St, has minstrels gallery near bedroom used by Prince Charles Edward, drilled troops on North Inch (1745): North Inch now park, golf course and sports ground.
The beauty of Perth lies in area beside river Tay and bridges; boating, fishing. Perth's cattle market world famous.

Scone, 3 m N: Stone of Destiny said to have been Jacob's pillow at Bethel. Became coronation stone of Scots king. In 1297 Edward I of England took it to Westminster Abbey to put under Coronation Chair where it has stayed since except when Scottish nationalists stole it 1950. Good Scotsmen say Westminster stone a fake, real one is buried in Scone. Scone Palace, home of Earls of Mansfield, 19th-century house on site of abbey; fine furniture, china; gardens. Open May–Sept.

A9, keep on old A9 when new road forks right, Bankfoot, Birnam, Dunkeld A9 to Pitlochry, into town, avoiding new A9 bypass just completed (26 m)

Bankfoot: old inn left stranded by diversion of A9, renamed Hunters Lodge (tel Bankfoot 325). Won BBC Scotland's Best Pub Grub award '79; try fisherman's platter. Bar dish £2.20; good hot bar food; high tea £3.60; dinner card £5–7.50. BB £10–15.

Dunkeld House (tel 243): charming house built for Duke of Atholl 1900. 100-acre garden, woods; overlooks river Tay with 1½ m beat owned by hotel; super salmon fishing. Dinner FP £5.50; card around £15. BB £16–21.50.

At Pitlochry, Craigard Hotel, Strathview Terrace (tel 2592): lovely position in nice garden with views. Comfortable and cosy; dinner £7; BB £11.50. Shut Nov–Mar.

Green Park Hotel, Clunie Bridge Rd (tel 2537): superb peaceful position on loch side; lunch £3.50 (local salmon in season) dinner 4-course £6.95, buffet Sun eve. Bar dinners; card £6–7. Good value. House wine £3.90/litre. BB £13.50–£16.

Dundarach Hotel, Perth Rd (tel 2862): long-established comfortable hotel; lunch FP £4; dinner 4-course, good value £7; fair wine choice; BB £11–12.

Craigcrack Hotel, West Moul Rd (tel 2399): modern extension to old house; well furnished and decorated; dinner 4-course £6.70; wines from £3; BB £10–12. Shut winter.

Birnham Wood was a slope of fine oaks in Shakespeare's day, when Macbeth heard the prophecy that he would reign until it came down to Dunsinane (hill 12 m SE); now scrub oak and silver birch. Here on holiday Beatrix Potter wrote picture letters which grew into *Tale of Peter Rabbit* and *Jeremy Fisher*.

Dunkeld: peaceful little town; remains of medieval cathedral prove Victorian belief that ruins can be lovely; old houses nicely restored by National Trust. Deer roam round here; salmon abound in Tay.

Pitlochry: time has changed this once utterly peaceful little town in lovely setting of loch, river, mountains and woods. Its Festival Theatre, starting in tents and now in a fine new building, increased its summer tourist trade; Damming of river Aldour made a new loch, Faskally, for power boats, fishing and sailing, with a spectacular salmon ladder where you can see through windows the salmon climbing to their spawning grounds. These crowded Pitlochry, especially with foreign tourists. Now a new wide A9 bypass is complete and some of the traffic at least is diverted. A lovely place, at best outside summer months. Salmon fishing in loch; trout in many nearby waters.

A9 Blair Atholl,
Dalwhinnie,
A899 Laggan,
(39 m)

At Loch Tummel, Strathtummel, Port-an-Eilean Hotel (tel Tummel Bridge 233): very quiet; in 20-acre garden, woodland; on loch shore. Boats, fishing. Bar lunch; dinner FP £6 (trout, salmon). BB £11–13. SB. Shut end Oct–mid Apr.

At Blair Atholl, Atholl Arms (tel 205): fine solid old Highland hotel; dining room with musician's gallery built 125 years ago by Duke of Atholl for balls and official dinners. Meals good value. Dinner £6; BB £9.75–10.75.

At Loch Tummel (left on B8019) is Queen's View, one of Queen Victoria's favourite views; trees have grown up now and though view is good you get better one a little further on near Tressail. Nice run alongside loch; can return on opposite side of loch past Tummel Falls but road narrow.

Pass of Killiecrankie: bloody victory for Jacobite cause of James VII (James II of England) when Graham of Claverhouse trapped General Mackay's army in narrow pass. Graham was Viscount Dundee – 'Bonnie Dundee' of Walter Scott's ballad. He was killed in the battle.

Blair Atholl: village on Garry river with superb scenery. Blair Castle built 1269 by Duke of Atholl; altered often till present castle – bits dating from 1269 to last century. In 130,000-acre estate, with pleasant gardens; present Duke still lives there; one of the most interesting castle interiors I have seen, from arms in entrance hall to magnificent furnishings, rooms, pictures, tapestries. Duke commands private army of 20 officers, 75 other ranks; given official recognition by Queen Victoria. He is head of Murray Clan. When Protestant Georgian troops took the castle during Charles Edward Rebellion, Lord George Murray laid siege to his own home – failed to take it.

A86
Newtonmore,
old A9
Kingussie,
Kingcraig, into
Aviemore village
(new A9 goes
behind village)
(23 m)

At Newtonmore, Ard-Na-Coille (tel 214): former millionaire's shooting lodge with superb views over Strathspey to Cairngorms; wonderful salmon and trout fishing nearby; near Cairngorm ski slopes. Family run. Dinner FP £7.50; BB £9.40–11; DBB £14–15.

Pines, Station Rd (tel 271): family-run licensed hotel; home baking; value. Dinner £4–5; BB £7–8; DBB £10.50–11.50.

At Kingussie, Osprey (tel 510): small hotel, comfortably furnished, recommended by my spies for service, value, cooking (though little choice) and good wine choice (130 wines £3.50–30). Local smoked and fresh salmon and trout; high-praised venison casserole. Dinner FP £6.50; BB £10. Shut Nov 1–Dec 26.

Duke of Gordon (tel 302): local fish, game and meat with good sauces. Dinner FP £6; BB £12–13.

Wood'n'spoon (tel 488): home cooking and baking; filling 'skiers' soups, venison burgers, trout, salmon, steaks; self-service, open for snacks or meals 10am–9.30pm, so useful to active people such as skiers, walkers, sailors, fishermen; friendly; sensible wine list from £3.20; meals £3–6.

At Kincraig, Ossian Hotel (tel 242): ordinary-looking little family-run hotel known for good cooking. Very friendly. Six members of family look after guests. Chef Johnny

Newtonmore: MacPherson country; ancient clan gathering place in mountains on 2350-ft Creag Dhu, which is their rallying cry; Cluny MacPherson hid for years in a cave on this wild, steep mountain after '45 Rebellion. Clan museum in Newtonmore has broken fiddle of James MacPherson, who played it on way to gallows and broke it before he died. Now a pony-trekking centre.

Kingussie: tiny neat 18th-century town; Highland Folk Museum has most interesting items from past, including Highland black-house, with hole in roof for chimney (open May–Sept).

Highland Wildlife Park: 260 acres where animals which disappeared from Highlands centuries ago have been reintroduced (bison, brown bear, wolves, beaver, antelope, reindeer) to live with animals still there but rare (wildcat, pine martens, St Kilda Soay sheep, true wild Highland cattle and birds such as ptarmigan, golden eagle). Many seen without leaving car.

Kincraig: all round here wonderful mountain, forest scenery, small lochs, streams and river Spey rich in salmon, trout; superb country for walkers, hill walkers, fishermen, sailing, canoeing, bird watching, pony trekking; Cairngorm Gliding Club at Glenfeshie (near Kincraig offers superb chance to learn gliding, adjacent hills give wonderful

Rainbow, son-in-law, was 2nd chef on P&O liner *Canberra*. People living for miles around come to eat. Dinner card around £7; £10 with chef's speciality lobster thermidor. House wine £3.75.

At Loch Alvie, just before Aviemore, Lynwilg Hotel (tel 207): my favourite eating place around here, but I still cannot pronounce it. Everything home made, including bread; try local dishes in season – salmon, trout, venison, hare; dinner card £5–7.50. BB £11–13.

Winking Owl: favourite eating-drinking bar of ski instructors and Aviemore Centre staff. Many good Scottish dishes but my favourite is local salmon with Dieppoise sauce. Good bar snacks and lunches. Dinner around £6.50. Wines from £3.90/litre (Soave, Valpolicella).

lifting conditions. Skiing, 'curling' in winter; superb area for open-air enthusiasts any time of year, but check winter driving conditions, especially off A9. Sailing on Loch Insh. Loch an Eilein has car park and nature trial along wooded shores. Castle on little isle supposed to have been used by notorious Wolf of Badenoch, outlawed son of Robert II of Scotland, but doubtful. On right towards Aviemore on old A9 is trout farm; amazing sight to see trout thrashing water into 'boiling cauldron' at feeding time.

Aviemore: Centre was opened to try to make jobs and bring money into depressed Highlands. Chance to learn sailing, canoeing, riding and trekking, skiing, ice-skating (big indoor rink). Scottish ice game of curling, swimming (indoor pool); indoor entertainment; ski schools and ski hire; hotels from family chalet hotel, Freedom Inn with downstairs restaurant, to starred hotels. Centre has Clan House where computer helps anyone with Scottish blood trace family history and tartan.

Down B8951, past Coylumbridge, is Loch Morich, good dinghy sailing.

Glenmore Forest Park starts here. Reindeer herd set up 1952; plenty of local deer about too; road leads to chairlifts up Cairngorm ski slopes; at top is Ptarmigan, highest restaurant in Britain. Strathspey Highland Steam Railway still runs from Aviemore to Boat of Garten.

old A9, right fork
on A95, left on
B9150
Carrbridge new
A9 Inverness
(31 m)

At Carrbridge, Dalrachney
Lodge (tel 252): friendly
family-run hotel; produce
from garden; lunch £2.15;
dinner £4; BB £6; DBB £9.50.

At Inverness, Glen Mhor, 9
Ness Bank (tel 34308): looks
a little forbidding but
comfortable, splendidly run
by real expert. Overlooks
river Ness and theatre. Room
prices vary enormously
according to room and
season. Super breakfasts;
good fish, shellfish, game;
outstanding wine list. Bar
lunches; dinner FP £7.50;
pre-theatre high tea, BB
£8.50–25 SB (good: 1–3
nights).

Kingsmill Lodge, Culcabock
Rd (tel 37166): little pricey
but a fine hotel; converted
from early 18th-century
house, formerly home of
Provost of Inverness; modern
wing; 12 big old family
rooms, 13 new modern
rooms with large bathrooms
and fine pine furniture. Good
bar lunches, card £2.50–3;
dinner FP 3-course (residents
only) £6.50; 4-course FP
£8.25 card around £9. Always
one old-fashioned pud –
treacle, bread and butter etc.
BB £17.50–25.

Bishops Table, Eden Court
Theatre (tel 723): you don't
have to be going to the
theatre; popular eating place,
nice outlook, good cooking.
Buffet lunch up to £3; dinner
FP £6.90; card around £10.
Try venison in Marsala
sauce. Run by ex-staff
manager Claridges, London.
Interesting wines.

Old A9 wanders and twists
below new road; views not
as good.

Carrbridge: holiday skiing
capital until Aviemore Centre
took over. Now quiet again
except in ski season. Man
who started it, Karl Fuchs,
still runs ski school and hotel
with help of his son who
made superb effort for
Britain in winter Olympics.
Landmark, permanent
museum of this area, very
interesting.

Inverness: one of my
favourite cities; atmosphere
and people warm.
Caledonian Canal joins lochs
and waterways to connect
Moray Firth on this east
coast with Oban on the west
coast – and you can hire a
boat for the trip (a great
one). Loch Ness almost runs
into city. Ferry across Beauly
Firth leaves you 14 m from
Dingwall (Route 9). This
Kessock Ferry takes you to
Black Isle, very protected,
one of Britain's sunniest
spots; nice small forest and
coastal small roads.

Inverness Castle fairly
modern but good views from
its hill. St Andrew's
Cathedral built 1866, carved
pillars, modern glass
windows. Beautiful new Eden
Court Theatre, with superb
expanding stage; lawns to
loch; incorporates former
bishop's palace. Shows from
ballet, opera, drama,
symphony concerts to jazz,
pop, music hall. Players' rest
room, Green Room, in
former bishop's private
chapel.

suggested diversion round Loch Ness A82 Drumnadrochit, Fort August (33 m)

See Route 9.

back on A862, B852 Foyers, Inverfarigaig, Dores, Inverness (30 m)

Foyers: site of Britain's first hydroelectric scheme 1896; lovely waterfall, dropping 90 ft into rocky pool, then river races through woods to Loch Ness. Inverfarigaig is start of 3 m forest walk.

A9 B9006 Culloden, Nairn (16 m) A96 Forres (10 m)

Nairn: Clifton Hotel, Viewfield St (tel 53119): I seem to be the only person who has visited Nairn yet never been to the Clifton, and I shall put that right; many reliable friends *have* been. Gordon MacIntyre is known in wine circles, showbusiness circles and among my friends as a splendid eccentric, running a splendid hotel. Victorian house with fine Victorian décor; classic

Culloden: so sad, this moorland; on stormy day in 1746 Charles Edward, seeking George II's throne, thrust 5000 wet, march-weary Highlanders into hopeless battle against experienced Duke of Cumberland's troops. 1200 Highlanders slaughtered. Sad graves; films and charts of battle.

Nairn: nice resort, fine sands. Attractive fishermen's quarters, streets to harbour.

cooking of local salmon, trout, duck, game, Scottish beef, lamb. Winter enlivened by plays and music when hotel otherwise shut. Meals average £10 with wine; wonderful wine list of 140 bins; BB £15.30. Shut mid Nov–mid Mar.

Carnach Country House, Delnies, Nairn (tel 52094): 7½-acre grounds overlooking Moray Firth; good traditional cooking, dinner: summer for residents FP £5.75; FP 4-course £8. Sensible wine list. BB £8.85–11; DBB £14.60.

Cawdor Castle (5 m SW): Shakespeare made it scene of Duncan's murder in *Macbeth*.

Fine medieval building; central tower dates from 1454; drawbridge.

Rait Castle (3 m S B9101); 13th-century built by Comyns Clan on ground disputed with Mackintoshes. Comyns asked Mackintoshes to dinner in 1442 to kill them; Mackintoshes tipped off; killed their hosts.

Forres: Shakespeare made this the site of Duncan's royal court. Witches' Stone marks place where three witches accused of causing death of King Duffus were burned in AD 965. Just off Nairn-Forres Castle in Darnaway Castle, built 1810 around 15th-century hall of Mary Queen of Scots.

very small distance from town A940, left on small road through Altyre Woods to Rafford right on B9010 to Dallas Forest right on small road past Tor Castle to Dallas; small road left outside village to Upper Knockando right on B9102 Grantown on Spey (32 m) B970 Nethy Bridge small road left, left again to join A939 right to Tomintoul, Cock Bridge, Rinloan (36 m)

At Grantown on Spey, Craggan Mill (tel 2288): owner-chef Bruno Belleni cooks venison and spaghetti carbonara, lasagna or local salmon equally well; meals card £6.50–8.50 (no lunches in winter); wines from £3.50 nice Barolo.

At Tomintoul, Gordon Arms (tel Tomintoul 333); old inn; lunch from £3; dinner from £5; BB £8.50–9.

Glenmulliach Restaurant (tel Tomintoul 356): all the great Scottish dishes; 3-course lunch £1.95; high tea £2.45; card around £7 (smoked salmon, venison, apfelstrudel £6.55). Wine list. Shut Dec. Open, weather permitting, rest of year.

Nice drive through little-known area of forests and rivers.

Grantown on Spey: Sir James Grant built it 1776 as centre for linen industry; salmon fishing, walking, skiing. attractive wide streets, granite buildings, old bridge.

Nethy Bridge: in fine walking, fishing, exploring country. Rare ospreys nest near at Loch Garten.

Tomintoul, 1160 ft up in Grampians, claims to be highest village in Highlands. Tomintoul restaurants open 'weather permitting' Jan–March. Visitors come to fish in summer, ski in winter (Lecht Ski Centre).

**B976 Crathie,
A93 Braemar
(14 m)**

At Braemar, Mar Lodge (tel 216): built in Edwardian days as hunting lodge for Duke of Fife and Princess Louise, daughter of King Edward VII. Lunch from £5.50; dinner from £7; BB £10.50–15; shut Nov–Apr.

Invercauld Arms (tel 605): partly 16th-century and luxurious. Residents' disco; piping and Scottish dancing displays sometimes arouse house ghost. Hotel has 9 m salmon-fishing stretch on river Dee, so salmon, with Angus beef, are chef's speciality. So is duckling Braeside (sauce of Drambuie and heather – you can't get more Scottish); beautiful cooking; chef a judge at national Hotel and Catering Exhibition; dinner FP 4-course £7.25; also card; fine wine list from £3.50. BB £10–18.50. SB spring, winter, autumn.

B976 sometimes impassable in winter (use A939 Ballater road).

Crathie: Balmoral Castle, family holiday home of Royal Family where, by tradition, they are left in peace. Prince Albert bought the 11,000-acre estate and had built the Baronial Hall which he helped to design. 15th-century house there was called Bouchemorale – Gaelic for 'majestic house'. Gardens open to public May, June, July, except Sun or when Royal Family staying.

Braemar: Deeside village 1100 ft up among heather-covered hills with Cairn Toul (4241 ft) to west. Royal Highland Gathering here each September, usually attended by Queen. Winter sports area. Castle built by Earl of Mar 1628; burnt by Farquarsons 1689, rebuilt 1748. Underground pit prison. Open Easter-early Oct.

**A93 Spittal of
Glenshee, B951
Kirriemuir (42 m)**

Spittal of Glenshee Hotel (tel Glenshee 215): Scottish dishes and Malaysian curries (welcome here in winter); modern hotel a boon to many travellers. Meals FP £5.50; card around £7.50; BB £7.50–12.50.

At Kirriemuir, Thrurns, Bank St (tel 2758): owner May Simpson demonstrated her near-legendary clootie dumplings on BBC TV, tourists flock to try them. Dinner 4-course £5.75. Bar lunch £2.50. BB £7–7.50.

Road climbs through Glen Clunie and over Cairnwell Pass – lovely, wild. New road down to Spittal of Glenshee avoids notorious Devil's Elbow – old road often snowbound in winter. B951 passes Kirton of Glenisla, pretty village on river Isla in remote, lovely glen.

Kirriemuir: little town of narrow streets, sandstone cottages on lovely slopes of Braes of Angus. Streams flowing into Esk river rich in trout. J. M. Barrie's birthplace (9 Brechin Road) is museum. Author of *Peter Pan* called his hometown Thrums in his stories.

A928 Glamis (6 m)	Strathmore Arms (tel Glamis 248): owned by Strathmore Estates, Glamis Castle. Taste of Scotland dishes; bar lunches; meals FP £4; card £7.75.	Glamis Castle: childhood home of Queen Elizabeth the Queen Mother, wife of George VI; birthplace of Princess Margaret (1930); home of Earls of Strathmore, and a royal home since 1372. House mostly dates from 1675, though square tower much older; oldest part is Duncan's Hall, setting for part of Shakespeare's *Macbeth*. Fine china, furniture. Lovely views from battlements. nine ghosts including Macbeth, 11th-century King of Scotland; one monster bricked up in wall 200 years ago; beautiful grounds; sundial with 84 dials. Open May–Sept, Sun and Thurs pm). Restored cottages in Kirkwynd with museum showing 200 years of farm life. Angus Folk Museum: open 1 May–30 Sept pm.
A94 Coupar Angus New Scone, local road right to Old Scone A93 Perth A90 Bridge of Earn, B996, A922 Kinross (16 m) M90 motorway to Forth Bridge (12 m) South Queensferry A90 Edinburgh (13 m)	At Kinclaven (4 m W Coupar Angus), Ballathie House (tel Meileour 268): in 2,000 acre park on banks of Tay; built around 1880 in French château style. Once had own railway station and chapel. Greenhouses and walled garden supply kitchen, salmon, trout fishing; golf nearby; Scottish, French cooking: dinner FP £9; also card. BB £21–24; lodge in grounds £17–18. SB winter. Shut 1 Dec–mid Jan.	2 m W Queensferry, Hopetoun House; truly splendid house, home of Hope family (Marquesses of Linlithgow). Built 1696, altered 1721 by William Adam and son Robert Adam; paintings include portraits by Van Dyck, Rembrandt, Canaletto. Grounds laid out like Versailles; fallow and red deer; rare St Kilda sheep; woodland and sea walks; lovely rose garden. Open 3 May–23 Sept pm, except Thurs, Fri.

Route 11

Chepstow – Brecon – Tenby – Pembroke – Aberystwyth – Llandrindod Wells – Hereford

Severn Bridge
Chepstow, B4235
Usk (12 m)

First Hurdle, 9 Upper Church St (tel 2189): owner was in wine trade, his wife cooked on TV; good wine list, imaginative cooking. Two cards: one grills, one French-style cooking (sensible idea). Lunch (roasts, chop steak) around £4; dinner card £3.50–7. Wines from £3.30. BB £7.50–8.

At Usk, Three Salmons, Bridge St (tel 2133): old inn where anglers gather, grown into rather pricey, fashionable hotel but good conversion. 28 of 31 bedrooms have bath or shower, TV, phone, teamaker. Dinner card around £9.50. House wine £4.40, good list; BB £13–19.50.

At Little Mill (towards Pontypool), Pentwyn Farm (tel Little Mill 249): 145-acre farm producing beef, corn, potatoes. Farm welcome, farm cooking. Sports and action within 5 m – canal cruising, reservoir sailing, fishing, swimming, squash, badminton, dry ski slope; and, of course, watching rugby. 16th-century farmhouse; outdoor heated pool; pretty bedrooms; views; bargain at £8.50 dinner plus BB. Bring own wine.

Chepstow. Normans built castle as base for advance into Welsh kingdom of Gwent (11th century). Spectacular pile on river Wye; lovely view from Castle Dell path leading from car park; overlooks river Wye (tidal here). Steep streets; famous racecourse.

Usk: on river Usk; angling centre, some of best salmon fishing in Britain. Recent excavations suggest Roman fort of Burrium was sited here; livestock market. Peaceful area.

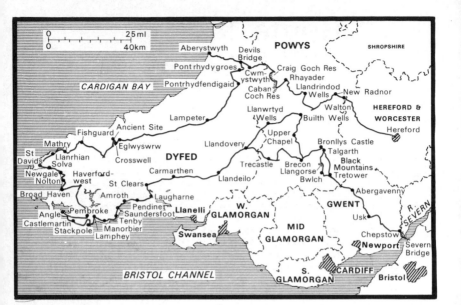

A471, A40
Abergavenny
(10 m)

Abergavenny Hotel, 21 Monmouth Rd (tel 3802): two chefs – Italian and Welsh. Home-made lasagne and cannelloni; Welsh lamb; lunch (including roast) £2.15; bar snacks, dinner card £6–9. BB £8–9.

Angel, Cross St (tel 2613): Trust House Forte, 'country kitchen' idea of various set dishes and menus. American style, with weights given of steak, even trout, lamb; chicken, not my kettle of scampi, may well suit 'plain eaters'. Nice friendly place with friendly manager. Beds £14–21; breakfast £1.75–3.25 extra.

Abergavenny: high hills to walk and climb, river Usk for fishing, canal nearby for cruising. Swimming pools, bowling green, pony trekking. Museum in 11th-century castle ruins includes beer mat signed by Rudolph Hess, Hitler's deputy, who flew over to Britain to talk peace in 1941, in hospital in Abergavenny 1942–5. Ruined castle had violent history; Norman, Braose, took it back, invited all Welsh chiefs to Christmas dinner and killed them while they were 'at meat'. Later got his own deserts from England's King John.

In 1215 Llewellyn, Welsh hero, took the castle; later it was knocked around during uprising of another Welsh hero Owen Glendower; but it took Cromwell – castle demolition expert – to destroy it.

(alternative 1 Abergavenny– Brecon) A465 Llanfihangel Crucorney B4423 left for mountain road to Gospel Pass through Llanthony, Capel y Ffin, Hay on Wye (15 m)

At Llanthony, Abbey Hotel (tel Crucorney 487): in part of old priory; dishes from Spain, Morocco, Mexico, Japan, Portugal on card. Wales offers Cawl Lafwr soup (seaweed and fish stock), local trout, Caerphilly turkey (with ham, Welsh cheese), vegetarian nut roast. Meals card around £6; shut Mon, Sun eve. BB £6–7.50. Shut Jan–Mar.

At Hay on Wye, Black Horse (tel 820841): Dorothy Adler, former civil service catering adviser, and her chef not only cook well but will show

Beautiful mountain run; we meet many of them on our two Welsh routes but this is outstanding. Not to be taken lightly in bad weather. If misty, there is little point in going this way, so take alternative 2 (page 202) through Llangorse.

Llanthony: pony-trekking centre, in Vale of Ewyas, farming land by river Honddu beside Black Mountains. Priory started here in 1108 by Hugh de Lacey, powerful lord of Hereford who decided suddenly to leave the rat race; took with him Henry I's

Hay on Wye
continued

you how to do it; courses in cookery, crafts, wine making, beauty care held periodically. Try salted duck cooked in cider, with cider, cream and onion sauce; lamb baked in pastry. Most comfortable hotel; partly 13th century; Cromwell slept here – a change from the Stuarts. One family room, 17th-century, has two extra beds in its gallery. Dinner card around £8; BB £10.30–15.67.

Effy's, Frank Lewis House (tel 820625): three girls run it: Ellie (actress, playwright), Helen (singer, pianist, Latin scholar), Neffy (artist, 'pleasure seeker – very single', she says); Effy's jams, chutneys much sought after. Salmon from Wye, lamb, pork from local farms, local game pie, coddled duck eggs. Open noon–midnight daily, but book. Lunch £4, dinner £7. Wines from £3.70 include La Clape '77 £4.

chaplain and the Constable of England. Walter Landor, the artist, bought it (1811). Prior's house now an inn.

Hay on Wye: market town, many narrow, winding streets; Lord Hereford's Knob (2263 ft) rises from Black Mountains to S, with Hay Bluff. River Wye dramatically rock-strewn here. Richard Booth's second-hand bookshop, started 1963, now second biggest in world, spread to old fire station and castle. All a stone's throw from English border. Hang gliding on Hay Bluff.

A438 Glasbury, Talgarth B4560 Llangorse, Bwlch small road back to Llangorse Lake (south side), joining A40 just before Brecon

At Glasbury, Three Cocks (tel Glasbury 215): varying reports of this famous inn, run when I last went by a member of French Hine brandy family, now by experienced hotel-keeper Barry Cole. Some amused, others not, by his party piece of reciting menu. Most comfortable, well-run hotel but my envoy disappointed with mallard duck dish 'too much thyme and skin, too little duck'. (Wild duck notoriously dodgy.) I shall try venison in damson wine sauce (sounds super!). Starters highly praised.

Glasbury: canoe hire on Wye (tel 210); big village on both sides of river.

Talgarth: small market town in lovely setting at foot of Black Mountains; Hywel Harris, a founder of Methodism, born here; after failing to get ordained in Church of England became wandering preacher. Set up communal farm and craft centre at nearby Trefecca. Died 1773.

Llangorse: 4 m round, second largest natural lake in Wales. Shallow reedy shoreline but superb for

Dinner card around £11.50, £9 with more limited choice. Good wine list. BB £10.50–12.

Old Barn Inn (tel Glasbury 215): new, in splendid old barn opened by Barry Cole opposite Three Cocks. Truly rural décor; good value meals and snacks. Beef 'n beer casserole, shepherd's pie, chicken in red wine. Play area (darts, pool), children's swings, etc; good non-alcoholic cocktails for drivers. Real ale; house wine £3.50. Meals card £3–6.

At Talgarth, just off A479 2 m, Penyrheol Farm (tel Talgarth 711409): Ann Powell is fully trained farmer, farming 135 acres (cattle, sheep). Cooks well – special dish Welsh lamb in Marsala wine. Dinner £3.50 good value; BB £5; DBB £8–8.50; children welcome (pony to ride); central heating.

Trewalter Farm (just off B4560 Talgarth-Llangorse) (tel Llangorse 662): glorious scenery, 1 m lake. 230 acres cattle, sheep, soft fruit; Wales Tourist Farm award. Children welcome but no pets. Open March–Dec. Home cooking. BB £6; DBB £9.

At Llangorse, Red Lion (tel 238): inn used by locals; good home cooking, imaginative use of vegetables, local trout; well-decorated bedrooms all with bath or shower, good value. Hot fresh bar snacks; dinner card around £7. BB £8.50–12.65. SB (2 nights).

sailing, canoeing, fishing, water skiing and caravans. Hamlets dotted around.

Bwlch: lovely views around village.

Brecon: surprising more people do not know it; cathedral city, beautiful, interesting. Set where Usk river meets Honddu. St John's priory church built 12th century, not made a cathedral until 1923. Early English choir and nave; side chapels dedicated to trade – tailors, weavers, tuckers, fullers, corvizors (shoemakers). Working at a trade in Wales is still a social asset, not a stigma, as in parts of England. Welsh snobberies are different. Wise people in Brecon – in war between Stuarts and Parliament, they wanted nothing to do with it, so they slighted (made ineffective) the castle so that neither Cromwell nor Charles I could use it; it wasn't Brecon's quarrel. Fine Georgian, Jacobean town houses (Sarah Siddons, the actress; John Aubrey, antiquarian; Hugh Price, founder of Jesus College, Oxford, lived in them). Calvinist Methodist chapel, seating 800, is attractive. Museum of South Wales Borderers regiment from 1689 to after 1945 (anti-terrorist campaigns in Malaya, Borneo); relics of many battles including 1879 Zulu War, defence of Rorke's Drift, when 9 of regiment won Victoria Cross in 24 hours.

Brecon
continued

Doorway to Brecon Beacons National Park, with high bald hills where sheep roam, thick forests planted recently, running waters rich in trout. Becon Y Gear, 5-acre Roman fort from AD 75; some walls clearly seen; garrisoned by Spanish cavalry; excavated 1924 by Sir Mortimer Wheeler, popularizer of 'digging' on TV.

Monmouth and Brecon Canal ends here; dug 1797–1812, it was neglected for years; now section Brecon-Monmouth restored for pleasure boats (for hire).

(alternative 2 Abergavenny–Brecon) A40 Bwlch, Llangorse Lake, Brecon (17 m)

White Swan, Llanfrynach (tel 276): near canal; casseroles, home-made country pies; meal card £6–8. Bar meals.

Main road, can get crowded.

---

from Brecon B4520 Upper Chapel B4519 left, left on small road to Llangammarch Wells, Llanwrtyd Wells (26 m)

At Llangammarch, Lake Hotel (tel 202): where river Irfon meets Gammarch; barium in the spring water made it once a thriving little spa for treating heart and rheumatic conditions; pump house fell into decay; this one hotel survived. New owners have modernized; anything could happen by the time you get there; steep 9–hole golf course in 45-acre grounds already in use; trout lake stocked with fish up to 6lb; tennis court, croquet lawn. Pump house due to offer spring water soon (and sauna, solarium); swimming pool planned. Bedrooms already have TV; hotel grounds a delight. Lunch FP £3.50; dinner FP £7.75; 5-course very good value. BB £9–15.50. SB off season.

Lovely views in good weather; artillery range warnings.

At Llanwrtyd Wells, Dol-y-Coed Hotel (tel 215): claims to be one of most beautifully situated hotels in Britain; even after touring Scotland, I agree. Beside river Irfon, quiet; free trout fishing for guests, also two rods on Wye. Log fires, home cooking, fine value. Meal plus cheese £5. BB £13.25; April, May, June DBB £13. Rooms with own bath extra.

Llanwrtyd Wells: in 1732 a frog was seen leaping about in strongly sulphurous waters; what was good for frogs was good for humans, so little spa was launched. Now lure is pony-trekking and gorgeous scenery around river Irfon.

A483 Llandovery (11 m) A40 Llangadog A4069 in 100 yd branch right on small road to Myddfai on the Plas Glasevin back on to A40 Llandeilo (12 m)

At Llandovery, Llwyncelyn Guest House (tel 20566): homely, comfortable; dinner £5.50; BB £7.50–9.

At Llangadog, Plas Glasevin (tel Llangadog 238): beautiful old house, comfortable; run by ex-TV producer (Cardiff) and wife who presents Welsh language programmes. They all speak English! Good cooking in either language, all fresh produce. Dinner FP £6; 5-course normal FP menu £9; house wine (own shipping Burgundy) £4.75/litre; Welsh nights: harp music, folk songs. Fun, good meal and wine £6.50. Nice grounds. BB £12–17.45; DBB £18–22.

At Llandeilo, Cawdor Arms (tel 823500): beautifully furnished, all bedrooms with bath, TV, phone, hairdrier; well run inevitably pricey; dinner FP £9, card £12, light lunch dishes £2–3.50. BB £17–22.

Plough, Rhosmean (on A40) (tel Llandeilo 823431): fresh Towy salmon, local trout, venison, jugged hare, wild duck in season. Italian management, so also excellent Italian dishes. Meals card £6–9. Shut Sun.

Llandovery: George Borrow author of *Wild Wales* (1862) thought it most pleasant town he had met; now market town with cobbled square; fishing.

Llandeilo: nice hilly town on river bank; Elizabethan poet Spenser in *Fairie Queene* put Merlin's cave in local hills. Merlin was born in Carmarthen (in Welsh, 'Merlin's City').

Dynevor Castle: same family held it from 9th century; ruins of original on cliff above river; present building 17th century.

B4350
Carmarthen
(15 m)

At Nantgaredig, Cothi Bridge Hotel (tel 251): on river banks; country hotel, lovely views, comfortable. Dinner FP £4.95, card £6.50. Wine from £3. BB £11–16. SB (weekends).

Carmarthen: some streets left from medieval days. Romans also occupied this site on River Towy, which is longest river in Wales (68 m). Dairy farming valley.

A40 St Clears
A4066
Laugharne
Pendine (23 m)

Laugharne (pronounced 'Larne'): in a little Georgian boathouse on a cliff walk near the castle lived Dylan Thomas. He is buried in the churchyard with a simple cross. He denied that Laugharne was the town of *Under Milk Wood* but local people give a dramatic performance of it every three years; charming place. Muddy foreshore. Ruined castle, mentioned in 1195; captured by Llewellyn 1215; captured in Civil War by General Laugharne, Parliamentarian who switched sides to fight for Charles I. Castle has gone, but the General is apparently still around; he rows himself naked across the river estuary, in a coracle using peaked hat as an oar. Even Dylan didn't do that.

Pendine Sands: 5 m stretch of sands between dunes and hills, now flanked by caravan sites. Here in 1924 Sir Malcolm Campbell broke world land speed record at 146.16mph. Then Parry Thomas was killed when his Leyland car Babs crashed, buried itself in the sand. It stayed there until 1969, then excavated for restoration. In 1933 that remarkable lady Amy Johnson flew from here solo across Atlantic.

A4066 Amroth,
Saundersfoot
Tenby (9 m)

At Saundersfoot, Glen Beach, Swallow Tree Rd (tel 813430): families welcome; cabaret room with entertainment; superb seafood (chef used to dive for shellfish). Dinner FP £5.25; card around £7 (lobster extra). BB from £10.50.

Royal Lion (tel 2127): 300 years old. fish, meat, veg fresh daily. 2-course FP lunch £2.75; dinner 4-course £5–6, also card. Good wine list from £3.49. BB £11–14; shut Nov–Apr.

Cambrian Hotel (tel 812448): fine position on quayside, views of bay, courtyard patio, beer garden, wine cellar bar; very nicely furnished, all bedrooms with bath, TV, teamaker; known for mini holidays, weekends, at special rates. Dinner card around £7. BB £14–18; DBB £18–22. SB.

Tenby has hotels of all shapes and sizes; popular resort:

Royal Gate House, White Lion St (tel 2255); big; fine views; four bars; dinner card. BB £7–17.

Imperial, Paragon (tel 3737): biggest, best known in Tenby; built into ancient walls; some bedrooms superb, all comfortable. Most furnished as bedsitters with balcony. All except two with private bath. Dinner 4-course FP £6.25; card £10. Good wine list. BB £14.50–22.50. DBB from £18.50. Shut Nov–Mar.

Amroth: sandy shore reached over bank of shingle; at low tide blackened stumps of prehistoric forest are seen. In 1943 beaches of Carmarthen Bay used for D-Day. Landing rehearsals for invasion of Europe. At Wiseman's Bridge, Gen. Eisenhower, Gen Montgomery and Winston Churchill met to watch manoeuvres.

Saundersfoot: attractive boating, fishing resort. Harbour packed with leisure craft in summer. Flanked by sand beaches, some shingle and rocks. Rocky to north; Saundersfoot late in becoming resort as, until recent years, coal boats used harbour and steam engines hauled trucks of anthracite across quay.

Tenby: old hideaway, has become very popular with help of motorways through England. Two beaches, yachting centre, sub-aqua school, water skiing; golf, sheltered harbour; secluded coves between cliffs northwards; town well protected, so warm sun-trap. Sand beaches south behind dunes. Maze of narrow streets in old town. St Catherine's Island now a zoo; Caldey Island, 2½ m offshore, frequent summer boats, has ancient Cistercian monastery; monks make perfume from island's flowers. Caravan parks have spread around this coast and Pembrokeshire – possibly too many, especially static sites.

A4139, B4585
Manorbier back
to A4139
Lamphey B5484
Freshwater East;
small road to
Stackpole on to
B4319 Angle
(23 m)

Manorbier: castle (1325) with church, moat, dovecote, ponds, mill; typical Norman barons' residence. Built by Gerald de Windsor (*not* Royal Family – different Windsor); he married Ness, so lovely she was called 'Helen of Troy of Wales' because her beauty caused bloodshed and hate between Normans and Welsh. She was abducted by Owain, son of Prince of Powys. One of her sons, Gerald of Wales became priest, went round Wales recruiting for the Crusades, wrote account of Wales invaluable to history. Castle open Apr-Sept. Manorbier has sand beach but also many caravans.

Lamphrey: Robert Devereux, Queen Elizabeth I's very own Earl of Essex, born in Bishops' Palace, spent boyhood here. Built mostly 13th/15th centuries, one of seven palaces of Bishops of St David. Neglected for centuries, restored gradually. Henry Earl of Richmond, stayed on way to Bosworth, battle which made him Henry VII of England.

Freshwater East: sandy beach backed by low dunes; caravans. Stackpole Quay, visited occasionally by small boats; reached only by path from village.

Angle: one-street village leads to muddy shingle beach in bay, but West Angle Bay is nice sandy cove, between cliffs, low-tide rock pools.

B4320 Pembroke
A4139 Cleddau
Bridge
Haverfordwest
(21 m)

At Haverfordwest, Pembroke House Hotel, Chez Gilbert Restaurant (tel 3652): Gilbert Lacroix, chef-patron, ran a restaurant in South France at 17, came to Britain as au pair, was chef to a peer and cooked for guests such as Royal Family, PM Macmillan and his shooting parties; now breeds horses and rabbits; cooks splendid classic French dishes plus a few 'façon Gilbert'. Italian spoken – and French. Dinner around £8; BB £12.50–15. SB good discounts.

Pembroke: mighty castle on ridge, with water on three sides; walls of keep 20 ft thick; Normans thought it impregnable; their base for invasion of Wales; Henry VII born here. Cromwell took it, dismantled defences. Pembroke is corruption of Welsh word 'Penfro' – 'land's end'; Normans, English and Flemish weavers settled so area called 'Little England Beyond Wales'. Home of families such as Meyricks and Owens. Pembroke has two 13th-century churches on its main street.

B4341 Broad
Haven small
road to Nolton
Haven, Newgale,
A847 Solva, St
Davids (22 m)

At Croesgoch, off A487, 6m from St Davids; Trearched Farm (tel Croesgoch 310): 139-acre arable farm; 8 bedrooms; garden games for children; children's

Series of sandy beaches along this coast, flanked by cliffs, many with streams beside beach. Broad Haven most popular; Druidston beach reached by steep track

St Davids
continued

reductions when sharing parents' room. BB £5.20–6; DBB £8.63–9.50. SB (autumn, spring). Unlicensed.

Druidston, Druidston Haven (tel Broad Haven 221): clifftop, small hotel in 20 acres above sand beach reached by steep paths (for fit people only). Interesting cooking but meals a little pricey. Dinner around £8.50; wines from £3.58. BB £12. Closed Nov.

At St Davids, Grove, High St (tel 720341): perfect Regency house in local stone, a joy to look at; country cooking using local sea and land food, some home-produced, Family run. Dinner £5.75; house wine £3.15; BB £9.50–16.

Old Cross, Cross Square (tel 387): charming 18th-century house, very good value; splendid fish, including lobster; all bedrooms with bath, teamakers. Dinner FP £5.30, card around £7. BB £9.75–16.50.

St Nons (tel 720239): nice hotel. All bedrooms have bath; David Burns cooks very well, local fish, crab, lobster; buffet lunch £3.15, dinner FP £7.50, card £10. BB £13–17. SB out of season. St Non was St David's Mum.

Whitesands Bay Hotel (tel St Davids 403): on headland, very good value. Good cooking, try lettuce soup, stuffed pork with walnuts in pastry. Child listening, launderette, drying room. Some bedrooms in annexe 500 yd from hotel. Bar lunches, dinner, residents' FP £5; FP general £7.50. BB £12–13.50.

(surfing); Nolton Haven has nice beach but bathing dangerous when ebb tide halfway out; Newgale for surfers; boards for hire. Solva in fjord-like creek between steep green slopes; boating centre.

St Davids: named for patron saint of Wales; Britain's smallest city. St David born AD 530. Cathedral built in valley so that marauders could not spot it from sea. Top of tower can be seen from city square; not an exciting place except to a Welshman, to whom it is a holy city. Second to Rome for British pilgrims until the death of Becket made Canterbury the holy shrine. Not beautiful, this area, but captivating, with soft high light and long, spectacular sunsets. Great coastal park runs either way from Whitesands Bay with fine seascapes and coastal scenes.

A487 Llanrhian, Mathry, Fishguard (17 m)

At Fishguard, Bistro and Compton House Hotel (tel 873365): attractive; dishes with a difference (Welsh lamb steak in juniper); dinner card around £8.50; house wine £3.95/litre (Nicolas); BB £9.

Fishguard: Lower Town is old fishing village; small harbour, rows of cottages, steep headland; zig-zag paths down to rocky coves. Dylan Thomas's *Under Milk Wood* filmed at Lower Town in 1971. Royal Oak Inn on square recalls splendid military fiasco when Irish-American Tait, with expeditionary force of French and Irish ex-convicts, landed with help of French fleet in 1797 to take Bristol, but seasickness in foul weather landed him at Fishguard where they mistook a group of Welsh girls in red cloaks and tall hats for guardsmen and surrendered at Royal Oak. In churchyard is memorial to Jemina Nicholson, lady who captured a lot of Frenchmen by threatening them with a pitchfork: last foreign invasion on British soil. Scot Paul Jones from Dumfries, privateer and 'Father of American Navy', landed during War of Independence and got away with ransom. Local girls must have had an off-day!

B4313 for 5 m, small road left through gorge, rejoining B4313 to New Inn left on B4329 small road left to Pentre Ifan back on to B4313 at Crosswell right on A487 to Eglwyswr (18 m) A487 Cardigan A484 Llechryd, Genarth to Newcastle Emplyn A475 Lampeter (38 m)

At Eglwyswr, Serjeants Inn (tel Crosswell 271): handsome village inn; home cooking; dinner around £5; BB £7–7.50.

4 m W Eglwyswr, at Boncath, Pantyderi Farm (tel Boncath 227): Jones family work 500-acre farm and run guest house. Lovely 16th-century house; swimming pool; bar; trout lake and 1 m river fishing. Trekking centre with 800 acres riding land. Also self-catering cottages. Dinner FP £3.50; BB £7. A bargain – nearly kept it to ourselves!

At Cenarth, Coracle Café: Fresh salmon sandwiches with home-made bread, delicious.

At Newcastle Emlyn, Emlyn Arms (tel 710317), overlooks lovely Teifi river; modernized 18th-century coaching inn; trout and salmon – to catch and eat. Meals FP £4–5.50; card from £6.30; house wine £3.30; BB £10.50–18.25. SB (many, including fishing weekends).

Good views.

Pentre Ifan: Stone Age burial chamber built 2000 BC; huge capstone weighing about twenty tons supported by four upright stones.

Eglwyswr: St Wrw buried in chantry chapel in Tudor times; people would not allow anyone else to be buried there because she was a virgin and would not want bedfellows; attractive village.

2 m right off A487, just over A478 is Cilgerran Castle, in ruins. Painting of it by Turner in Tate Gallery, London. Here on river Teifi and at Llechryd, coracles used for salmon fishing; boats like ancient Britons used made of hides stretched over wickerwork frame; treated with pitch, propelled by single paddle.

Cardigan: quiet market town in estuary; port until silting-up; great salmon, trout fishing; old seven-arched bridge; covered market; wildlife park, of local animals; river cruises from Prince of Wales Quay. Superb scenery in this area. Teifi is lovely river.

Llechryd: coracles still made here; old nine-arched bridge over Teifi; nice older houses.

Cenarth: Teifi flows through woods, then in small rapids where you can see salmon jumping to reach spawning grounds in season; watermill. Fishing museum; art gallery – Welsh artists – open Easter–Oct.

Newcastle Emlyn: market town in double loop of meandering Teifi river. Splendid fishing. Ruined fortress knocked down and rebuilt several times over centuries until Cromwell's troops finished it off. Detour 3 m along B4334 (Henllam road) to woollen industry museum (Drefach Felindre; open Apr-Sept except Sun).

Lampeter: several valleys meet by Teifi; once famous horse fair but now lively market. St David's College, founded 1822, to help boys who could not afford Oxford or Cambridge to become Anglican clergy.

B4343 Tregaron,
Pontrhydfendigaid,
Pontrhydygroes,
Devil's Bridge
(30 m)

Tregaron: George Borrow in *Wild Wales*, also author of *The Bible in Spain*, thought this town set against dark mountains looked like scene from Andalucia. He stayed at Talbot Inn. Tranquil country until near Devil's Bridge, one of Wales's most popular tourist sights.

At Pontrhydfendigaid: ruins of abbey (Strata Florida) built 12th/13th centuries.

At Pontryhydygroes: Hafod estate (Forestry Commission), 18th-century mansion with priceless collection rare books, and two million trees round it, planted by William Jones. In 1807 fire destroyed mansion and books.

Devil's Bridge: Devil built first bridge in 12th century; it spans deep, rocky, thickly wooded gorge of river Mynach near where it meets river Rheidol; second bridge

Devil's Bridge
continued

built on top of that in early 18th century; third metal bridge built 1901; all still here. Gorge 500 ft deep, Mynach falls 300 feet to meet spectacular falls of Rheidol. You can see it from road bridge, but better from the bottom; 91 ft zigzag descent; viewing platform down there for five separate falls. Devil, it seems, met a girl, Megan, whose cow had somehow got over the ravine; offered to throw a bridge across for her on condition that he could have first living creature to cross it; thought she would rush across for her cow. But she threw a crust across first and a poor hungry dog dashed across bridge to get it. Not a very *British* act, but she was saved. Devil's Bridge is terminus of Vale of Rheidol Railway to Aberystwyth – 12 miles through magnificent scenery, climbing to 600 ft narrow gauge, pulled by British Rail's last steam locos.

B4120
Aberystwyth
(11 m)

Aberystwyth – resort; accommodation of all sorts. Information Centre at Eastgate has bed booking service (tel 612125):

Belle Vue Royal, Marine Terrace (tel 617558): 150 years old, same family ownership as Edwardian Metropole. Fair value. Welsh chef; local fish, traditional Welsh dishes; lunch FP £3, dinner FP £6.25, card £7–10; interesting wines; BB £12.25–14.

Cambrian Hotel, Alexandra Rd (tel 2446): useful; value;

Like most university towns, Aberystwyth seems eternally young; oldest part of university is Victorian Gothic building on promenade, because it was built as hotel. Railway pioneer Thomas Savin built it, intending to give week's free holiday there to anyone buying return ticket from London – the spirit of Freddie Laker, but Savin's scheme never got off the ground. Prince Charles studied at university here, 1969. In university is Welsh Plant Breeding station, producing strains of cereal

bar meals, dinner FP (roasts) £4.50, card £6–7 (Thur, Fri, Sat).

Julia's, 17 Bridge St (tel 617090): one of several interesting restaurants in Aberystwyth. Ambitious and good cooking; try guinea fowl in red wine with cassis and cream. Lightish lunches up to £5; dinner FP 5-course French provincial cooking £8.25; card around £10 with wine. Simple but sensible wine list; house wine £3.95. Shut Sun, Mon.

Caprice, 8 North Parade (tel 612084): cheap, good value. Nice crab salads. Lunch FP £3; dinner FP £3.75; card, main dish £2–4. Wines £3.45. Shut Sun, Weds; winter evenings.

and grass; much seed exported.

N on Penglas Hill is Welsh National Library, around six million books including oldest Welsh manuscript; castle built 1277, now ruin laid out as gardens with view over Cardigan Bay. Better view from top of funicular at end of promenade.

A44 Ponterwyd, A4120 Devil's Bridge B4574 Cwm Ystwyth Drovers Road to Elwan Valley right Craig Coch Reservoir, Caban Coch Reservoir B4518 Rhayader (42 m)

Old Drovers Road, narrow, with passing places, through Abergwesyn Pass (if winter conditions bad, go long way round from Aberystwyth on A44). Elwan valley: five dams built of stone 1904, forming four main lakes, reservoirs supplying Birmingham. Hold 21,780 million gallons. Trout fishing, but no sailing or water sports allowed. Drovers' Road one of most spectacular in Britain; used 18th-19th century by drovers taking cattle to London, Midlands. Climbs to 1600 ft, gradients 1 in 4; descends into three-river valley; some scenery like desert.

Rhayadar: reservoirs as lakes, river Wye and other streams full of fish have turned little market town into holiday area; hills around with paths for walking, pony trekking. Pretty town centre.

| A44 right on A483 Llandrindod Wells (11 m) | Griffin Lodge, Temple St (tel Llandrindod Wells 2432): nice little hotel run by two former civil servants; friendly, good plain cooking in residents' menu, more elaborate 4-course menu. Dinner FP 3-course £4.50; FP 4-course £5.50. BB £7.50–8.50. | Llandrindod Wells: attractive as a spa, once a leading resort of Britain. Charles II first popularized it. 700 ft up, it has wide streets, pleasant 19th-century houses. Modern treatment at Rock Park baths. Interesting museum includes world collection of dolls; fine collection of old bikes and trikes back to 1850s. |
| A483 Crossgates, A481, to A44 turn right through New Radnor Walton over English border Kington A411, A438 Hereford (41 m) | | At Crossgates, Guidfa Guest House (tel Penybont 241): family atmosphere in house owned by former domestic science teacher with four children; AA Best Guest House award 1979. Real country cooking. Wine cheap. You are a house guest here. Dinner FP £4. BB £7–8. |

Route 12

**Leominster – Aberystwyth (meets Route 11) –
Dolgellau – Llanberis – Anglesey – Denbigh –
Llangollen – Leominster**

Leominster
(pronounced
Lemster)

Strasbatch Farm (tel
Leominster 2673): lovely
14th-century black-and-white
farmhouse; sheep, horse
stud; heated pool. river;
rooms with bath. BB £6.50–7.

Royal Oak, South St (tel
2610): old coaching inn;
serves prime Hereford beef,
venison in red wine, honey
roast duck; good hotel bar
meals; dinner card £7.50.
Wines reasonable; French
house wine £3.30. BB £11–
13.50.

In England; hops, wool,
apples, cider; Hereford cattle
(still exported) helped to
improve beef all over the
world. Monks of Leominster
bred Rylands sheep 600
years ago, famous for wool;
exported to Australia, New
Zealand, South America.

A44, right on
A4110, left on
B4362 Presteigne
(14 m)

Bull Hotel (tel Presteigne
488): owner-chef Dunkirk
veteran, ex Trust House Forte
manager. Inn is 400 yd from
England. All bedrooms have
shower, central heating.
Dinner FP £4.75; card from
£6. BB £9.25–12.50.

Radnorshire Arms (tel
Presteigne 406): historic
black-and-white house, once
home of Christopher Hatton,
one of Elizabeth I's
favourites. Inn since 1792;
priesthole found 1875 with
diary (since lost) of RC priest
hidden there for two years.
Hot bar meals around £2.80,
lunch FP £3.75, dinner FP
£3.95; BB £16–22.75; SB
Trust House Forte.

On Wales–England border:
boundary is river Lugg.
Presteigne is smallest county
assize town in England and
Wales. Gentle hill walking up
to 1000 ft, pony trekking.
Black-and-white timbered
houses; once had 30 inns.
Curfew still rings at 8pm but
not enforced! Gruesome
story on tombstone of
servant girl hanged in 1805
for murdering her baby; the
father who had persuaded
her to do it sat on jury which
condemned her.

A4355 Knighton,
B4346 Llanbister,
A483 Llananno,
small road W to
Pantydwr, B4518
Llanidloes (34 m)

At Knighton, Heartease Farm (tel Bucknell 220): pleasant, friendly; farmhouse cooking – Welsh lamb. BB from £7; DBB from £12. Shut 1 Nov–1 Apr.

At Llanidloes, Trewythen Arms (tel 2214): during 1839 Chartist riots, police from London billeted here; local Chartists stormed it, took three policemen hostage, plus an ex-mayor, defied attempts by 50 other police to dislodge them. Now a friendly, peaceful place. Local lamb, steak and kidney pie; dinner FP £4.50. BB £8–10. SB.

Knighton: lovely little town seemingly hanging from hillside in Teme valley. High hills around; lovely walks. Offa's Dyke, built by Offa, King of Mercia, AD 748 to mark Wales–England boundary and keep Welsh in Wales, runs alongside town; ditch, earth bank 30 ft high. Splendid Victorian Gothic railway station.

Llanbister: known for unusual church with total-immersion baptistry and for old family argument of the Vaughans in 15th century. John killed David; David's sister Ellin dressed as a man, went to Llanbister archery contest, missed the target and shot John dead – bullseye!

Llanidloes: town of character; lovely 1609 half-timbered market hall, arcaded; many uses in its time from local lock-up to Quaker meeting house, workingmen's club, library. Shop fronts showing symbols of trades. River Severn (source 8 m E) meets river Clywedog under bridge.

| A470, A44 Dyffryn Castell, A4120 Devil's Bridge, Aberystwyth (35 m) | Devil's Bridge, Aberystwyth – see Route 11. | Dyffryn Castell is usual starting point for ascent of Plynlimon Hills, 2469 ft, for sources of Severn and Wye rivers.

Devil's Bridge, Aberystwyth – see Route 11.

Route meets Route 11 here. |
| A487 Talybont, Machynlleth (18 m) | At Machynlleth, Wynnstay Hotel, Maengwyn St (tel 2289): once home of Wynn family, now unpretentious Trust House Forte hotel; dinner FP £5.75; card £6.50–10. BB £11–20. | Machynlleth: charming town; at meeting place of several old coach roads, once had 24 inns and big sheep trading centre; before that Owen Glendower crowned Prince of Wales here in 1404. Brother-in-law David tried to kill him; Owen forgave him and he lived to become hero of Agincourt. Now inns fill with anglers fishing river Dovey for salmon and sea trout. |
| A493 Pennal, road right through Happy Valley A493 Tywyn (14 m) | At Pennal, Llugwy Hall (tel Pennal 228): in 40 acres, gardens to banks of Dovey; all bedrooms with bathrooms; lamb, game in season, crab, prawns – all local; dinner from £7.50; BB £12–18. | Tywyn, once called Towyn, changed to avoid confusion with other Towyn. Talyllyn narrow gauge railway runs from here to Abergyndwyn. Run since 1866, steam; lovely scenery. Town flanked by Cader Idris mountain. Too |

At Talyllyn, Tynycornel Hotel (tel Abergynolwyn 282): 56 years in same family; owns Lake Talyllyn; trout fishing reserved for hotel guests; boats, dinghy sailing, windsurfing, canoeing, tuition, courses. Magnificent scenery. Lunch around £3, dinner FP £6.50, card £7–8. BB £13–17.

many caravan sites; crowds in little resort in summer.

A493, B4405, Abergynolwyn, A487 Dolgellau (19 m).

At Dolgellau, Golden Lion, (tel 422579): said to have been Wordsworth who wrote 200 years ago: 'If ever you go to Dolgelley/Don't stay at the Lion Hotel/There's nothing to put in your belly/ And no one to answer the bell'. The Halls, whose family have had the Lion since 1926, and chef John Riley, here 22 years, have succeeded. Mind you, there are teasmade machines in the bedrooms, but I prefer real maids. A good inn. Meals card from £5, average £7; 48 wines £4– 14. BB £12.50–21. SB.

Glyn Farm Guest House (tel 286): two farms, total 710 acres; Welsh mountain sheep, Black cattle; own trout fishing; 300-year-old house, low beams, during dry spells (they have them in Wales) baths may have to be limited. Simple traditional meals of lamb, beef etc. Dinner £3; BB £5.50.

La Petite Auberge, Smithfield St (tel 870): I have not tried it but envoy reports good, genuine French cooking, especially trout and turbot dishes. Dinner card around £7.50. Wines good but not cheap. Shut Sun.

Dolgoch Falls; 125 ft fall, splendid.

Abergynolwyn: mountain terminus of Talyllyn railway; Lake Talyllyn 3 m along B4405; Cader Idris (2927 ft) to north. Myth says anyone who sleeps on mountain will wake blind, mad or a poet. Name means 'Chair of Idris' or 'Arthur's Seat'.

Dolgellau (Dolgelley when I was young): rather sombre-looking town of dark local slate; Welsh speaking; for fit walkers with five paths to peak of Cader Idris, and famous Precipice Walk circling high ridge 2 m N; through woodlands, meadows; fine views of Cambrian mountains. Owen Glendower assembled Welsh Parliament here, signed alliance with French.

Bontddu: village produces the gold for royal wedding rings, including those of Queen and Princess of Wales.

Dolgellau
continued

At Bontddu on A496 W,
Bontddu Hall (tel Bontddu
661): luxury hotel, yet
reasonable prices. One of the
best in Wales. Beautifully
furnished, attractive garden,
superb views. Fine cooking;
try Welsh lamb with cider
and rosemary sauce, local
salmon in pastry with lobster
sauce, crail stuffed with
pâté in pastry, Madeira
sauce. 'Eat and Eat' lunch
buffet FP £3.95; bistro dinner
FP £7.50; gourmet dinner FP
5-course £10.50 (lobster,
game). BB £7.50–18. SB.

Gwernan Lake Hotel (tel
Dolgellau 288): guests say
it's unique – Austrian
gasthaus, Scottish fishing
inn, French family hotel
rolled into one in lovely
Welsh mountain scenery by
lake. Isolated, with all you
need except showgirls. Very
good cooking. Dinner £7.40;
BB £10.50–11.50. SB. Shut
mid Oct–Easter.

A470 Ffestiniog
Betws-y-Coed
(32 m)

At Betws-y-Coed, Old Court House (tel 534): all court houses should undergo same conversion! Where prisoners stood in fear and magistrates handed out sentences is delightful split-level dining room where Joan Smart artist-chef provides cooking and décor. Very good value; dinner FP 4-course £4.75, good sweets; house wine £2.40. BB £6.50–10.

Craig y Dderwen (tel 293): lovely stone-built house overlooking river Lledr. Well furnished; all bedrooms with bath, TV, teamaker; family run; excellent food – local trout, salmon, game (some from own shoot). Fishing, pony trekking, Outstanding hotel. Lunch from £4.50 (also bar meals), dinner from £6. House wine £2.25. BB from £10. SB.

Park Hill Hotel, Llandrwst Rd (tel 540): attractive little Victorian house, lovely views, pleasant décor; delicious food (try jugged hare, pheasant dishes); dinner FP £5; wines from £3.15; BB £9.50–11.50.

Gwydyr Hotel (tel 217): enlarged when railway came (100 years ago); in the same family 150 years; remarkable value, owns exclusive fishing rights over 15 m rivers and some lake. Salmon expensive, of course (£14.50 a day; £60 a week); trout fishing reasonable. Comfortable hotel, homely atmosphere, fine plain cooking; lunch card around £2.50, dinner FP 4-course £5, wines £4.20–6.80; BB £9.25–10.25.

Festiniog: local bard in time of Owen Glendower, Red Rhys of Snowdon, wrote songs calling for extermination of the English. Many have done the same, from Bruce to Napoleon, Philip of Spain to Hitler. We're still not exterminated. Many strange stories of warfare and love, bloody raids and retribution, about this beautiful valley. Blaenau Festiniog, nearby, has famous slate quarries. Cynfal waterfalls below Festiniog (spectacular; 300 ft); nuclear power station S, with cooling-water lake excellent for fishing (trout, perch); visits possible to station (tel 076 687 331).

Ffestiniog Railway (built 1836 to service slate quarries) runs from 3 m W of town to Porthmadoc Harbour. At Blaenau tour by loco-pulled train into Llechwedd quarry in which 19th-century slate-quarry workings reconstructed; very interesting. Nearby Gladfa Ganol Mountain Centre; mountain of slate, part of 42 m of tunnels, is museum and gallery; you can split slate, take panoramic walks, see grotto; restaurant.

Betws-y-Coed: very beautiful narrow wooded valley; too many people midsummer. Painter David Cox popularized it with Victorians; three rivers meet – Conway, Lledr, Llugwy; superb waterfalls, especially Swallow; attractive bridges.

A470 Capel Curig, A4086 Llanberis, Caernarvon, A487 Menai Bridge to Anglesey (34 m)

At Capel Curig, Bryn Tyrch Hotel (tel 223): two ex Trust House Forte managers, one from Grosvenor, Park Lane, run comfortable hotel efficiently. Bar snacks. Dinner FP £5.50. House wine £3.25. BB £9.75–10.75.

At Llanberis, Royal Victoria (tel 253): good plain cooking, value; but in view of hotel's name, surprising that owner speaks of 'traditional Welsh fare' – roast beef, Norfolk turkey, grapefruit Florida, grilled gammon, fried scampi! Dinner FP £5.40; BB £11.65; SB.

Gallt y Glyn (tel Llanberis 370): for climbers and families; in grounds is 'bunk house' with own wc, shower, sleeps 6; give children bunk-house freedom while you sleep in comfort in hotel. Dinner FP £5.50 (good value); card around £7.50. Fair list 50 wines from £3.30. BB £11–13.50. DBB £15.50–18. SB

At Caernarvon Muriau Park Hotel, South Rd (tel 4647): useful, reasonable prices; Spanish chef. Meals, card £2–6; BB £7.50–8.50.

Black Boy, North Gate St (tel 3604): home cooking; lunch FP (good value, choice of roasts) £3; dinner FP £5 (good choice, usually with trout, sometimes salmon); BB £7.50–9.75.

Menai Bank Hotel, North Rd, (tel 3297); friendly, comfortable, family run. Dinner FP £4.25; wine £2.75–4.50; BB £7.80–8.60.

Capel Curig: heart of Snowdonia National Park. Ringed by mountains of Snowdon range; climbing, fishing centre. Plas y Brenin (National Mountaineering Centre) near village. 4 m along Bangor road, short mountain path leads to Idwal National Nature Reserve. At Pen-y-Gwyrd on Llanberis road: inn used by Hunt's and Hilary's team practising for Everest ascent in 1953.

Llanberis: small village; walking, climbing centre – Llanberis Pass, Snowdon. Easiest walk up Snowdon to summit (3½ m, 3560 ft) starts here, or easier still by train – Snowdon Mountain Railway (1896); 5 m winding track along precipice, return trip 2 hours. Other routes up Snowdon of varying difficulty, some for good climbers only; three go from Llanberis Pass, of which easiest is miners' track following cart tracks made when copper mines worked. Check before you go on any route, even easiest, for weather prospects, and leave message at hotel or in car about route and time you left.

Two lakes by Llanberis: Padarn, Peris, jumping with trout. Flat railway from old Donorwic quarries by Lake Padarn. Narrow gauge, steam; two lakeside stopping places for picnics or exploration.

Caernarvon (or with 'f'): castle and town founded by Edward I 1283 after defeat of Welsh princes. His son, born here, presented to Welsh as Prince of Wales. Owen Glendower, who called himself Prince of Wales, attacked it unsuccessfully twice (1403–4). Prince Charles invested as Prince of Wales here 1969 – still called 'foreign prince' by Welsh nationalists. Superb castle, open to public. Roman settlement AD 78; legend says Emperor Maximus met world's most beautiful woman Helen here and married her. Opposite castle, statue of Lloyd George, Prime Minister and MP for Caernarvon for 50 years – gesticulating, of course!

Anglesey – A545 Beaumaris, B5109 Pentreath, A5025 Benllech, Amlwch, Valley y Fal, A5 Holyhead (41 m)

At Beaumaris, Henllys Hall (tel 810412): I have not, alas, been to Val Williams' 'monkery' but my Welsh spy thinks very well of it, so do BBC viewers. 40-acre estate; manor house was Franciscan monastery for 20 years. Beautifully organized now, with swimming pool, 'health place' (sauna, sunbeds, steam bath, massage); children's dinner menu; sea fishing; some entertainment, dances. All dishes home made; local fish. Dinner card £4–7; FP 4-course £6; BB from £10.

Wern Y Wylan, 4 m from Beaumaris (tel Beaumaris 810398): in beautiful isolated spot on small hill over sandy beach; Cdr Hamilton Ridler and family run pleasant little restaurant with flats and

Menai Bridge: Museum of Childhood; fascinating one-man collection of old toys; alas, I'm old enough to remember some as new toys. Some still play tunes. Bridge 155 years old; great tribute to Telford, world's greatest bridgebuilder, son of a Scots shepherd with little academic training.

Beaumaris: named in Norman-French personally by Edward I, who built castle there; was masterpiece of military architecture; it was never used for fighting. Beaumaris is pleasant tiny resort, some sand at low tide; yachting centre. Gaol of 1829, including last punishment treadmill used in Britain and condemned cell, is tourist attraction.

Anglesey
continued

suites (all with kitchenettes). Meals average £6; flats sleep 1–6; from £7/night per person. Restaurant shut Sun.

At Benllech, Bay Court, Beach Rd (tel 2573): bright, modern, good service; horse riding opposite; fishing, golf, nearby. Dinner FP £4.50; card around £5. BB £11–14.

Hafod Wyn, Tyngongl (tel 2357): good value; family run, plain cooking; early 4-course dinner £4; dinner card £3.50–5.50. BB £8–9.50. SB.

Benllech: little resort with long sandy beach to Red Wharf Bay; 4 sq m of sand at low tide, but watch incoming tide – rapid. Red Wharf was shipbuilding village.

Holyhead: on Holy Island, joined to Anglesey by causeway; port for car ferries to Ireland. Sailing, including navigation school for yachtsmen. In 2000 BC boats from Ireland brought axes; 1500 BC Irish gold landed. Zigzag path of 360 steps down to bridge across to rocky isle of South Stack, with lighthouse, ledges where seabirds breed, caves where seals live. North Stack has caverns, one with 70 ft arch called Parliament because of continuous chatter of birds in summer.

B4545 Trearddur Bay, Valley y Fal, right on A5, A4080 Rhosneigr, Aberffraw, Mallreath, Newborough, Plas Newydd, Llanfair PG Menai Bridge (39 m)

Trearddur Bay Hotel (tel 0407): most pleasant hotel, handsome building, comfortable; linked to sailing club. Next to beach; good views. Lunch FP £4; dinner FP £6.60; BB £15.50–26. SB.

At Rhosneigr, Maelog Lake Hotel (tel 810204): pleasant inn, nice position; meal from £4.60; BB £8.

Dolphin, Morfa Hill (tel 810302): not cheap but excellent cooking; chef trained at Tante Marie school. Good sauces, sweets. Dinner £8. Wines fair prices; shut Sun.

Trearddur Bay: two beaches, secluded coves, sailing; pleasant place except for jets from RAF Valley nearby flying low; necessary but noisy.

Rhosneigr: over 3 m sands, rock outcrops make sheltered coves.

Aberffraw: cluster of houses, where in 5th century Britons rallied to fight Saxons. In AD 870 Rhoderick made village capital of North Wales kingdom, remained so until Llewellyn the Last died in 1282. More sandy coves.

Newborough Warren: nature reserve; one of Britain's biggest stretches of sand dunes. Farmland and port until 14th-century storms swept sand over it; wild flowers include orchids, wild thyme, dune pansies.

Plas Newydd: Marquis of Anglesey's superb 18th-century home, gardens, park, woodlands, bordering Menai Strait; family still live there; many splendid military historical mementoes; huge wall painting of Battle of Waterloo where first Marquis led cavalry. Better still is mural in dining room by Rex Whistler. Open April–Oct.

Llanfair PG = Llanfairpwllgyngyllgogerych wyrndrobwllllantysiliogogogo ch, name of the village, written on its station name board in full.

A5 Bangor, Tal-y-Bont, A55 Conway (16 m)		

A5 Bangor, Tal-y-Bont, A55 Conway (16 m)

At Conway, Castle, High St (tel 2324): two old inns joined; alas, Victorians gave it red-brick front in 1885, also large murals with Shakespearean themes by Dawson Watson. Good antique Welsh furniture, china in public rooms; Trust House Forte. Dinner FP £6; also card. Room only £14–20 per person (breakfast extra). DBB £18.50 (2 nights or more).

Alfredo's, Lancaster Sq (tel 2381): Italian-owned restaurant; fine Italian cooking, plus English dishes. Home-made pizza in another world from usual British frozen or boxed. Home-made pasta; try cannelloni Romana (filled with cream cheese, ham, beef, spinach, topped with wine, cheese sauce). Lunch FP £3.25 (roasts); dinner FP 4-course £7.50; also card.

A5 desperately crowded on this stretch in summer, but no reasonable alternative to Bangor.

Bangor: Bishop's Garden, by cathedral, contains Bible Garden with every flower, shrub, tree mentioned in Bible. Town a maze of little old streets, difficult for traffic.

Penrhyn Castle (just off A5): built 1827 in new Norman style; lovely gardens, woods; collection 1000 dolls; industrial railway museum (old locos); stuffed birds, animals; open Easter–Oct.

Conway: most Welsh now call it 'Conwy' but I use old form because we backward English, Scots, Americans know it by that name. I shall be in trouble with Welsh, majority of my Welsh friends know little Welsh – about enough to sing the national anthem at rugby internationals.

Conway
continued

Conway Castle best known of Edward I's string of castles across North Wales. He was glad of it when in 1294 Welsh rebels took Caernarvon castle and he fled here to withstand a siege. Possible to walk ½ m round its 15 ft thick walls, with eight drum towers, 21 half-circle towers. Telford's superb suspension bridge blends beautifully. Robert Stephenson built tubular bridge 1822; road bridge built 1958.

Aberconway House, Castle St: 14th-century timber-framed with town history exhibition back to Roman times; open Apr-end Sept. Plas Mawr, High St: one of best Elizabethan town houses in Britain; wonderful banquet hall 1580; home of Royal Cambrian Academy of Art.

A470 Bodnant Gardens (6 m)

Two Tal-y-Bont within few miles; this one on B5106, 2 m SE of Bodnant Gardens – The Lodge, Tal-y-Bont, Conway (tel Dolgarrog 534): useful comfortable modern motel; baths to all bedrooms; traditional cooking; fresh local fish, meat, most veg from own garden. Dinner: resident's FP £6; FP 4-course £7.95; card around £8–9. BB £12.50–15; DBB £17.50 (2 days min).

Bodnant Gardens: among finest in Britain; 120 acres, magnificent camelias, magnolias, rhododendrons, trees; lovely views of Snowdonia. Superb terraces, little bridges, old mill and pond. Incredible care taken over every plant; every rhododendron flower picked off by hand to stop seeding! Incredible displays of colour; remarkable laburnum arched 'tunnel' over road. Started 1875 by Henry Pochin, ancestor of Lord Aberconway; now National Trust but family still care for it; open mid Mar-end Oct.

---

local roads S
Eglwys Bach,
Llanddoged join
A548 left, right
on B5382
Denbigh (27 m)

Llanddoged: lovely views from village over Conway Valley; nice church with two-deck pulpit; sacred well called Ffynnon Ddoget.

Denbigh: 467 ft above Clwd Valley; delightful town; castle, 1282, with museum honouring explorer Stanley, who found Dr Livingstone in Africa ('Dr Livingstone, I presume?'). Born below castle wall, real name John Rowlands; workhouse as a boy, rebelled, ran away to sea; became reporter with *New York Herald*, which sent him to find Livingstone. Stanley got a knighthood.

A525 Ruthin,
A525, A542
Llangollen
(25 m)

Ruthin Castle Hotel (tel Ruthin 2664): this is the medieval castle, with modern plumbing, and the old inn; a proper way to absorb history. Fine grounds. Old medieval banquet hall; Britain's original; £7.50 (4-course with wine); more modern meals in dining room: lunch £3.95; dinner FP 4-course £6.50 (very good); also card; wines from £3.50. BB £16.50–18.50.

At Llangollen, Chain Bridge Hotel (tel 860215): alongside river; specializes in luscious salmon. Meals from £5.50; wine from £3.28. BB £11–16.

At Rhewl, NE Llangollen, Rhydonnen Ucha (tel Llangollen 860153): pleasant farmhouse; BB £5.50–7; DBB £8.50–10. Shut end Oct–Easter.

Gales Wine Bar, 18 Bridge St (tel 860089): meals £3.50; wines from £2.95; 150 wines available; BB £6. Shut Sun, Mon end Oct–start June.

Ruthin: delightful town; castle was medieval fortress taken over by Edward I; now hotel. Many timber-framed buildings: Myddleton Arms is 500-year-old inn. In 14th-century Church of St Peter is carved oak panel presented by Henry VII to Welsh families who helped him beat Richard III.

Vale of Llangollen, one of the most beautiful areas of Britain. Llangollen town sits astride river Dee, rich in salmon which leap under four arches of St Asaph's stone bridge. A542 goes through Horseshoe Pass, past remains of Cistercian abbey Valle Crucis 1202. Pass can be crowded in summer, impassable in bad winters. Horseshoe Falls built by Telford 1795 to dam water for his remarkable aqueduct carrying Shropshire Union Canal. It is 2 m E at Acrefair, 120 ft high, 1070 ft long, 19 arches. Wonderful views from boats on canal too. Trips from Llangollen. Canal Museum on wharf; old locos, carriages at station. International Eisteddfod held in Llangollen since 1947.

| A5 Chirk A5, A483 Oswestry (12 m) | At Glynceiriog, on B4500 from Chirk, Golden Pheasant (tel Glynceiriog 281): one of best-known, best-loved hotels in Wales; has fine informal atmosphere with good service; Turners have owned it 35 years; also have farm helping to supply kitchen; local trout, lamb, salmon, lot of game in season; lovely fresh sweets. Horses and ponies to ride; fishing. Charming furnishings; all bedrooms have bath; beautiful country; dinner £7.50; BB £16.50. SB Nov–May.

At Oswestry, Wynnstay Hotel, Church St (tel 5261): Trust House Forte; nice Georgian house, once posthouse called Cross Foxes; bowling green there for 200 years (summer bowling weekends). Well-known restaurant, Garden View, lunch around £4.15; dinner FP £5.50; card around £7.50; imaginative dishes. BB £14.25–22.75. DBB £18.50. | Chirk: just in Wales; river marks boundary. Another castle – built by Roger Mortimer 1310; lived in by Myddleton family since 1595; fine park with famous gates. Open Easter–Oct, pm, not Mon, Wed, Fri.

Oswestry: English, according to 1535 Act of Union, but a lot of locals speak Welsh. Anglo-Welsh punch ups for possession went on for centuries; burned twice in 20 years in 13th century. Attractive market town between meadowland and wild hills. Wilfred Owen, poet of First World War, born here. |
| A 483 Welshpool, A483, B4385 Montgomery (10 m) | At Welshpool, Moat Farm (2 m S just off A483) (tel 3179): busy dairy farm 250 acres; calves, dogs (working and ornamental) for children; 17th-century house, large; guests have own oak-beamed dining room with log fire, own TV lounge. Six guests max. Pretty garden, views. Super value; farm cooking; no licence; BB £6; DBB £9 with 4-course meal. Shut winter.

Royal Oak, The Cross (tel 2217): real old market town | Welshpool: back in Wales; market since 1263; still held on Mondays, dealing in livestock from wide area. Probably Europe's largest sheep sales. Georgian houses; Anglicized town – refused to help Owen Glendower; fought with English.

Llanfair Caereinion railway opened 1903, shut by British Rail 1956, run now by volunteer enthusiasts; open to visitors in summer; superb little steam locos from Austria, Britain and West Indies. |

inn. Meals: FP £3.75; card £6.50; wines from £3.35, 41 bins, five countries. BB £7.50–10.

Garth Derwen Hotel, Buttington (edge Welshpool) (tel Trewern 238): on A458; bright décor; friendly. Speciality ham and eggs. Dinner £4.30–6.25; wines from £2.85. BB £7.50–10.

At Montgomery, East Penyllan Farm (tel Montgomery 245): fine old red-brick farm; farmhouse cooking. BB £4.50; DBB £6.50.

Powis Castle: medieval, on hill overlooking river Severn; good condition; beautiful Dutch gardens from 1690, remain unspoiled. Open June–Sept Weds-Sat. Gardens Mon also.

Montgomery: reminds me of Italian towns; main street so wide it is like a square; little steps and quaint corners; buildings of each period, Tudor, Jacobean, Georgian, Victorian jumbled up. 13th-century, with later restorations and a strange robber's grave: John Davies, hanged for murder he swore he did not commit, said that to prove his innocence no grass would grow on his grave for 100 years. That was in 1821. Today a bare cruciform patch is on the grave.

A490 B4385
Bishops Castle
A488 Knighton

Bishops Castle: in England; Three Tuns in Salop Street brews its own beer. House on crutches, Tudor with overhanging upper storey supported on two posts.

A4113, A4110,
A44 Leominster

Knighton (see beginning of route) is back in Wales. Recross border into England on road to Leominster.

Index

Arthur Eperon
Travellers' Italy £2.50

A whole variety of holiday routes to guarantee that you eat, drink, explore and relax in the places the Italians themselves would choose. The best places to sample local speciality foods and wines, spectacular scenery, facts the history books won't tell you, as well as the magnificent beaches and art treasures you'd expect. Arthur Eperon is one of the best-known travel writers in Europe and has an extensive knowledge of Italy and its food and wine. With an introduction by Frank Bough.

Travellers' France £2.95

Six major routes across France, taking in the best restaurants and hotels, visiting the most interesting out-of-the-way places. This detailed and up-to-the-minute handbook is for the traveller who wants more out of France than a mad dash down the motorway. Each of the six routes across the country is illustrated with a specially commissioned two-colour map, and includes a host of information on where to eat and drink, where to take children, where to stay, and how to get the most out of the towns and countryside.

John Slater
Just Off for the Weekend £2.50
Slater's hotel guide

The bestselling author of *Just Off the Motorway* has selected more than a hundred places to stay, with details of what to see and walks to take, specially recommended pubs and restaurants – and all within a Friday evening's drive from one of England's big cities. With an introduction by Anna Ford.

You can buy these and other Pan books from booksellers and
newsagents; or direct from the following address:
Pan Books, Sales Office, Cavaye Place, London SW10 9PG
Send purchase price plus 25p for the first book and 10p for
each additional book, to allow for postage and packing
Prices quoted are applicable in the UK

While every effort is made to keep prices low, it is sometimes
necessary to increase prices at short notice. Pan Books reserve
the right to show on covers and charge new retail prices which
may differ from those advertised in the text or elsewhere